THE
MUSEUM

# THE MUSEUM

## ONE HUNDRED YEARS AND THE METROPOLITAN MUSEUM OF ART

## BY LEO LERMAN · INTRODUCTION BY THOMAS P. F. HOVING

### A STUDIO BOOK · THE VIKING PRESS · NEW YORK

To Mina Curtiss, who painstakingly read this manuscript, making detailed suggestions for its improvement: I owe her a greater debt for this prodigious service and her unstinting help throughout these now many years than any gratitude expressed here can possibly repay.

To the late Pascal Covici, of The Viking Press, who lovingly encouraged my bookish ways for many years, plying me with delicious luncheons whilst assuring me that one day he would "get a book out of me." In a sense he has.

And most especially to Gray Foy, without whose constant attention this book would not be.

Frontispiece by Richard Kalvar

First published in 1969 by The Viking Press, Inc.
625 Madison Avenue, New York, N.Y. 10022

Published simultaneously in Canada by
The Macmillan Company of Canada Limited

Library of Congress catalog card number: 70-87252

Printed in U.S.A.

# CONTENTS

# INTRODUCTION

For thousands of New Yorkers, the Metropolitan Museum of Art is not only the symbol of the cultural life of New York City; it is also the object of an intense and lifelong affection. Not every New Yorker fell in love with the Museum as a three-year-old, as Leo Lerman did, but like Mr. Lerman millions have found it a source of delight and mystery ever since their first visit.

That New Yorkers should love this museum was perhaps foreordained. The men who conceived the Metropolitan Museum had in mind that it should be a very special kind of gift to the people of New York, but the story of the Museum has become one long saga of bounty from the people of New York in return. The story begins with some New York families summering in Europe in 1866 who gathered in the Bois de Boulogne to celebrate the Fourth of July. To them John Jay first addressed his suggestion that the time had come to found a "National Institution" devoted to art. The story continues through the gifts and bequests of many of these families and their descendants, who were soon joined by scores of families like them. All of these families collected great works of art or contributed generously with the present and future needs of the Museum in mind.

Today the gifts are coming still, signs of both affection and pride in New York's great cultural center. But the gifts would have no meaning if each year the Museum did not attract the devotion of more and more visitors from all walks of city life. Indeed, each year, as life in New York becomes more demanding, the need for the kind of

OPPOSITE: The great hall of the Museum as it was in the 1920s.

refreshment which only the Museum affords becomes more necessary to its visitors. And if at times on a crowded Sunday I fear the Museum will suffocate in the embrace of the thousands swarming over it, when peace and order return on Monday, the Museum seems renewed rather than exhausted by the attentions it has been paid.

Leo Lerman's visits have spanned half a century. Happily, while he was visiting— and long before—the Museum was doing a better job than most American institutions of keeping track of its history. When Mr. Lerman came to write this book, he found in the storehouses within the Museum a full and rich archive, and he has spent many hours scrutinizing the thousands of photographs, prints, pamphlets, catalogues, and books the Museum has filed away over the years.

The whole story is not here; it would be a superhuman task to tell it all. But the outline, suggestions, and many of the fascinating details that Mr. Lerman gives his readers are an admirable account of what one hundred years of affection can do to infuse a wealth of human culture into one city's life.

*Thomas Hoving*

OPPOSITE: Music-lovers enjoying a free concert in the Jade Room, Trustee Heber R. Bishop's ballroom setting for his jade collection.

# I

# ALL FOR ART

## 1866–1879

1866–1879

In the spring of 1864, while Sherman burned his way through Georgia and Grant fought indecisively the Battle of the Wilderness, art-fancying New Yorkers assembled in the Fourteenth Street Armory and outbid each other in the cause of patriotism. Thousands of Yankees plunked down over a million dollars to vie at auction for one hundred and ninety-six paintings and to gape at some three hundred and sixty works of art at the Metropolitan Fair Picture Gallery, as its industrially and socially important planners (mostly Union League Clubbers) had titled this splendidly aesthetic and financially remunerative occasion. And the chatter at the Fair which was held in aid of the United States Sanitary Commission (and thus to benefit the National Army's sick and wounded) was as much about war as about art. But, in a year, the war technically ended and Art (with a capital A, indeed) prevailed. It was precisely the right moment, that postwar era—1865–1869—and New York City, bustling rich, was precisely the right place for it to happen.

"New York is nobly supplied with Hospitals and Libraries, but she lacks one Institution essential to a great civilized metropolis—a permanent free Gallery of Art." Henry Theodore Tuckerman, poet, essayist, biographer, critic, art's own American champion, knew definitely what he was writing about when he made his special plea. And he proceeded to write, and to publish in 1867, his 637-page *Book of the Artists: American Artist Life; comprising Biographical and Critical Sketches of American Artists; Preceded by an Historical Account of the Rise and Progress of Art in America; with an Appendix containing an Account of Notable Pictures and Private Collections*. Early on in this amazingly shrewd, omnivorous appraisal, Tuckerman sums up the art-museum–ripe moment:

> The surprise and delight exhibited by the thousands of all degrees, who visited the Picture Gallery of the Metropolitan Fair, has suggested to many, for the first time, and renewed in other minds more emphatically, the need, desirableness, and practicability of a permanent and free Gallery of Art in our cities. The third metropolis of the civilized world should not longer be without such a benign provision for and promoter of high civilization. Within the last few years the advance of public taste and the increased recognition of art in this country, have been among the most interesting phenomena of the times. A score of eminent and original landscape painters have achieved the highest repu-

OPPOSITE: Studying a model of the Pantheon, c. 1913.

tations; private collections of pictures have become a new social attraction; exhibitions of works of art have grown lucrative and popular; buildings expressly for studios have been erected; sales of pictures by auction have produced unprecedented sums of money; art-shops are a delectable feature of Broadway; artist-receptions are favorite reunions of the winter; and a splendid edifice has been completely devoted to the Academy, and owing its erection to public munificence,—while a School of Design is in successful operation at Cooper Institute. Nor is this all; at Rome, Paris, Florence, and Düsseldorf, as well as at Chicago, Albany, Buffalo, Philadelphia, Boston, and New York, there are native *ateliers*, schools, or collections, the fame whereof has raised our national character and enhanced our intellectual resources as people. These and many other facts indicate, too plainly to be mistaken, that the time has come to establish permanent and standard galleries of art, on the most liberal scale, in our large cities.

The time had not only come, but in the hearts of certain staunch, art-minded New Yorkers the most beautiful, vigorous baby of a museum, a museum beyond even the most fanciful imaginings of its progenitors, was already being born.

It all began in 1866, most unexpectedly but appropriately in Paris, in the Bois, at the Pré Catalan, at a gala Fourth of July dinner party of Americans. Some of those present were expatriates, some tourists, some were in government jobs, and others had flocked to Paris to make arrangements for the following year's Universal Exhibition,which they saw would be a golden opportunity for the reunited U.S.A. to sell to the world the glories of American industry, manufacture, invention, craftsmanship—even art: in short, the American way of life. This was the Second Empire's most effulgent moment: the waltzes could never stop, the gaslights never dim.

And it was in this heady climate that Orator-of-the-Day John Jay (indefatigable Abolitionist; Civil Service reformer; Minister to Germany and, later, Austria; grandson of the first Chief Justice of the United States John Jay) stood up, wineglass in hand, and addressed himself to the Minister to France, John Bigelow; Assistant Secretary of War Fox; Captain Beaumont of the monitor *Miantonomoh*, "now lying at Cherbourg"; U.S. Commissioner to the Universal Exhibition of 1867 Beckwith; the Reverend Doctors Hitchcock and Thompson of the Broadway Tabernacle; and all sorts of other patriotic celebrants of the ninetieth anniversary of the National Independence of the United States. There, in the large tent garnished with botanical caprices which the Prefect of the Seine contributed from his city's conservatories, beneath entwined American and French flags (in the red, white, and blue dancing-tent, portraits of George Washington and Napoleon III, Emperor of the French, confronted one another), John Jay voiced the sentiments of the day; stirred the genialities, gaily discoursing on "the American invasion of the Old World"; and then proceeded to pluck a fragrant flower from his ornate oratorical bouquet, brandishing the blossom assiduously under the Paris-art-sensitized noses of his fellow countrymen.

"The simple suggestion that 'it was time for the American people to lay the foundation of a National Institution and Gallery of Art and that the American gentlemen then in Europe were the men to inaugurate the plan,' " he wrote twenty-four years later, "commended itself to a number of the gentlemen present, who formed themselves into a committee for inaugurating the movement." And inaugurate it they did at once, pressing the Union League Club of New York to take immediate action "for the foundation of a permanent national gallery of art and museum of historical relics, in which works of high character in painting and sculpture and valuable historical memorials might be collected, properly displayed, and safely preserved for the benefit of the people at large."

Why was the Union League Club chosen to be midwife to the museum baby? This club, the city's third oldest, was strongly social-minded and powerfully Republican. In those new-money, postwar profiteering, Boss Tweed days, Republican meant liberal in the solid, old-fashioned sense. The Union League Club's five hundred or so members, veteran New Yorkers (Van Rensselaer, Beekman, Delano, Wetmore, Duer, King, Bryant are typical founders' names), *bon vivant* but hard-working statesmen, financiers, men of letters, and artists, were united not by snobbery but by a passionate desire to preserve the truths embodied in the Union fought for by their founding forefathers and so recently by themselves. And not only to preserve them, but to better them. And so John Jay, recently elected president of the club and now at home in New York between ambassadorships, entrusted the museum idea, the liveliest of babies, to the Union League Club's Art Committee. Publisher George P. Putnam was chairman; the other committee members were landscape painter John F. Kensett; sculptor J.Q.A. Ward (his are Central Park's *Indian Hunter and Pilgrim* and the gigantic *Washington* on the Sub-Treasury Building's steps in New York City); landscape painter Worthington Whittredge; portrait painter George A. Baker; painter Vincent Colyer; and art dealer, collector, and patron Samuel P. Avery.

On the evening of November 23, 1869, some three hundred men managed to make their way, through daunting weather ("museum weather" this was later called) to the Union League Club's theater on East Twenty-sixth Street—the club occupied Leonard Jerome's quasi-Georgian mansion on Madison Square. And here, at the invitation of the Art Committee, gathered some of the nation's eminences. There were artists, editors, architects, lawyers, merchants, writers, collecters, dealers, clergymen. There were representative members of the club itself and of the National Academy of Design, the Institute of Architects, and the New-York Historical Society. Along with its incomparable collection of local memorabilia and its library of Americana, the Society housed the only public art collection in New York City. The Century, Manhattan, and brother clubs; Columbia College and Cooper Institute faculty; the Park Commission; and, most necessary, the municipal government were all represented. The Union Leaguers never thought of the museum idea as their offspring: it was to be the city's, the nation's, the people's. When William Cullen Bryant, "the Nestor of our poets and journalists . . . who has been the counsellor, adviser and promoter of all projects for the encouragement of American art" (the *New York Evening Mail*), stood up, as president of the meeting, to make his address, the welcoming applause was as intense as the anticipatory silence that followed.

"We are assembled, my friends," said this seventy-five-year-old international eminence, "to consider the subject of founding in this city a Museum of Art, a repository of the productions of artists of every class, which shall be in some measure worthy of this great metropolis and of the wide empire of which New York is the commercial center." He went on to answer questions before they were asked. No rivalry was "contemplated, no competition"—thereby he assuaged the fears of the New-York Historical Society. Later, when it was suggested that the Society and the Museum merge, W. Nicholas Fish declared, "Some of the sponsors of the . . . Museum are not gentlemen," and both institutions remained independent. Wryly but meaningfully, Bryant suggested that the only competition would be "with similar institutions in other countries, and then only such modest competition as a Museum in its infancy may aspire to hold with those which were founded centuries ago, and are enriched with the additions made by the munificence of successive generations."

No one knew precisely how the Museum was to be achieved, but everyone knew that the public must first be roused. And then, without naming names, Bryant told enormous, unpleasant truths. "Our republic . . . is the richest nation in the world, if paying off an enormous national debt with a rapidity unexampled in history be any proof of riches; the richest in the world, if contented submission to heavy taxation be a sign of wealth; the richest in the world, if quietly to allow itself to be annually plundered of immense sums by men who seek public stations for their individual profit be a token of public prosperity. My friends, if a tenth part of what is every year stolen from us in this way, in the city where we live, under pretense of public service, and poured profusely into the coffers of political rogues, were expended on a Museum of Art, we might have, reposited in spacious and stately buildings, collections formed of works left by the world's greatest artists, which would be the pride of our country." Should political graft be diverted to art's gain, we could, Bryant assured his rapt fellow movers and shakers, garner "every stray statue and picture of merit" unwanted by individuals; "every smaller collection" owners could no longer "conveniently keep"; "every noble work by the artists of former ages . . . thrown upon the world."

There was much more, all pathetically true. Bryant compared the woeful museum desert of our mighty Republic with the glorious museum oases of such minor European kingdoms as Saxony, Spain, Holland, and Belgium. He expounded the plight of American collectors with no center to which to will their collections and no public walls upon which to hang commissioned paintings. He deplored the plight of American artists with no extensive public gallery in which they could hang their works and wherein they could learn from the works of others. Attrition would be the result, Bryant promised, as he significantly applied the lesson of the caged bird to the American artist. And on he went, his circumlocutions lapidary, in the taste of that day, but each ornateness was a solid stone cast unerringly. New York was bloated with postwar immigration: degradation stank more than the filth in the gutters. "It is in the labyrinths of such mighty and crowded populations that crime finds its most seductive and fatal snares, and sin is pampered and festers and spreads its contagion. . . . It is important that we should encounter the temptations to vice in this great and too rapidly growing capital by attractive entertainment of an innocent and improving character." The contemplation of Art, he assured them, could be the panacea. Art, Truth, Beauty . . . Religion, especially a belief in Christ the Consoler made very real by old and modern masters. . . . Bryant was a genuine, lovable product of that earlier America which doggedly realized its dream. But that dream, even four years after the bloodiest of fratricidal wars had been fought to preserve it, was becoming something else, something the Bryants of America could not tolerate. They would fight, these Bryants, with the weapons in which they believed—the good weapons, the constructive weapons—with even so improbable a one as a museum. . . . Others spoke.

Young Professor George Gray Comfort of Princeton, having spent six years abroad studying European institutions of art, discoursed most prophetically on exhibits, administration, loans of art works to the proposed museum, lecture rooms and public lectures, a decorative arts department (a most unusual notion at that time), educational work with children, benefits to the poor and to industry. Comfort even suggested that General Cesnola's Cypriote collection should not be permitted to go to a European museum. Richard M. Hunt, most notable architect of the time, told of the Society of Architects' recently formed Architectural Library of the City of New York, which the Society aimed to transform into "a museum like the Kensington Museum in London" (later the Victoria and Albert Museum), gathering into this New York museum, as the Kensington had already done, "a Loan Collection of Works of Art." Young architect Russell Sturgis, Jr., warned that collections of art were now vanishing swiftly into private hands from which they might be difficult to dislodge. The very popular Rev. Dr. Henry W. Bellows of All Souls' Church refuted this prophetically: "Who is to say when we, through the redundant wealth with which our property threatens to possess us, shall be able to outbid the world in any market for those great, recondite works of Art which are so necessary to the cultivation of every people? Who can say how soon we may find ourselves the largest and the safest offerers for the custody and protection of the highest of all works in the world?"

No one *could*, at that moment, answer Dr. Bellows' questions. But a committee immediately formed with first fifty, then one hundred and sixteen, members with a subcommittee of thirteen "to draw a plan of organization for a Metropolitan Art Museum Association and to nominate a list of officers." They met at the Century Club. They gathered in Samuel P. Avery's chambers. They corresponded relentlessly—with one another and with men of knowledge and taste at home and abroad. They discussed the Leipzig Museum, eleven years old; Berlin's National Museum, then being built; Nuremberg's Museum, wherein art's relationship to industry and other facets of German history was the central idea. London's South Kensington was extolled, as was Paris's Cluny, where applied arts of the Middle Ages were supreme. And they talked ceaselessly about who were "the fittest men to have charge of the enterprise."

The much-consulted Rev. Dr. Henry W. Bellows counseled that there be "men who can make provisional agreements with the Central Park Trustees." The *New York Evening Mail*, viewing Central Park commissioners on the committee, observed, "The cooperation of the Park Commissioners means . . . a site worth half a million dollars, whereon to erect a museum. . . ." The Rev. Dr. Bellows went on, ". . . men who can quietly collect the amount necessary to procure from the best architects we have, in connection with the best specialists in the history and proper elements of an Art Museum—a plan which can be presented in all its majesty and charm to the public and the men of wealth—and yet which can be built piecemeal, as it is needed, or just in advance of the need. . . ." How prescient was this remarkable Rev. Dr. Bellows! A plan "which can be built piecemeal, as it is needed." Here is the structural history of our Museum, accurately foreseen, before the sound of a single spade was heard or the smallest stone was ready to be set in place: one hundred years of persistent, triumphant flux clearly presaged.

Bellows' advice flowed on. Middle-aged men were needed to forward this work, inexhaustibly energetic, resolute, enthusiastic men, "and among them must be men of art-culture and positive art-knowledge." A board of trustees was indispensable, "not large eno' to allow factions within it . . . not so small that it will be a clique, and be wholly dominated by one master-mind." And most important, "The enterprise wants a Head . . . one man in whose soul the enterprise is a principal thing, and about whom the Trustees can rally and fire up with his courage and hope and determination." By January 13, 1870, the perfect head had been found.

John Taylor Johnston was middle-aged, seemed never to tire, was strong-willed, raptly enthusiastic, and, most important, was not only wealthy (banking and railroads) but used his fortune for art's sake. His marble mansion, the first of that aristocratic stone to be erected in the city, stood on Fifth Avenue and Clinton Place, later Eighth Street. And to the rear of this gleaming residence lay his stable, above which he had created his own private gallery of art. Here, one day a week, the public was permitted to come and to view, at leisure, one of the nation's unique (some said most important) collections of paintings. Frederick E. Church's *Niagara* and Winslow Homer's *Prisoners from the Front* held pride of place; for Johnston, unlike his fellow American collectors, was passionately devoted to living American painters. He bought their works and became their friend. His annual artists' reception, held in the gallery, was celebrated not only for the Ornaments of American Art who flocked to it but for the highly invigorating "artists' punch" lavishly brewed and dispensed by their host. This, then, was the man whom the Museum's committee cabled (he was abroad during all of the preliminary brouhaha) and who, sojourning on the Nile

Committeeman of New York's Museum, *could* say, since he and President Johnston, after borrowing the money on their own good names, had paid $116,180.27, including expenses, for the much-wrangled-over 174 victims of the Franco-Prussian War. "It was very magnanimous in Blodgett not to keep some of those fine things when he had it in his power," Johnston wrote. "I fear I couldn't have done it. I would have had at least to have taken out that Van Dyck, or perished."

But some of the trustees continued to excoriate Blodgett and even Johnston. "Fakes!" they shouted. "Frauds! Humbugs! Reckless extravagance!" Despite this ugliness among the Museum mighties, by May 3 over $250,000 worth of pledges were in the hands of the Museum's officers. Johnston and Blodgett were ultimately repaid; and the Museum owned its first collection. It also, by this time, had received its first gift, a Roman sarcophagus from ancient Tarsus, tendered by J. Abdo Debbas, a wealthy Turk who was American Vice-Consul in that city. The 1871 purchase collection's delights, acknowledged even today, included Franz Hals's *Malle Babbe*, a wild-faced, ruddy witch of a woman now well-known to generations of schoolchildren; Jan van der Heyden's delicate *Quay at Leyden;* Maartin van Heemskerck's portrait of his father; a brace of dependable Jan Fyt still lifes; *Beggars at a Doorway*, by a follower of Louis Le Nain (most popular during that heyday of anecdotal painting); a pair of hyperactive Oudry animal scenes; and Poussin's *Midas Washing at the River Pactolus*. The Italian group was headed by a shimmery Giovanni Battista Tiepolo study for the Wurzburg Palace mural painting, *The Investiture of Bishop Harold as Duke of Franconia in 1168*; and two serene early beauties by Guardi, *The Rialto* and *Santa Maria Della Salute, Venice*. There were, of course, misattributions, but time and ever-improving techniques of authentication sorted out Mr. Blodgett's brave venture, proving that he was not only courageous but canny. By 1872 the Museum had even gained international celebrity and respect through its 1871 purchase. In Paris, the *Gazette des Beaux-Arts* published two congratulatory, picture-descriptive essays, and the collection's *chefs-d'oeuvre* were etched by Jules Jacquemart (a tribute indeed) and published in London by P. & D. Colnaghi.

The Metropolitan Museum of Art now had its first collection and its first gift, and it had, through an act passed by the New York State Legislature, on April 5, 1871, the sure future of a home in Central Park, or in "any other public park, square, or place" in the city. This legislation also guaranteed the American Museum of Natural History a future "suitable fireproof building." But the officers of the Metropolitan Museum agreed that until a site had been agreed upon, interim housing would have to be found; their wonderful collection could not continue to remain in hiding in its Cooper Union storage. On December 1, the Museum's first home was leased. A typical, discreet Manhattan brownstone of the period, 681 Fifth Avenue, between Fifty-third and Fifty-fourth Streets, had given up family life and dedicated itself to the dance. Here, in Allen Dodworth's Dancing Academy, "where the poetry of motion had been taught to so many of the young men and maidens of New York," the Museum (in possession, for an annual stipend of $9000, until May 1, 1874) cut a skylight. A large hall, more accustomed to piano tinklings and the discreet swoop, whirl, and careening of the waltz, became an exhibition chamber. On the seventeenth of February, 1872, the press and artists were, most cordially, invited to imbibe punch, consume oysters, and view the pictures. On February 20 subscribers and friends would come, and on February 22 the public, it was hoped, would pour in.

What was to be seen? The 1871 purchase, of course, in all its glory (though some cracking and blistering had occurred), overflowing most gratifyingly from the big, skylighted hall to lesser rooms. John Taylor Johnston's choice marble, *The Last Days of Napoleon I*, by Vincenzo Vela (not the original, as its possessor explained, but "the marble is perfect"), drew all visitors. The Loan Committee fattened the proceedings with a small gathering of treasures such as a trio of confessionals and an excess of wall paneling, which were excellent examples of sixteenth- and seventeenth-century carved oak from a suppressed convent in Ghent. An Apollo, bestowed by a Westchester donor, caused merriment because, a mere three feet high, it was thought to be a midget Greek. And a Mr. Rowe graciously donated Schwanthaler's *Dancing Girl*, a Corybant by one of Munich's most sought-after sculptors. Johnston, writing to Blodgett (who was ill and recuperating abroad during these openings) commented, "It may be very fine, but eight feet of dance is a trial to the feelings. Hereafter, we must curb the exuberance of donors except in the article of money, of which latter they may give as much as they please." The Metropolitan Museum of Art was open at last, and all who came to see remained to cheer. "No one had imagined that we could make such a show," exulted Johnston, "and the disposition to praise is now as general as the former disposition to deprecate. We have now something to point to as the Museum, something tangible and something good." The truth of this statement was demonstrated in the Museum's first three months, during which six thousand visitors trooped up the stone steps into what had so recently been Allen Dodworth's Dancing Academy.

Among these fascinated votaries of art was a bearded, balding, quite lithe, twenty-nine-year-old gentleman-writer. As the *Atlantic Monthly's* art critic, Henry James had already evaluated an exhibition of French paintings in Boston. Now he applied his "painter's eye" (John La Farge's phrase) to the Metropolitan Museum's paintings collection. James placed this in true critical perspective for the cultured of his day, making it vivid to readers of his *The Dutch and Flemish Pictures in New York* even one hundred years later. In possessing the pictures, James wrote, the Museum had "an enviably solid foundation for future acquisition and development. It is not to be termed a brilliant collection, for it contains no first-rate example of a first-rate genius; but it may claim within its limits a unity and a continuity which cannot fail to make it a source of profit to students debarred from European opportunities. If it has no gems of the first magnitude, it has few specimens that are decidedly valueless." And after pages of appraisal, some of it amazingly accurate, all of it imbued with intense appreciation, James concludes, "We can, perhaps, not close our review more aptly than with the wholesome text that half the battle in art is won in the artist's conscience, that there are no easy triumphs, and that genuine charm is one of the deepest things in the world. . . ." James talks of the "wholesome moral eloquence" of the paintings and points out that "Imagination," which is lacking in many of the collection's minor works, "is not a quality to recommend; we bow low to it when we meet it, but we are wary of introducing it into well-regulated intellects. We prefer to assume that our generous young art students possess it, and content ourselves with directing them to the charming little academy in the Fifth Avenue for lessons in observation and execution."

Avid to profit from European examples, the art students came and copied away from nine to twelve a.m. on Wednesday, Thursday, and Friday mornings. On Monday, cleaning day, no visitors were admitted until seven o'clock in the evening, from which hour the collections could be savored, under gaslight, until ten o'clock. All other weekdays the Museum was open from nine a.m. to five p.m., and so many subscribers' tickets were distributed that almost everyone was admitted free. A catalogue was soon available, annotated by "foreign experts." But no professional staff was on the premises to aid visitors. Only George P. Putnam presided, unpaid, a volunteer superintendent, abetted by a man-of-all-work, a twelve-dollar-a-week assistant. This now-incredible situation was not actually the result of penny-pinching. "In 1870, when this Museum and the Museum of Fine Arts in Boston were founded," Francis Henry Taylor, Director of the Metropolitan Museum of Art, 1940–1955, told the Annual Meeting of the Corporation on January 19, 1953 (for the third successive year the Museum's attendance had exceeded two and a quarter million), "In 1870 . . . there was no museum profession. A handful of gentlemen—amateurs in the arts with a sense of history and a flair for criticism—shared the safe-keeping of our incipient public collections with a few imaginative archeologists whose rigidity, acquired mostly in German universities, had been softened by walking trips through classic lands."

Earlier in the century, Samuel Finley Breese Morse vitalized the history of art in a series of tantalizing lectures. Given in the New York Atheneum and the Academy of Design in 1826, Morse's lectures on the fine arts were the first ever to be heard in the United States. Several decades later, James Jackson Jarves, pioneer collector, art enthusiast, critic, journalist, diplomat, the American with the greatest eye for Italian primitives (a suspect taste at the time), wrote some unpleasant truths about the state of American art appreciation. Then in 1871, after selling his incomparable collection of early Italian masters for a pittance, Jarves established, with these marvelous works, a bastion for "pure art" in Yale. "Machine work," said Jarves sadly, "is the one great idealism of our prosaic civilization." After which he continued, his faith in no wise diminished, to attempt to fulfill his life's avowed purpose, the "diffusion of artistic knowledge and aesthetic taste in America."

At last, in the Seventies, Harvard awarded Charles Eliot Norton the first professorship, in any American college, in the Fine Arts. Also in the Seventies (1879) St. Louis created its Museum of Fine Arts, now the City Art Museum, and by 1880 Wellesley and Princeton had their own art centers, and Cincinnati its Art Museum. Chicago's Art Institute flourished from 1885. But not even these ardent pioneers could foresee a future in which a museum such as the Metropolitan would require at least a thousand workers to keep its doors open.

In 1872, the most urgent of museum matters was not, however, keeping faith with Art, for Art was being steadfastly cherished by the continued exhibition of the Museum's collection, by provision for young would-be artists, and, in the spring of 1872, by lectures presented in the Museum to the entranced trustees and their friends. Future trustee and Museum Treasurer Hiram Hitchcock read a paper about the discoveries in Cyprus of General Cesnola, a man who was soon to shape the Museum's future. And a month later architect, writer, and Museum founder Russell Sturgis, Jr., revealed the beauties and profundities of ceramic art. This was all very well for art, but what of a permanent Temple of Art? Manhattan Square (site of the Museum of Natural History) was in the offing, with the possibility of sharing a building or even occupying a separate structure there. The Executive Committee thought Reservoir Square (now Bryant Park) most desirable, for it was near the new Grand Central Terminal which Cornelius Vanderbilt, the richest man in America, was building, and it was also close to the theaters, shops, and restaurants surging ever northward. The park commissioners settled the matter explicitly. The Metropolitan Museum of Art would stand on Fifth Avenue but away to the north, almost in the country, it seemed, between Seventy-ninth Street and Eighty-fourth Street, on that calculated wilderness of land known as the Deer Park. The Museum's western limit would be the park's Drive, lively with riders in summer and thronging with sleighers in winter. The last miasmic pollutions from nearby Seneca Village, the biggest, most scabrous squatter colony in the park, would fade from Olmsted and Vaux's tree-fragrant air. By 1873 five million vines, shrubs, and trees would be planted in the park, and the bone-boilers' hovels, swill mills, hog farms, and pestilential squatters' dens would retreat across Fifth Avenue northward and eastward, there to congeal into noisome slums. There would be room to expand, to stretch, in the Deer Park. And already a marble palace stood, one of several, in "Marble Row" at Fifty-seventh Street and Fifth Avenue. On April 1, 1872, the Museum's trustees ratified the park commissioners' choice. Eighty-two years later this was still a good arrangement. "The Museum stands on City land in our best-known park," said the Commissioner of the Department of Parks of the City of New York, Robert Moses, in 1954. "It is privately endowed and run by independent distinguished citizens with some ex-officio public representation. It is financed by interest on its capital, by private contributions, and by City funds voted annually for upkeep for which the Park Commissioner is more or less directly responsible. The relationship between the City and the Museum has, by far and large, been a happy one from which the people of the city and the innumerable visitors have substantially profited."

But even before a spade could break a single clod of earth in the Deer Park the Metropolitan Museum of Art was on the move, to the south and 128 West Fourteenth Street, where what survived of the city's pleasure life lingered. (A catastrophic financial crash occurred in 1873, affecting the state economy and many of the nation's rich, and ground breaking did not take place until 1874.) Union Square and its purlieus were still New York's shopping and amusement center; the shift to Madison Square came four years later when the economic depression lifted and the nation's most tremendous expansion began. Then Broadway, from Eighth Street to Twenty-third, became "the ladies' mile," with New York's most enterprising drygoods shops lining it. Thirty-foot-high elevated railways sooted Ninth Avenue house fronts; soon chugging, smoke-spewing little monsters would be tugging their light-green cars along clattery elevated roadbeds on Second, Third, and Sixth Avenues, from five-thirty a.m. to midnight. Ten cents a ride, and all of the upper-story family life views you could fleetingly catch at the ten-mile-an-hour speed of these mechanical dragons! Midst grandeurs and squalors the locomotive and its four-car tail sped, while the downtown New York skies were thickly cat's-cradled with telegraph wires and newfangled telephone wires. "The sky, indeed, is blackened with them," a British visitor wrote in 1878, "and it is as though you were looking through the meshes of a net."

In 1873, the Museum's first expansion was caused by its urgent need for a larger albeit again temporary home. This was the beginning of those continual expansions, rehabilitations, adjustings, and maneuverings which were to occur within the rigidities of its Deer Park site. The Museum has never had sufficient room for its acquisitions, its ever-increasing personnel; it never will have all of the room it needs and will need. . . . What did the Museum acquire that caused its expansion? The Cesnola Collection of Cypriote Antiquities, over ten thousand items, "the most valuable and richest private collection of antiquities existing in the world." That is how General Cesnola described the results of his excavations on Cyprus, his opening of eight thousand ancient Phoenician, Greek, Assyrian, and Egyptian tombs, and a temple of Venus. He would not break up the collection, not even for the British Museum, the Louvre, or the Russian Museum in St. Petersburg. And it was most important to him that it be owned in America and forever under his own name. "I have the pride of my race," he announced, "and that of a Discoverer who wants his name perpetuated with his work if possible." Johnston worked out the finances through banker Junius Spencer Morgan, John Pierpont Morgan's father (son John, deeply involved in the creation of the Museum of Natural History, was to be the Metropolitan Museum's prime shaper), and Cesnola's trove was bought for an initial $60,000. With later additions the total cost came to $110,000, and within two years the Museum owned the collection, having paid for it by popular subscription. Quite possibly Cesnola could have sold the collection abroad for $200,000.

In an addendum to Cesnola's 456-page, enthusiastically detailed *Cyprus: Its Ancient Cities, Tombs, and Temples. A Narrative of Researches and Excavations During Ten Years' Residence in that Island*, published in 1878, Johnston exultingly sums up the purchase and the fledgling Museum's glory: "These collections contribute to modern knowledge a wider field of art and a greater amount of important material than has ever before been produced by any one discoverer. They form the most complete illustration of the history of ancient art and civilization, revolutionizing some of the theories of art . . . they determine the place of Greece in the history of art." He enumerated the categories of magnificence. The oldest sculptures extant "remodelled the history of that art." The inscriptions on the engraved cylinders "enabled scholars to complete" the wedge-shaped Cypriote language system, dead since the fifth century B.C. The statuary from Golgos; the collection of Archaic Greek fictile art; the Greek and Phoenician glassware; the finds from the temple vaults of Curium ("the most precious single discovery of ancient art ever made"); the ceramic art and vases (covering 2000 years and more of ancient history); the gems and massive gold jewelry, especially the armlets of Etevandros, King of Cyprus, 672 B.C. . . . All this was of an historical and artistic significance beyond most American belief—at least in the 1870s. "The Trustees of the Metropolitan Museum of Art," concluded Johnston, "cordially invite all scholars to a careful study of the Cesnola Discoveries, which will soon be permanently displayed in their new buildings in the Central Park."

There were, of course, cries of fakery. Cesnola, a tidy man, had concocted a loving technique for neatening some of his deities. He joined bits and pieces here and there with an adhesive concocted of honey and lime dust. As a result, when hot weather came, buzzing garlands and draperies of mesmerized flies festooned the more fractured ancients.

In the Eighties, a French dealer in antiquities, Gaston L. Feuardent, led the anti-Cesnola Collection attack. False restorations, artificial patinas on the bronzes, he thundered. A trustee-empowered, Cesnola-urged investigatory committee, utilizing all scientific means known and enlisting a wide variety of specialists, vindicated the General. But art critic Clarence Cook raised an accusatory voice even louder than Feuardent's. Cook concentrated on two statues, *Aphrodite and Eros* and *Figure Holding a Horned Head*. This duo, said Cook flatly, was "a fraudulent patchwork!" In a twelve-page editorial in *The Century*, Richard Watson Gilder said that Cesnola was "a liar, falsifier and fraud." The Museum had its first scandal on its hands, with the press throughout the nation joining in vociferously. The public was then invited to view the statues, unprotected by their glass cases, and in strong light. The public not only thronged to look, but it "washed, chiseled, cut, scraped, treated with caustic potash and other chemicals, brushed with wire brushes, and examined microscopically to their hearts' content. . . ." All agreed that the suspect couple was authentic. General Cesnola, amazingly silent until this moment, "published a brief and total denial of the charges against him and his collection." Whereupon Feuardent sued him for libel. A laymen jury ruled that the General had not libeled his traducer; the Museum expressed every faith in its General; and Americans everywere now definitely knew that in the City of New York there stood a Metropolitan Museum of Art and that it was absolutely essential to visit this hub of high-minded controversy. Sympathetic letters descended, so many olive-branch-bearing eagles, from the luminaries of American art appreciation and taste . . . from Professor Charles Eliot Norton, from James Jackson Jarves, from George William Curtis. Admiration came even from European monumentals such as A. S. Murray of the British Museum. But the General, his "high and delicate sense of honor" once impugned, never quite recovered.

Cesnola died in 1904 and about five years later Professor J. L. Myers, foremost authority on the art and civilization of Cyprus (and later Wykeham Professor of Ancient History at Oxford University), wrote of Cesnola's findings, "The collection, which is probably in any case the largest single collection of Cypriote antiquities, contains also a large number of examples of Cypriote art which are of the highest importance for the history and civilization of ancient Cyprus." Cesnola would, perhaps, have felt even more fully exonerated when, in the late 1920s, the Museum sold off at auction Cesnola collection duplicates for a happy total of $120,000. John Ringling lavished his circus and Florida real estate gains to buy the largest number of items for his museum at Sarasota.

Who was General Louis Palma di Cesnola? More professional army man than trained archeologist, and said to be a nobleman by birth, this Piedmontese graduate from the Royal Military Academy of Turin was an American phenomenon. A former Garibaldi Redshirt and Crimean War soldier, Cesnola emigrated to the United States. In New York he established a training school for officers (ancestor of the War College in Washington, D. C.) and became a known town character. Soon he was off to war for Union Forever. His training school helped in the ultimate Union triumph; he, himself, fought mightily; and, in 1865, President Lincoln rewarded him by appointing him Consul of the United States at Cyprus. Remote, removed from any worldly turmoil, convinced that in antique times all ancient races had sooner or later crossed one another's paths on that little island, Cesnola undertook the prolonged digs which ultimately made him world famous, even notorious, and brought him back to the United States of America, the nation he adored, and to the very young Metropolitan Museum of Art in New York, an institution he would command for twenty-five years as its first Director. In 1877, while the Museum was in its second home, the Douglas Mansion on West Fourteenth Street, Cesnola, who had unpacked the Cypriote collection piece by fragile piece and supervised the exhibition of the hoard, was appointed Secretary, succeeding William J. Hoppin in this unsalaried job. And just before the move to Central Park, the trustees made the Italian, antiquity-impassioned General their Director, or "manager"—with salary.

A portly man who loved good food and wine, Cesnola later established a popular restaurant in the Museum, complete with Italian chef, mirrored bar, excellent comestibles, and drink. On the majestic side, he wore pince-nez high and affirmative upon his aristocratic nose and parted his thick hair relentlessly right down the middle. Fiery-tempered to impetuosity, always hungry to learn and voracious to build the Museum into the greatest in the world, this self-made archeologist, this event-created, militaristic museum administrator (always wearing steel-heeled shoes to alert employees to attention galleries away) was typical of the best new Americans arriving by the thousands from northern and western Europe and, after 1883, from central and southern Europe. Here, then, was another basic pattern in the future fabric of the Museum: the heirs of the earliest American dream, working together for the general civic, social, and aesthetic good with apostles of the new industrial faith and with men come recently to America to pursue their own dreams.

What did Cesnola find in 1877, when he first undertook to help the trustees run the Museum? In the four years of its occupancy, the elegant, mansard-roofed Douglas Mansion bulged with treasures. The walls of its curving stair, the large gallery lighted from the roof, the soundly constructed coachhouse, every nook and cranny of the Museum breathed art, history, culture, beauty. Here were Cesnola's collections and the paintings of the 1871 purchase, row upon gleaming row, from wainscoting to ceilings high above. Hiram Powers' *California*, a modest Amazonian, neoclassic girl, originally named *La Dorada* when it was first conceived in Florence in 1850 by its soon-to-be world famous sculptor, was a cynosure. Not as celebrated as Powers' *Greek Slave*, this sister sculpture nevertheless enticed the public by being much to the taste of the period's passion for classic antiquity, especially as it was heroically and smoothly sculpted in glistening white Carrara marble. *California* also attracted notice because it had ornamented, for twelve years, the Astor Place mansion of William Backhouse Astor. Payment of a reputed $7500 for the statue added to Mr. Astor's *réclame* as a modern Medici. And such was the success of the naked marble girl in his home, that Mr. Astor, it would seem, did not fully realize its implications until Tuckerman, in his *Book of the Artists*, pointed out, "Evidently the sculptor's idea is to contrast the fascination of form with the sinister expression of the face—the thorn concealed in the right hand with the divining rod displayed in the left—and thus illustrate the deceitfulness of riches. It is a singular coincidence that such an allegorical statue should adorn the dwelling of our wealthiest citizen." In 1872, Mr. Astor moved his mansion north to the Thirties and gave the sculpture to the Museum. *California* became the Museum's first sculpture gift, the precursor of the 354 pieces, by 176 Americans, enumerated in the Museum's 1965 catalogue, *American Sculpture*.

Here in the second home of the Museum was Henry Peters Gray's *Wages of War*, a large, melancholy, storytelling painting of a romantic-classical Roman scene. Gift of "several gentlemen" in 1874, this little-known New York City painter's somewhat naïve canvas (finished in 1844 or 1845) became the Museum's first painting gift and was the vanguard of the 1250 pictures by some 625 American artists, which in 1965 were in the Museum's collection, one of the most comprehensive surveys of the nation's native painting talents. It was Cesnola who, in 1877, first urged the Museum trustees to make a collection of early American art. And there were other American paintings. The Museum owned thirty-eight works by John Frederick Kensett, a Museum founder, Hudson Valley painter, and one of the inaugurators of that golden-glow school. Given by the artist's son, all the canvases (some unfinished, but all landscapes painted during Kensett's last year, 1872) arrived at the Museum for the artist's memorial exhibition in 1874, a one-man display which established a long-lived Museum tradition of posthumous accolades to American artists. Not in the Kensett memorial, but even more typical of his essential American lyrical art, is his Indian-summer-haunted *Lake George*, which came to the Museum in the Maria DeWitt Jesup bequest in 1915.

*The Nine Muses*, nine separate canvases, the most famous of the 1432 portraits Giuseppe Fagnani was said to have painted in the last thirty-three years of his life, captivated all beholders. Disguised as the Muses, nine American high-society belles, whom everyone knew by name, clearly demonstrated that American pulchritude was as classic as any to be found in Europe. Fashion and chauvinism, plus the artist's glorious reputation as the most sought-after society portraitist of his day and the legend of his Americanization (born in Naples, he had become an American citizen at the height of his European glory), combined to make viewers of *The Nine Muses* thrill with delight. Many years later, in 1911, the Muse Polyhymnia, Mrs. Francis E. Barlow, wrote to the trustees, "I think they all look like ladies on prune boxes and they have very little value."

There was much more already in the Museum or scheduled to be shown on loan before the move to Central Park, and almost all of it was proudly listed in the first general guide to the collections, circa 1875: a bust of William Cullen Bryant; a large canvas filled with the quiet, Indian-legend beauty of New York State crags and waters by the Hudson River School painter Asher B. Durand; Houdon's astute portrait bust of Benjamin Franklin; two hunting scenes, twilight panels by, it was certain at that time, Piero di Cosimo; the Cogniat arms and armor collection; Samuel P. Avery's excellent Oriental pieces and William C. Prime's pottery and porcelain collections; the Castellani collections of antiquities and majolica recently exhibited at the 1876 Centennial Exhibition in Philadelphia. It was hoped that some benefactor would purchase this European cache for the Museum. No one did, but it fascinated visitors for an entire year in the Douglas Mansion. The Andrew MacCullum collection of lace and embroideries was on loan display, available for munificent purchase. Sighed over by all females (for this was a lace-mad, embroidery-crazed era) and studied carefully by textile workers, the collection, "a number of early sixteenth-century Italian embroideries—drawnwork, cutwork, colored drawnworks in silks, in part from the Grecian Islands under the dominion of Venice, and all fragments of transitional *punto in aria*"—ultimately became the Museum's. Thus the Textile Study Room, one of the world's great repositories, was started.

To the west of the capacious entrance hall, reproductions of works of art in the South Kensing-

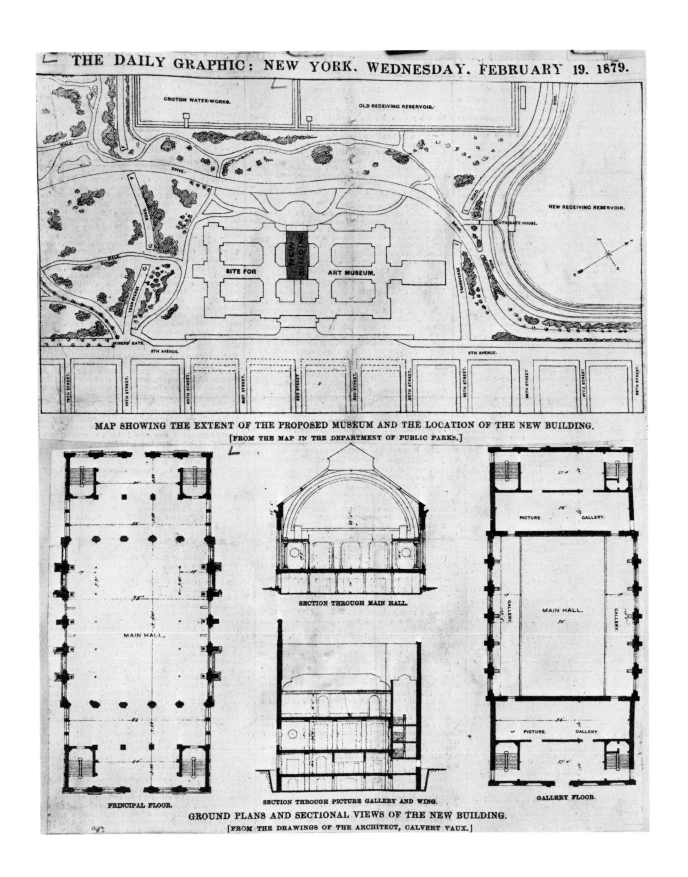

MAP SHOWING THE EXTENT OF THE PROPOSED MUSEUM AND THE LOCATION OF THE NEW BUILDING.
[FROM THE MAP IN THE DEPARTMENT OF PUBLIC PARKS.]

SECTION THROUGH MAIN HALL.

MAIN HALL.

PRINCIPAL FLOOR.

SECTION THROUGH PICTURE GALLERY AND WING.

PICTURE. GALLERY.

MAIN HALL.

PICTURE. GALLERY.

GALLERY FLOOR.

GROUND PLANS AND SECTIONAL VIEWS OF THE NEW BUILDING.
[FROM THE DRAWINGS OF THE ARCHITECT, CALVERT VAUX.]

Calvert Vaux's map and ground plans published in *The Daily Graphic* in 1879.

ton Museum, London, created a distinguished atmosphere of foreign travel at home while also testifying to a firm friendship between the British institution and the American. Here also were the Museum-owned copperplates engraved for Audubon's *Birds of America*. And in the Old Masters Picture Gallery, Jacquemart's ten etchings "from some of the most Valuable of these Paintings" were on sale at $25 for the series. In Room G, a revolving stand offered for sale photographs of Museum objects. These now evocative photographs were furnished by trustees Prime and Hoe, at their own expense but for the Museum's profit. And Tiffany and Company were exclusively empowered to reproduce Museum favorites. Seeds of future Museum services and departments were being planted abundantly and wisely.

Secretary Cesnola and the trustees shared the joys of the overflowing Museum and the tangle of economic and policy-making problems. Purchases of works of art and costs of running and moving the Museum had greatly depleted the original $250,000 subscription fund. Although the country was emerging from its four-year-long depression, money was still difficult to come by. In 1873 the legislature had passed an act enabling the Park Department to apply annually to the Museum's maintenance a sum not to exceed $15,000. That was a help. Admission charges were imposed. Much against the trustees' desires (for it was always their intention to maintain a free Museum) a toll of fifty cents was asked. Attendance dropped, and in three months the charge was lowered to twenty-five cents per person, and Mondays were free. Soon after, Thursdays also became free days, and the trustees were overjoyed to tell anyone who cared to read their 1875 *Annual Report* (the first of these reports had appeared in 1872) that the average daily free-day attendance had been 577! It was then decided that the Museum should be available to working people, those who couldn't come during the day. At first the Museum was opened from seven o'clock to ten o'clock Tuesday, Thursday, and Saturday evenings, and subsequently only on Mondays and Saturdays, with the former entrance-free. But the workers did not turn out in sufficient numbers to help meet the expense of keeping the Museum open at night, and the plan was abandoned for some years.

The trustees did, however, have reasons for self-congratulation and happiness in their Museum. In seeking to defray running expense, they decided to create a new membership class, especially attractive to persons who could not afford to become either Fellows or Patrons of the Museum. Annual memberships were offered. For ten dollars a year an Annual Member received an admission ticket for two persons, whenever the Museum was open, and bids to all receptions the Museum's officers gave for Museum events. Some six hundred enrolled. *The Ninety-Eighth Annual Report*, for the fiscal year 1967–1968, gives a total membership, in the twelve current classes, of 22,868. Back in 1876, six hundred annual members represented six hundred affirmations of faith in the Museum. Also deeply gratifying were the Museum's educational efforts. Art students from Cooper Union, the Brooklyn Art Association, the Art Students League (founded in 1875), and many with no school affiliations were given free tickets and did use the Museum constantly. Entire classes

Century Club, 109 East Fifteenth Street,
JANUARY 11TH, 1870.

SIR:

I beg to enclose to you a copy of the Constitution of the *Museum of Art Association* of the City of New York, adopted by the Provisional Committee on the 4th inst.

I am instructed to notify you that, in accordance with the provision contained in Article II, the *first annual meeting* will be held, for the purpose of electing officers for the ensuing year, and transacting such other business as may come before them, at the *Century Club*, as above, on Monday, 17th inst., at 8 o'clock P. M.

By order of the Chairman.

THEODORE WESTON,
Sec'y Provisional Committee.

To Mr. *C. Putnam*

ABOVE: Theodore Weston. ABOVE RIGHT: Invitation to the Museum's first official meeting.

The Century Club, where the members of the Provisional Committee sometimes met.

LEFT: John Jay, president of the Union League Club. His enthusiasm gave the museum idea its initial impetus. Portrait by Jared B. Flagg, American, 1820–1899. (Courtesy Union League Club) BELOW: The Union League Club's headquarters on Madison Square Park. Drawing by Franklin Wittmack. (Courtesy Union League Club)

ABOVE: Theater of the Union League Club on East Twenty-sixth Street, where on November 23, 1869, William Cullen Bryant proposed a museum "which would be the pride of our country." (Old engraving)

The Tiffany and Company store in Union Square. The second story was offered for a loan exhibition in 1871.

Among the early officers and trustees of the Museum were (left to right) Eastman Johnson (Courtesy The Century Club), Russell Sturgis, George P. Putnam, William Cullen Bryant, John F. Kensett (Courtesy The Century Club).

LEFT TO RIGHT: Alexander T. Stewart, Frederick Law Olmstead, Joseph H. Choate, John Q. A. Ward, and Samuel P. Avery. All were actively engaged in the founding of the Museum.

Detail of Roman sarcophagus from Tarsus, given by Abdo Debbas in 1870, the first gift received by the Museum.

*The Hatch Family.* Eastman Johnson, American, 1824–1906. Oil, dated 1871. Gift of Frederic H. Hatch, 1926. The painter received $1000 for each "head" in the painting, including the new baby.

RIGHT: *Catharine Lorillard Wolfe.* Alexandre Cabanel, French, 1823–1889. Oil, dated 1876. Bequest of Catharine Lorillard Wolfe, 1887. BELOW RIGHT: *Beggars at a Doorway.* Follower of Louis Le Nain, French, seventeenth century. Oil. Purchase, 1871.

*Lake George.* John Frederick Kensett, American, 1818–1872. Oil, dated 1869. Bequest of Maria De Witt Jesup, 1915.

ABOVE: *St. Rosalie Interceding for the Plague-Stricken of Palermo.* Anthony van Dyck, Flemish, 1599–1641. Oil. Purchase, 1871. RIGHT: *The Investiture of Bishop Harold as Duke of Franconia, 1168.* Giovanni Battista Tiepolo, Italian, 1696–1770. Purchase, 1871.

da Vinci, along with many tributes to the fair sex, both human and bovine. It was a happy time for cows on huge canvases. Among the lenders was Henry Gurdon Marquand, future prodigal benefactor and next president of the Museum. Frederick E. Church and John La Farge sent works, and S. F. B. Morse's daughter sent his beautiful portrait *The Muse—Susan Walker Morse*. This characteristic painting (Miss Morse posed for *The Muse*) was bequeathed to the Museum in 1945, but the first Morse work to belong to one of the permanent collections was a model of his most important invention, the recording telegraph. Today this instrument might well be exhibited as a work of art.

The greatest loan exhibition in the Museum's first decade developed through a desire to show what New York City could offer, in fine art, while the 1876 Centennial Exposition in Philadelphia was attracting fair-goers from, it was hoped, all over the world. In cooperation with the City's National Academy of Design, the Museum mounted a summer show (the first in its long history of related events) of 580 paintings from fifty-eight private collectors, all of them in New York. Part of this mammoth display was to be viewed in the Museum, part in the Academy. Modern European paintings predominated—French, German, English—but about one-fourth were by American artists. For some 220 days, from June 23 to November 10, some 154,441 determined art lovers meandered through the Museum and the Academy, purchasing 46,033 catalogues and leaving the cooperating institutions net proceeds of almost $38,000. Of that windfall, the Museum took forty per cent, the Academy received sixty per cent, and everybody agreed that this had been a long, lucrative, heartening summer. The Philadelphia Exposition and the New York art exhibits had clearly demonstrated what a "go-ahead" country this U.S.A. was. At the Centennial Exposition, the Corliss steam engine, the greatest in the universe, and a hand from Bartholdi's unfinished Statue of Liberty shared visitors' astonished attention with manifestations of John Ruskin's and William Morris's concern with industrial arts. As Americans trudged through the resplendent Centennial grounds in Philadelphia's Fairmount Park, and trailed through the priceless exhibits borrowed from America's self-made aristocracy at the Metropolitan Museum of Art and the National Academy of Design in New York City, they realized that the United States of America had come a long, marvelous way in one hundred years. Contentedly they went home to their modern pea-soup-and-brown-gravy-colored parlors, their crimson-plush sitting rooms where smooth Carrara marble glowed in sorrowing female shapes among the aspidistras and where the paintings upon the walls revealed rural vistas or told endless, carefully articulated tales of historic or mythic woes. They sank upon their rigid Eastlake sofas and chairs and thought of what they had seen: the miracles of modern ingenuity and taste. And they were all for Art, especially when Art was Success' own and ever-enhancing bride.

An even more momentous occasion occurred in the Douglas Mansion on February 14, 1879. On the evening of this very special Saint Valentine's Day, "a stalwart crush" made it almost impossible for trustees and other Museum officers (William Waldorf Astor to Cornelius Vanderbilt, Jr.), artists, members of all classes, city dignitaries, and the press to take one final look at the now celebrated collections of the Metropolitan Museum in their second New York home. The Museum was, at last, moving north to its permanent glory, the very modern Ruskin Gothic edifice so adventurously designed by Park Department architects Calvert Vaux and J. Wrey Mould. (Museum architecture itself was now one hundred years old, architect Simon Louis du Ry having created the first structure designed as a museum, the Fridericianum in Kassel, between 1769 and 1779.) So in they came, in prodigious crowds, New York's mightiest. And it was a "bully" time, as Teddy Roosevelt (his father was a recent Museum officer) would have put it, for rejoicings and congratulations.

LEFT: *Midas Washing at the River Pactolus*. Nicolas Poussin, French, 1593–1665. Oil. Purchase, 1871.
RIGHT: Henry James. As art critic for the *Atlantic Monthly*, he reviewed the Museum's first exhibition in February 1872. (Courtesy The Century Club)

BELOW: *The Rialto*. Francesco Guardi, Italian (Venetian), 1712–1793. Oil. Purchase, 1871.

OVERLEAF: The opening reception, February 28, 1872, in the temporary quarters at 681 Fifth Avenue. (From *Harper's Weekly*)

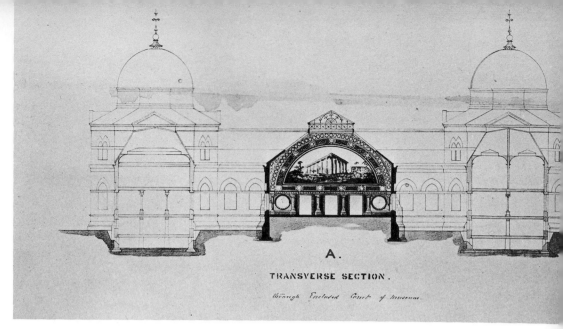

A.
TRANSVERSE SECTION.
through Enclosed Court of Museum.

LEFT: Calvert Vaux (1824–1895). ABOVE AND OPPOSITE: Elevation and floor plans for the first Museum building by Calvert Vaux and J. Wrey Mould.

The city had survived the $200,000,000-and-more ravages of Boss Tweed and his ring. And now William Marcy Tweed, who, it must be remembered, had helped push through the Museum's charter, was dead, having justly expired behind bars in the Ludlow Street jail. A booming economy was blossoming over the bogs of the 1873–1877 financial depression. Every day more and more immigrants poured out of shipholds into slums which were becoming more awful than those in Naples. But these "foreigners" were cheap labor, helping to ease an ever-grander American way of life. Intimations of refinement and culture (the most popular of words in the late Seventies) flourished. And while the pleasure-loving heart of the city beat most gaily in Madison Square, where soon one of Charles Francis Brush's 6000-candlepower electric arc lights, atop a 160-foot pole, would annihilate night and be visible sixteen miles away, society was installing itself again in the gas-lighted lower reaches of Fifth Avenue and from Thirty-fourth Street northward. At that Olympian juncture, A. T. Stewart's neo-Renaissance pile on the southwest corner confronted Mrs. Astor's palace on the northwest, newish-money vis-à-vis oldish-new. Three-quarters of a mile up the avenue, religion was being monumentalized in a shrine as Gothic as any to be found in Europe, the almost-finished St. Patrick's Cathedral. When so much was so good for so many, who in the world could recall the scorching words published in 1866 by the New York weekly, *The Round Table*? "A strange craziness is abroad in the land. Some mysterious spirit of evil has led our people into the blindest, wildest infatuation . . . wild and foolish speculation. . . . At least half the people are living beyond their means."

The trustees of the Museum did have ample reasons for joy. The world, as reflected in the Museum's very existence, was altruistic, even pure. The *Annual Report* for 1879 elucidates:

The Metropolitan Museum of Art has been in existence nine years. . . . These nine years have advanced the young Institution to a position of vastly greater power and prosperity than its most ardent well wishers could have expected in such brief time. Its collections have been purchased without a dollar of public aid. They are the gift of a small number of persons, forming the membership of the Museum, to the millions of inhabitants of the City and State. The labors of the Museum, which have been constant and arduous, have been carried on by the Trustees in person, who have freely given of their time to the Institution; and, it is not improper to add, these Trustees have contributed to the funds of the Institution and the purchase of its present valuable collections, about one-fourth of the entire amount expended.

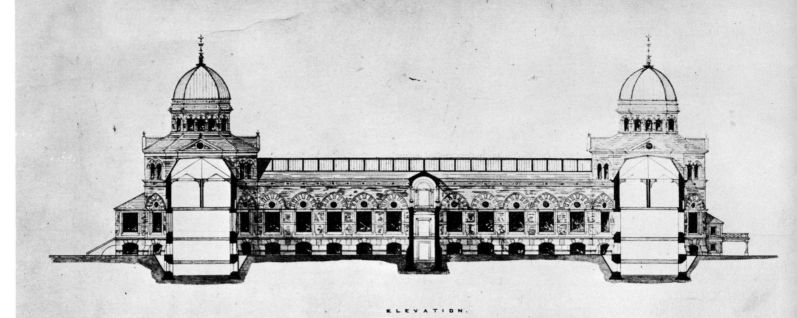

ELEVATION.

PLAN OF SECOND STORY.

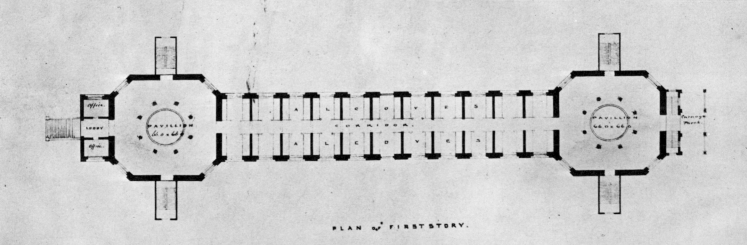

PLAN OF FIRST STORY.

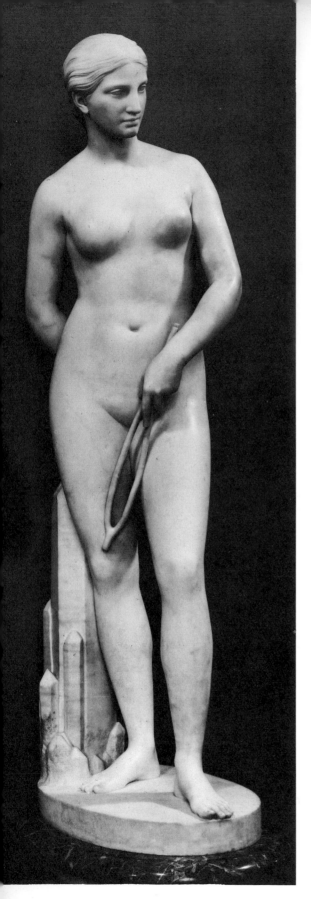

ABOVE: *California*. Hiram Powers, American, 1805–1873. Marble. RIGHT: An appeal to the legislature for financial aid.

OPPOSITE: At left, *Wages of War*. Henry Peters Gray, American, 1819–1877. Oil, dated 1845. Gift of several gentlemen, 1873. At right, *Benjamin Franklin*. Jean Antoine Houdon, French, 1741–1828. Marble, dated 1778. Gift of John Bard in 1872. Below, the former Douglas Mansion on Fourteenth Street, the second home of the Museum.

## To the Honorable, the Legislature of the State of New York:

1873

The Trustees of the METROPOLITAN MUSEUM OF ART respectfully represent,

That they have been duly incorporated by the Legislature of the State of New York, by Act passed April 13, 1870, for the purpose of establishing and maintaining, in the City of New York, a Museum and Library of Art; of encouraging and developing the study of the Fine Arts, and the application of arts to manufactures and practical life; of advancing the general knowledge of kindred subjects, and to that end of furnishing popular instruction and recreation.

That they have raised, by subscription, for the purposes of said Museum, about two hundred and fifty thousand dollars—a large part of which has been paid for the purchase of works of art, which are now in their possession:

That in April, 1871, the Legislature passed an act which has not been altered or repealed, by which the sum of $500,000 was authorized to be raised by the Department of Parks to erect a building for the Metropolitan Museum of Art within the Central Park, or some other of the public lands belonging to the City:

That the Department of Parks has not yet commenced the erection of said building, and your Memorialists believe that several years must elapse before said building will be ready to receive their collections:

That your Memorialists have in the meantime hired two large buildings for the reception and exhibition of the works of Art belonging to the Museum, and those which have been loaned to your Memorialists:

That for the rent of said buildings, and for the necessary expenses of preserving and exhibiting these collections there will be required annually at least the sum of Thirty Thousand Dollars:

That, these exhibitions will be virtually free to the people, subject to such restrictions only as the custody and preservation of the collections, and the rights of the subscribers to the fund shall impose; and that the said Museum will be as important and beneficial an agent in the instruction of the people as any of the schools or colleges of the city, and will also afford the most refining and, at the same time, innocent recreation for the public that can be provided:

Your Memorialists further respectfully represent, that the subscribers to the Museum fund having expended a large sum of money in the purchase of these objects for the public benefit, and having obtained the loan of other most valuable objects, also for the public benefit, and without any possible private advantage or profit, it is only just and proper that the expense of preserving and exhibiting these collections shall be borne by the people of the city, and should be supplied by the tax levy.

Your Memorialists, therefore, respectfully request that there shall be added to the sum to be raised by tax, for the year 1873, for the City and County of New York, the sum of thirty thousand dollars, to be paid to the Treasurer of the Metropolitan Museum of Art for the time being, for the purposes above mentioned.

And your Memorialists will ever pray.

JOHN TAYLOR JOHNSTON, *Pres't*,    THEODORE WESTON, *Rec. Sec'y*,
SAMUEL D. M. BARLOW,    RUSSELL STURGIS, *Corres. Sec'y*,
HOWARD POTTER,    LUCIUS TUCKERMAN,
HENRY G. MARQUAND,    ROBERT HOE, JR.,
JOSEPH H. CHOATE,    WM. C. PRIME,
WM. J. HOPPIN,    R. M. HUNT,
SAM'L P. AVERY,    D. HUNTINGTON,
   RUTHERFORD STUYVESANT.

On motion the meeting the adjourned

Theodore Weston
Rec Secty.

46

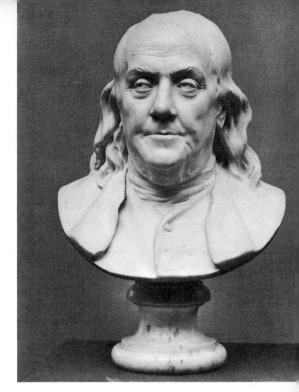

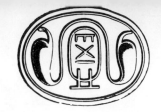

For six weeks Director-Secretary Cesnola and the trustees themselves packed up the Museum's belongings. Most active of the Museum officers were its Vice-President, William Cowper Prime, journalist, educator, lawyer, authority on numismatics and old porcelains (his *Pottery and Porcelain* had just appeared, and in five years he would be Professor of Art at Princeton), and William Loring Andrews. Bibliophile, founder of the Grolier Club and the Society of Iconophiles, Andrews, with a little bundle of books, would soon lay the foundations of the Museum's library, which, by 1970, would hold some 170,000 volumes and service more than twenty thousand readers. Pack away they did, cheerfully reviewing the past, speculating on the future. Even balancing the budget did not seem an impossibility, although Cesnola would have to cope with a depleted exchequer until 1883. But the legislature was helping nobly. It had appropriated $500,000, to be used in erecting the Central Park building. An enduring lease had been drafted by Joseph Hodges Choate. This Museum trustee was one of the most important lawyers of his day, a future Ambassador to Great Britain, and the most popular of after-dinner speakers, noted for his humanitarian and cultural endeavors.

The City of New York owned the new Museum building and, unless it was damaged by fire, would keep it in repair. The Museum was to be the building's only tenant, owning all the collections in it. In turn the Museum promised to be open from ten a.m. "until half an hour before sunset, on four days in the week, and on all legal or public holidays except Sundays, free of charge, and on the remaining days on such terms of admission as they saw fit, provided that professors and teachers of the public schools of the city or other free institutions of learning in the city should be admitted to every privilege of the Museum granted to any other persons." The legislature passed an act enabling the city to appropriate $30,000 to help the Museum move and make the structure in the park habitable. Without this sum the Museum, although it had kept the building costs within the half million appropriated for construction, would not have been able to move.

And the move was made at last to that single, stark, cathedral-like edifice on the Deer Park land, a big, gambrel-roofed, lavishly skylighted, gas-lighted, chimney-studded, ruddy-stoned structure whose glittering windows were surmounted by decorations of massive stone slabs like gigantic raised eyebrows. The days of the trustee-committee-run Museum were over, fading ever more swiftly as cart after cart trundled away, each vehicle so painstakingly loaded by the men who had gathered these treasures into the Museum that not a single breakage occurred.

The high-heaped wagons and vans jogged into the future along smooth, rich avenues and up roads as rutted and bucolic as any in country places. Their destination was a tomorrow none of them would know, a Museum in which well over four hundred thousand objects would occupy endless, ever-changing galleries and rooms. An Egyptian temple thousands of years old would rise at one end of this Museum, and a special building housing the arts of the ancient cultures of Oceania, Africa, and the Americas at the other. And far to the north, on a hilltop overlooking the Hudson River valley, would stand The Cloisters, a fine patchwork of medieval monuments and modern construction crammed with medieval riches, almost all given by a Rockefeller. At least a thousand schoolchildren would be bused each day to the Museum. How the original founders would have rejoiced at *that*. But above all, these determined men would have understood, with a quiet amusement and slightly rueful appreciation, that the creation of a living museum, the Metropolitan Museum of Art in New York, is a continuum, forever a beginning.

OPPOSITE: General Louis Palma di Cesnola, first Director of the Museum, 1879–1904. BORDER: motifs from the Cesnola Cypriote Collection.

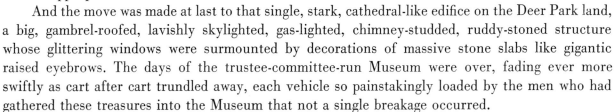
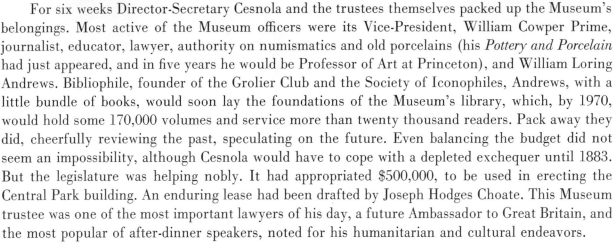

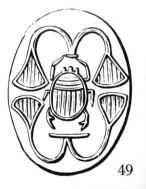

*Auction Sale in Clinton Hall, New York City, 1876.* Ignacio de León y Escosura, Spanish, 1834–1901. Oil. Gift of the artist, 1883.

ABOVE AND RIGHT: *Return from the Hunt* and *Hunting Scene*.
Piero di Cosimo, Italian, 1462–1521?. Gift of Robert Gordon, 1875.

*Landscape: Scene from "Thanatopsis."* Asher Brown Durand, American, 1796–1886. Oil. Gift of J. Pierpont Morgan, 1911. The painting was inspired by William Cullen Bryant's poem.

ABOVE: Interior views, *The Metropolitan Museum in 14th Street*, dated 1881, and (OPPOSITE) *Entrance Hall, the Metropolitan Museum When in 14th Street*. Both by Frank Waller, American, 1842–1923. Oils. Purchases, 1920 and 1895.

ROOM H.

Frank Waller
1881

ΠΟΛΥΜΝΙΑ

ABOVE: Cover of a brochure for the Industrial Arts classes established in 1880. ABOVE RIGHT: *The Daily Graphic* recorded activities in the woodworking and metalwork classes. RIGHT: John Jacob Astor, an early Benefactor of the Museum.

OPPOSITE: *Polyhymnia, Muse of Lyric Poetry* (Mrs. Francis C. Barlow). Joseph Fagnani, American, 1819–1873. Oil. Gift of an Association of Gentlemen, 1873. Mrs. Barlow, née Ellen Shaw, was one of nine American debutantes who posed for Fagnani's portraits of the muses.

LEFT: Impression of the seal stone from an engraved carnelian ring, which shows Eros carrying a girl. Fifth century B.C. ABOVE: Chariot. Detail of a Mycenaean Krater, 1400–1375 B.C. Both Cesnola Collection.

ABOVE: Part of the Cesnola Collection of Cypriote antiquities, purchased by popular subscription, 1874–1876, on display in the Museum. RIGHT: Early Kassite cylinder seal, sixteenth/fifteenth century B.C., in the Cesnola Collection. FAR RIGHT: Impression from the seal.

Central Park, 1895. The West Drive near Seventy-second Street. (Photograph by Byron, courtesy Museum of the City of New York)

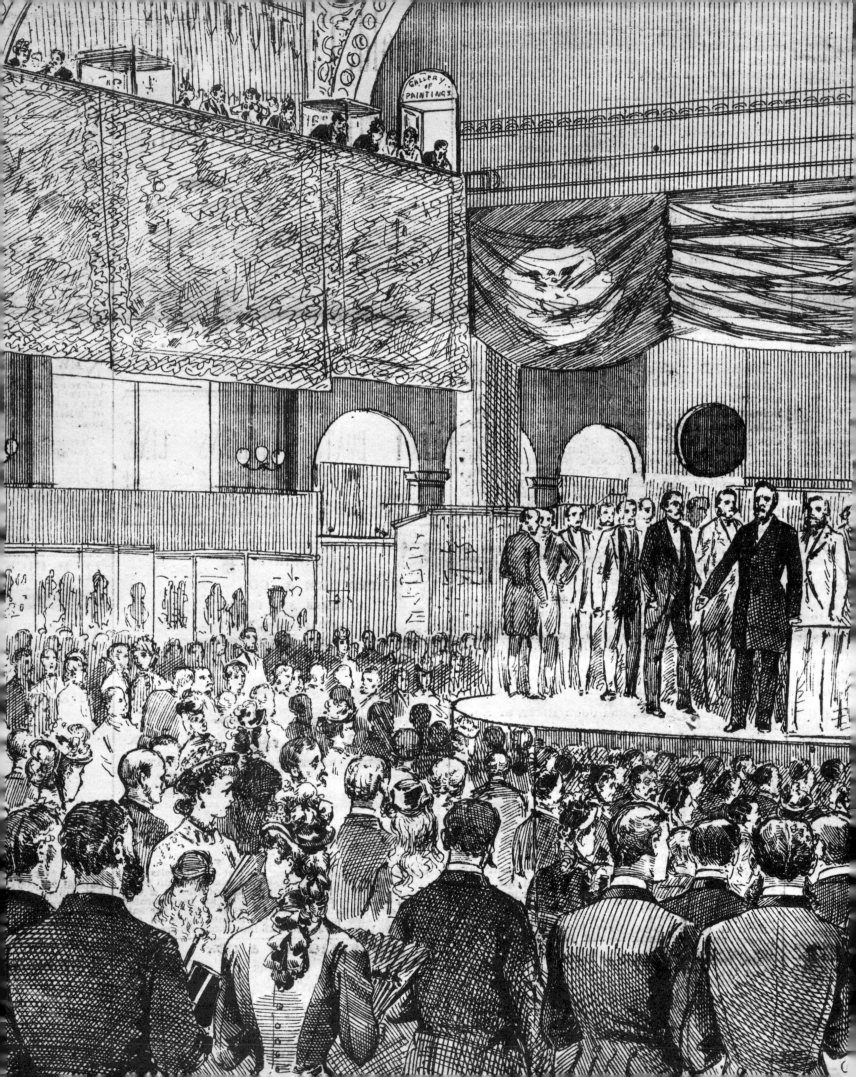

# II
# THE NORTHERN SUBURBS
## 1880–1899

## 1880–1889

It was a decade of grand dedications and gala openings. Paladins of church, state, society, and the arts rushed, silk-hatted and frock-coated, from glorious new institution to institution, proffering prodigious bouquets of homage. The majestic prelude to the decade's joyful solemnities sounded on May 25, 1879, when St. Patrick's Cathedral, its exterior reminiscent of Cologne's cathedral, its interior of Amiens', officially opened its neo-Gothic portals on Fifth Avenue. Then, on February 22, 1881, George Washington's one hundred and forty-ninth birthday, thousands gathered in Central Park, just west of the new Museum building, to view the presentation of "Cleopatra's Needle." Originally erected in ancient Heliopolis, the Romans re-erected it in Alexandria. And now the good will of the Khedive of Egypt, who gave this gift to the City of New York, plus almost $100,000 from William H. Vanderbilt for the "Needle's" transport, skillful piloting by Lieutenant Commander Gorringe of the United States Navy, and technical and artistic advice from the Metropolitan Museum of Art (which was rewarded by the Lieutenant Commander with two of the Roman crabs that had once supported the obelisk), combined to make New Yorkers feel that the city was, indeed, becoming cosmopolitan, almost like London or Paris.

Not a month passed without a glittering function, each pointing the way to an even more golden future. President Chester A. Arthur, Governor Grover Cleveland, and battalions of dignitaries opened the Brooklyn Bridge. It was the longest in the world, the first to use steel cables, and someone even declared that "it was a perfect work of art." Mr. William Henry Vanderbilt, rebuffed by old-guard New York society, now retaliated by taking it over. When the Metropolitan Opera House, financed by Vanderbilts, Jay Gould, Henry Clews, and others, opened on the evening of October 22, 1883, the new plutocracy was there *and* the old (Astors, Belmonts, Goelets), people whose total wealth was said to amount to over $500,000,000. The William K. Vanderbilts gave a costume-ball housewarming to inaugurate their new Fifth Avenue Richard Morris Hunt château (Blois was its inspiration), and Mrs. Astor had to ask for an invitation. New York had its first cable cars, electric lights, and bullfights. It had its Great Blizzard of 1888, and its bitter depression of 1886. Its first skyscraper, silk merchant John L. Stearns' thirteen-story Tower Building at 50 Broadway, withstood a hurricane in 1889, and in a year the sixteen-story Pulitzer Building opened close to Brooklyn Bridge's Manhattan terminal. And from 1886, "Miss Liberty," as the French

OPPOSITE: President Hayes addressing the fashionable throng at the opening ceremony. (Illustration from *The Daily Graphic*)

# Metropolitan Museum of Art,

## CENTRAL PARK.

## ORDER OF THE CEREMONY

OF OPENING THE MUSEUM.

### On Tuesday, the 30th of March, 1880,
At 3.30 P. M.

1st.—Prayer, by - - The Rev. Henry C. Potter, D. D.

2d.—Delivery of the Building to the Trustees, by the President of the Public Parks, - - Mr. James F. Wenman.

3d.—Acceptance of the Building on behalf of the Trustees, by the President of the Museum, Mr. John Taylor Johnston.

4th.—Address on the History and Future Plans of the Museum, by - - - - - Mr. Joseph H. Choate.

5th.—The President of the United States declares the Metropolitan Museum of Art, open.

The Band will play till half-past six o'clock, while the assembled company view the halls and contents of the Museum.

*The doors of the Museum will be closed at 6.30 P. M.*

ABOVE AND RIGHT: Pages from the official program.

*Guide Books to the various Departments of Art are now ready, and others in course of preparation.*

## Situation of the Museum.

The Museum is in Central Park, and fronts East on Fifth Avenue and Eighty-second Street, and West on the carriage drive in the Park, which skirts the East side of the Reservoir.

The Museum may be reached by this carriage drive in the Park, by the horse railroad of the Fourth and Madison Avenues, or by the Elevated Railroad on Third Avenue, from the station at 84th Street.

The Museum will be open to the public on the first of April.

Admission will be free on four days in the week, namely, on Wednesday, Thursday, Friday and Saturday, from 10.30 A. M. to 6 P. M.

On Monday and Tuesday an entrance fee of Fifty cents will be charged, except to members and holders of tickets.

L. P. di CESNOLA,
*Director.*

*P. S.—In order to display properly the pictures so liberally lent to the Museum for the opening Loan Exhibition, it has been found necessary to remove temporarily from the walls a number of the Pictures owned by the Museum and to devote the East Wall of the East Picture Gallery to the Works of the late Wm. M. Hunt.*

The first Museum building in Central Park, as it was in 1880.

people's 225-ton, 305-feet-1-inch gift to the Americans was lovingly named, stood, torch in hand, lighting the way for the immigrant hordes pouring in—more than twice as many immigrants as in any two consecutive previous decades.

The new plutocracy, the old guard, and the immigrants—one New York institution involved them all and even intermingled them closely. The Metropolitan Museum of Art, its trustees representative of the first two social strata, opened its doors wide to the third. And these doors were very new in March 1880 when the Museum was at last permanently installed in the Park. The press came on March 29, for a private view. The official opening was a day later, at three-thirty in the afternoon, after a reception and one o'clock luncheon given by John Taylor Johnston at his marble mansion. " 'Can you believe it?' cried one dignified trustee to another, slapping him heartily on the back. 'Can you realize that the thing really exists?' " Some four thousand people crowded into the still unfinished building and saw that it not only existed but that it was well-prepared to flourish. Joseph H. Choate assured them of this in his address, "The History and Future Plans of the Museum."

On March 30, 1880, the *New York Evening Post* gave a shrewd appraisal of Press Day and Opening Day in the Park: "The formal proceedings throughout were notable for the absence of all the vain glory and boasting which are sometimes thought to be inseparable from Yankee oratory, the modest, simple, and yet sufficient words in which President Hayes declared the institution to be open for the purposes of 'free, popular art education' being in entire accord with all the pre-ceding exercises." On March 29 the *Post* had reported,

> The Hanging Committee had done the most remarkable and admirable work ever seen in this country at a public exhibition of paintings. The features of this work are con-spicuously two: the system of bold or delicate and suggestive balancings, and the com-mingling of Americans and foreigners without respect to persons. You walk through the two large western galleries and you feel that American art is not so bad after all, because you see that it stands up like a man by the side of its fellows and neither blushes nor faints. . . . The eye is really not shocked to find a Gérôme balancing an Eastman Johnson, a Troyon balancing a William Magrath, a Bouguereau balancing a Henry A. Loop.

So the 1871 purchase of 174 paintings was to be seen along with a special exhibition of fifty-five works by the late William Morris Hunt: his *Girl at a Fountain* would become part of the Museum's collection in 1908. And there was a dazzling loan collection of over 250 paintings from almost one hundred collectors, including ten celebrated canvases from William H. Vanderbilt's more than one-and-a-half-million-dollar collection. James Jackson Jarves had written, "it has be-come the mode to have taste. Private galleries in New York are becoming almost as common as stables." Mr. Vanderbilt had both a gallery and stables, and when it came to the Metropolitan Museum of Art he had a generous heart. Here, "under that immense roof which from the outside is so suggestive of a hothouse," was General Cesnola's Cypriote collection and in "long rows of glass cases . . . loaned curiosities in porcelains, manuscripts, missals, gold ornaments, *repoussé* and chased work, carvings, bronzes, Limoges enamels, and what not." There was more, much more, and all of it fascinating to the congratulatory first-day public. "You can take any standard work on Cyprus, Greece, Italy or Japan, and pick out your own illustrations for it in the Metropolitan Museum," exulted the *New York Evening Post* on that frigid, howling March day in 1880. And during the next six months Cesnola noted 295,872 pleased visitors, "as reported to me by a policeman who counted them."

Now that the Museum was both permanent and popular, gifts and bequests became increasingly frequent. The first bequest (in 1881) was $50,000 worth of "Curiosities, Antiquities, and Works of Art" from Trustee S. Whitney Phoenix. The first money bequest in the Museum's history came in 1883 and totaled more than $100,000. It came from Levi Hale Willard, a New York businessman, who willed that it be "applied to the purchase of a collection of models, casts, photographs, engravings, and other objects illustrative of the art and science of architecture." When augmented three years later by a $10,000 gift from banker Henry Gurdon Marquand (the Museum's second president, 1889), the Willard bequest founded the Museum's enormous models and casts collection. Trustee Cornelius Vanderbilt (grandson of the Commodore) bought James Jackson Jarves's collection of almost seven hundred old-master drawings which he immediately gave to the Museum. At the A. T. Stewart sale, on March 25, 1887, Vanderbilt paid $35,000 for Lot #217, and in consequence the Museum received Rosa Bonheur's *The Horse Fair*. As recently as 1946, Curator of Paintings Harry B. Wehle wrote, "Few if any of the Museum's paintings have had such wide popularity together with solid claims to the respect of connoisseurs." Lot #210, in the Stewart sale, went to Judge Henry Hilton for $66,000, and soon the Museum displayed another internationally celebrated acquisition, Meissonier's *Friedland, 1807*. From Jarves the Museum joyfully received his collection of antique Venetian glass, some of which was recently authenticated as antique French, and from Marquand, the hundreds of Syrian and Roman pieces in the Charvet Collection of Ancient Glass. Thomas Eakins gave his oil painting *The Chess Players*, and William Loring Andrews bestowed his ample accumulation of Seymour Haden and James A. Whistler etchings which became the Print Department nucleus.

The Museum's Egyptian collection began substantially with the sale of Cesnola Cypriote duplicates to Governor Leland Stanford of California, the funds received from this being spent for antiquities which the Egyptian government was selling off as duplicates from the Museum at Boulac. Now the Metropolitan Museum showed Egyptian treasures such as could be seen nowhere else in the world save at Boulac. Lucy W. Drexel, because her late husband, John, wished it, added over two thousand Egyptian, Greek, and Near Eastern objects, and forty-three ancient musical instruments. Mrs. John Crosby Brown, having been charmed into becoming one of the most avid collectors of musical instruments by the sound of a flute in the streets of Florence one day, now gave the Museum 270 remarkable examples. Subsequently Mrs. Brown and her son brought their entire gift to over three thousand items, and the Museum possesses perhaps the world's most comprehensive instrument collection. John Jacob Astor gave Mrs. Astor's laces (at her request), and the Museum was inundated for decades with gifts of extraordinary laces, embroideries, textiles, and costumes. Miniatures, precious boxes, other *objets d'art* in gold, crystal, enamel came from the Misses Sarah and Josephine Lazarus, and the Museum purchased a treasury of Babylonian and Assyrian cylinders and seals from their eminent collector, Dr. William Hayes Ward.

But an art museum in the days before J. P. Morgan gave his great decorative art gift (after 1900) meant paintings and statuary; drawings, engravings, etchings, prints, and classical antiquities. The taste of the times is best represented by three collections the Museum received during the late Eighties. From George Ingraham Seney, lawyer, philanthropist, and collector, came twenty contemporary oils, including Carl Marr's *Gossip*, American George Fuller's *And She Was a Witch*, and canvases by such giants of the epoch as Israëls, Mauve, and Millet. But it was the Catharine Lorillard Wolfe collection of 143 paintings, bequeathed in 1887, which epitomizes what art lovers of that day thought most beautiful amongst contemporary works. Miss Wolfe, the only woman on the Museum's original subscribers' list, now became the first woman to make a really magnificent contribution to the Museum's collections. She not only gave Pierre Cot's *The Storm*, Corot's *Ville d'Avray*, her own portrait by Cabanel, and canvases by practically every current fashionable French "master," but also instructed that her paintings be housed in a fireproof gallery and left a $200,000 fund for the care of the works and for additions to the collection, stipulating that they always be "modern oil paintings either by native or foreign artists." With its first self-supporting gift, the Museum later bought "moderns" such as Renoir's *Madame Charpentier and Her Children*, Cézanne's *Poorhouse on the Hill*, Daumier's *Don Quixote*, Goya's *Bullfight*, Delacroix's *Abduction of Rebecca*, Whistler's *Théodore Duret*, Manet's *The Funeral*, and many others, the Wolfe Fund even helping to purchase Monet's *La Terrasse à Sainte Adresse* in 1968.

The era's basic conviction that there was no master like an old master was more than magnificently confirmed, in the decade's very last years, when Henry G. Marquand presented at least thirty-five spectacular examples, including Van Dyck's *James Stuart, Duke of Lennox and Richmond*, Vermeer's *Young Woman with a Water Jug*, works by Hals, and others attributed to Rembrandt, Rubens, and Gainsborough. Among the Marquand gifts was *Saltash*, by that recent old master, J. M. W. Turner. And Turner, an Impressionist precursor, leads directly to the most astonishing gift of paintings received by the Museum in the Eighties: Edouard Manet's *Boy with a Sword* and his *Woman with a Parrot*. Presented by a local eclectic collector, Erwin Davis, these Manets were the first to enter any American public collection. Along with the Manets came a third gift from Mr. Davis, Jules Bastien-Lepage's typically Seventies-Eighties *Joan of Arc*, which today astounds Museum visitors even more than the Manets.

With these gifts, bequests, and purchases, plus many others too numerous to mention, the constant Museum problems of space and personnel (but, paradoxically, not funds—the Museum was not in debt from 1882 to 1889) grew increasingly acute. The Museum was also embarked on such cherished projects as an industrial art collection (which failed) and the industrial art schools. The latter, aided financially by $50,000 from a public-spirited Massachusetts man and by the expertise and time of Edward C. Moore of Tiffany and Company, triumphed for over a decade, ultimately employing thirteen teachers to instruct young people and adults, workers, and teachers "in Color; Design; Modeling; Free-hand, Architectural, Cabinet, and Mechanical Drawing" and all sorts of allied fields, including carriage drafting and plumbing. With a $500 appropriation, the Museum art library was officially founded, and William Loring Andrews, bibliophile and trustee, became the first librarian. By 1883, the library had an endowment fund of $5000 from Heber R. Bishop, who later gave the Museum his huge collection of jades and other Chinese objects as well as a replica of his ballroom in which to house them.

Trustees' meetings were long throughout the Eighties: there was always so much to be done. The loan exhibits project, for example, took an unprecedented turn in 1884 when George Frederick Watts, R. A., sent a sizable sampling of his works from London, at the request of "several gentlemen," to the Museum. This was the first international loan exhibition ever held in America, and so many came to view it that it had to be held over for an additional six months. In May 1886 American contemporary art took over at the Museum when the Society of American Artists held its Eighth Annual Exhibit and Sale. The first big showing of modern American art consisted of 120 canvases and some sculpture, and only the new, iconoclastic generation was on view: Hassam, Sargent, Ryder, Thayer, Saint-Gaudens, Chase, La Farge, and Weir. Revolution was in the air, and, while some of the trustees did not pretend to like what they saw, almost all of them felt that the Museum was obligated to permit the public to see and make up its own mind.

The Museum's possessions and activities proliferated. In 1880 the property value of the collections was about $480,000; in 1888, the Museum's collections were valued at over $2,250,000. The time had come to break the Museum up into departments, all under the over-all supervision of Director Cesnola, who worked closely with the trustees. Curator George H. Story headed the new Department of Paintings; Curator Isaac H. Hall, the Department of Sculpture; and Curator John A. Paine, the Department of Casts. There were now additional helpers throughout the Museum. There was also a telephone; the first typewritten letter had been dispatched; electric light was installed. There was even a new wing to the south, Wing B, and a new entrance to the whole building. A still newer wing (C) was under way to the north. There was a new president, Henry G. Marquand, while John T. Johnston had been elected Honorary President. A general endowment fund had been created by William H. Vanderbilt's bequest. New men were on the Museum's Board of Trustees, men important in the Museum's future: Darius Ogden Mills, J. P. Morgan, Robert W. de Forest.

In Edith Wharton's *The Age of Innocence*, her chronicle of New York high society at just about this period, Newland Archer, scion of old New York, arranges an assignation with Ellen Olenska in "the Art Museum in the Park":

> Avoiding the popular Wolfe Collection, whose anecdotic canvases filled one of the main galleries of the queer wilderness of cast-iron and encaustic tiles known as the Metropolitan Museum, they had wandered down a passage to the room where the Cesnola antiquities mouldered in unvisited loneliness.
>
> They had this melancholy retreat to themselves, and seated on the divan enclosing the central steam-radiator, they were staring silently at the glass cabinets mounted in ebonized wood which contained the recovered fragments of Ilium.
>
> "It's odd," Madame Olenska said, "I never came here before."
>
> "Ah, well –. Some day, I suppose, it will be a great Museum. . . ."

## 1890–1899

The Museum's third decade began with a conflict of such violence that it pitted trustees against one another and set the whole city to taking sides. The cause of the altercation was as old as the Museum itself. Should the Museum open on Sundays? This question involved religion, morality, money, and the Museum's basic purpose. The Lord's Day was inviolable, kept that way by strict attendance to churchly duties, enormous Sunday dinners, and a barrage of blue laws which forbade stage plays, athletic contests, and even secular concerts. Ranged against Museum open Sundays were all who considered the institution more a place of amusement than education: the American Sabbath Union, the Presbytery of New York, the Ladies' Christian Union, the New York East Conference of the Methodist Episcopal Church, many clergymen of all denominations, and some trustees who also feared that open Sundays would alienate possible Museum benefactors. Other trustees argued that keeping the Museum open would fulfill original intentions while working for the religious, moral, social, and aesthetic good of every New Yorker. The most powerful state and city departments and boards wanted it, even increasing appropriations to help defray expenses or threatening to withhold funds should the Museum not open on Sundays. Newspapers howled for it, holding high cartoon carnival at the expense of the trustees, and the *New York World*, Pulitzer's

VOL. XXIV.—No. 617.  NEW YORK, JANUARY 2, 1889.  PRICE, TEN CENTS.

"What fools these Mortals be!"

Puck

KEPPLER & SCHWARZMANN, Publishers..  COPYRIGHT, 1888, BY KEPPLER & SCHWARZMANN.  PUCK BUILDING, Cor. Houston & Mulberry Sts.

## THE METROPOLITAN MUSEUM.

"It is intended as much for the humblest artisan as for the most refined lover of the fine arts."—*Henry G. Marquand.*

And this is how the workingman enjoys the Museum on his only day of liberty. — *PUCK.*

newspaper, even offered $2500 to help pay Sunday costs. But most of all eighty thousand citizens petitioned for it, thirty thousand of them raising $4000 to help their Museum.

"The people are the chief support of the Museums [the American Museum of Natural History was also involved in the controversy, with its president furiously opposed to opening], and we expect to live in the future as in the past by their bounty," a trustee raged. "Nothing can in my opinion be more shortsighted than to ignore them, to defy their wishes, and to deny to them the full enjoyment of the Museums which they can never have if they are closed all day Sunday."

The trustees remained unsure. Meanwhile the Museum of Fine Arts in Boston and the Cincinnati Museum instituted open Sundays. Finally on May 18, 1891, in a meeting which was more like a series of cloudbursts, the resolution that "the Museum be opened free to the public every Sunday from one p.m. until a half hour before sunset" was reported upon, fought over, voted upon and lost, petitioned personally by the *New York World* and "A Committee of Citizens," reconsidered, and passed. Vice-President William C. Prime, a long-time trustee, resigned; a $50,000 bequest was forfeited; and expenses mounted (mitigated somewhat by an appropriation of $70,000 and income from two pay days) while Director Cesnola, the curators, and all other employees had to be on hand each Sunday afternoon "to answer questions, keep order, and protect the collections." From May 31 to November 15, 1891, an encouraging 150,654 people swarmed into the Museum on Sundays, some thirty per cent of the total attendance from January 1 to November 15 of that year. At first, according to General Cesnola, these ardent art lovers were the kind "to be seen in the Dime Museums on the Bowery." They handled what they could reach, tore at objects, broke them, carried them off. They spat on the floors, ate their lunches where they fancied, and generally cavorted like mobs on a spree. But time and usage eliminated the curiosity seekers, and Sunday afternoons were taken over by the "respectable, law-abiding, and intelligent" workers and young people coming on that day more than on any other.

The Museum settled down, coping with its customary problems which, reflecting the world outside, became ever more complicated. The city was expanding, the Museum was expanding—nothing, it seemed, could stop the progress of either. It was a time of great wealth and wild extravagance. The heavily carved tables of the rich were banked with orchids and loaded with solid gold dishes. Fortunes, more sizable than any the Museum had yet received, were lavished on the weddings of dollar princesses to European titles and on balls at which American plutocrats waltzed and galloped in elaborate cotillions, impersonating the kings and queens of Europe past or even the Spirit of the Electric Light. In Chicago, the Columbian Exhibition blazed a white mirage upon Lake Michigan's shore, while Louis Sullivan, in whose office Frank Lloyd Wright was apprenticed, cried out against the fair's architectural excesses, derived by Richard Morris Hunt and his colleagues from the Renaissance *palazzos* of Venice and Florence and the ancient grandeur that was Greece's and Rome's. "The damage wrought to this country by the Chicago World's Fair will last half a century," Sullivan assured anyone who would listen. It is doubtful that anyone at the Metropolitan Museum of Art, in New York, heard Mr. Sullivan's prophecy, for it went unheeded. Mr. Hunt was the *doyen* of fashionable architects, and he was to design, before he died in 1895, the future Wing D, the Museum's long-awaited Fifth Avenue front.

President Marquand and some of the trustees were genuine connoisseurs; many of them loved works of art; almost all of them were well-to-do, if not fantastically rich; and every one of them knew precisely how much Museum membership could mean culturally and socially. They decided to establish a new membership class and to arrange higher fees for the others. To become a Benefactor required a gift or bequest of $50,000; the combined Patrons and Fellows in Perpetuity

OPPOSITE: *Puck* takes sides.

71

class cost $5000; and a mere thousand dollars made one a Fellow for Life. Really large bequests could even guarantee a certain immortality. By the end of 1893, the Museum benefited from at least eleven thriving funds, including the Vanderbilt; an Astor; one from Mrs. Amelia B. Lazarus, the Jacob H. Lazarus Traveling Scholarship for painters; and the George W. Callum for the purchase of casts. Gifts and bequests augmented existing collections and created new ones: 976 Egyptian and Coptic textiles; 296 Egyptian antiquities; the Stele of Zaut, a remarkable Egyptian treasure; a bounty of Syrian enameled glass and Mohammedan metalwork and decorative objects from Edward C. Moore, president of Tiffany and Company. Fourteen additional old masters came from Henry Gurdon Marquand, who also donated 455 European porcelains and hundreds of other works of art during the decade. Cyrus W. Field gave his collections relating to the laying of the Atlantic cable. The Museum acquired 772 pieces of Japanese pottery; Rodin's *St. John*; an Aztec tile; 166 pieces of arms and armor; 538 classical antiquities; 289 antique spoons; excellent tapestries; Sargent's portrait of Marquand; and two collections most evocative of the fashionable taste of that era, 2138 Japanese textiles and 182 superb pieces of Tiffany glass, all given by the H. O. Havemeyers, who became two of the Museum's greatest benefactors.

The Museum opened its own restaurant and its own bicycle room. This was the heyday of the "wheel," and even Lillian Russell pedaled Central Park on a gold-plated, mother-of-pearl-handled, diamond-ruby-sapphire-and-emerald-studded gift from Diamond Jim Brady. John La Farge, the most famous stained-glass designer of his day, an eminent muralist, easel painter, educator, and experimenter in the arts, gave a series of lectures in the Museum. And in 1894 the loan show of American paintings (140 oils, twenty-one miniatures, all pre-Revolution or no later than fifty years after those Independence-winning years) made art and taste-forming history. Nothing like it had ever been seen before anywhere. The Museum acquired Leutzé's *Washington Crossing the Delaware*, and to some this was like owning a piece of Betsy Ross's original American flag. Already in the collection were Matthew Pratt's *The American School*, a fascinating group portrait of American artists in Benjamin West's London studio; several beautiful Innesses (*Peace and Plenty* being a George A. Hearn gift); and a host of other important American works.

When the North Wing, Wing C, was opened on November 5, 1894, a day of terrible storms (the usual "Museum weather"), it was found that the entire ground floor of this structure, which made the Museum the same size as the British Museum, was to be given up to architectural models and figurative casts. A special committee was involved in securing them. Experts such as Henry Watson Kent of the Slater Museum, Norwich, Connecticut, and Edward Robinson of the Boston Museum (both to be powerful influences in the Metropolitan Museum later) were employed in gathering and advising on the collection, which by 1908 numbered 2607 items. Why were casts so important? Pierre Le Brun, architect, long-time purchasing agent and consultant for the Museum, assembler of the Willard Collection of Architectural Models, suggested an answer in an 1885 report. "Collections of casts are springing up in all the older communities, and they have a completeness and a unity not found possible in museums of originals. Such collections must undoubtedly in the future be the main dependence of our American fine-arts institutions. For although much of value still awaits the spade of the archaeologist . . . we cannot hope to stock [our museums] adequately with antiquities. Chances of acquiring valuable collections of originals are rare . . ."

Arthur Hoeber, in his *Treasures of the Metropolitan Museum*, published in 1899, seemed to agree with Le Brun. "Possibly no one, save the collector, can form any idea of the difficulty and expense attendant upon the obtaining of proper material for a museum in these days." Neither Le Brun nor Hoeber could see the incredible future of the Museum in the next two decades.

OPPOSITE: John Taylor Johnston, first President of the Museum, 1870–1879.

**1880–1889**

Façade of the 1888 addition to the Museum. At the left is "Cleopatra's Needle," the obelisk of Tuthmosis III from the Temple of Heliopolis. Egyptian, eighteenth dynasty. (Photograph by Pach)

ABOVE: The newspaper critics making their rounds. Engraving after a drawing by Clivedinst from *Harper's Weekly*. RIGHT: *Objects of Art from the Louvre*. Blaise Alexandre Desgoffe, French, 1830–1901. Oil. Bequest of Catharine Lorillard Wolfe, 1887, who commissioned the artist to depict some of her favorites.

OPPOSITE: Above left, *Weary*. James Abbott McNeil Whistler, American, 1834–1903. Etching. Gift of William Loring Andrews, 1883, first librarian of the Museum. Above right, *Girl at Fountain*. William Morris Hunt, American, 1824–1879. Oil. Bequest of Miss Jane Hunt, 1908. Below, *Friedland, 1807*. Jean Louis Ernest Meissonier, French, 1815–1891. Oil, dated 1875. Gift of Henry Hilton, 1887.

ABOVE: Case of cuneiform tablet. Ur 111, c. 2100 B.C. Purchase, Ward, 1886. RIGHT: *Henry Gurdon Marquand.* John Singer Sargent, American, 1856–1925. Oil, 1897. Commissioned by the Trustees, 1896. Marquand, second President of the Museum, was one of its greatest early benefactors. BELOW: Glass beaker. Cypriote. Seventh/eighth century. Gift of Henry G. Marquand, 1881. BELOW RIGHT: *A Child with a Cat.* Thomas Gainsborough, British, 1727–1788. Oil. Gift of Henry G. Marquand, 1889.

OPPOSITE: *Portrait of a Man.* Frans Hals. Oil. Gift of Henry G. Marquand, 1890.

JAR IN BLUE AND WHITE.

RING WITH EGYPTIAN DESIGN.

RING WITH CUPIDS.

SILVER OBJECT.

BRACELET WITH LIONS' HEADS.

PHŒNICIAN VASE—BUFF POTTERY DECORATED IN BLACK.

MEDEA

END OF A STONE SARCOPHAGUS.

TERRA-COTTA VASE. FROM DALI.

SIDE OF A STONE SARCOPHAGUS FROM AM

THE METROPOLIT

Pages from *Harper's Weekly* illustrating the main hall and miscellaneous treasures in the collection during the 1880s.

TERRA-COTTA HEADS—FROM TEMPLE OF APOLLO HYLATES.

GOLD OBJECT.

ENGRAVED SIGNETS WITH GOLD SWIVELS.

EGYPTIAN SCARABÆUS WITH SILVER SWIVEL.

JAR IN PALE GREEN.

HALL OF THE BUILDING.—PHOTOGRAPHED BY PACH.

BRACELET WITH ROSETTES.

GRÆCO-PHŒNICIAN VASE IN RED LUSTROUS WARE.

SIDE OF A STONE SARCOPHAGUS FROM AMATHUS.

TERRA-COTTA VASE FOUND IN A TOMB AT AMATHUS.

END OF A STONE SARCOPHAGUS.

FAR LEFT: *The Storm.* Pierre Auguste Cot, French, 1837–1883. Bequest of Catharine Lorillard Wolfe, 1887. Oil, dated 1880. Also known as *Paul and Virginia*, the painting was one of the most popular of the day.

LEFT: *The Crucifixion.* Cornelis Engelbrechtsz., Dutch. 1468–1533. Tempera and oil on wood. Gift of Coudert Brothers, 1888. BELOW LEFT: View of one of the painting galleries in the 1880s. The large painting at the left, *A Rehearsal in the Choir Loft* by Henry Lerolle (1848–1929), is one of the French artist's most important canvases. Oil. Gift of George I. Seney, 1887. BELOW: *Boy with Sword.* Edouard Manet, French, 1832–1883. Oil. Gift of Erwin Davis, 1889.

LEFT: Hunting horn. French, c. 1700. Elephant ivory. The Crosby Brown Collection, 1889. BELOW: *Joan of Arc*. Jules Bastien-Lepage. French, 1848–1884. Oil. Gift of Erwin Davis, 1889.

OPPOSITE: *Woman with a Parrot*. Manet. Oil. Gift of Erwin Davis, 1889.

LEFT: *Chess Players*. Thomas Eakins, American, 1844–1916. Oil on wood, dated 1876. Gift of the artist, 1881. BELOW: View of the Marquand Gallery, 1907, displaying many of the old masters given to the Museum by its second president during the 1880s.

ABOVE: *Ville D'Avray*. Jean Baptiste Camille Corot, French, 1796–1875. Oil. Bequest of Catharine Lorillard Wolfe, 1887. RIGHT: *George Washington*. Gilbert Stuart, American, 1755–1828. Oil. Painted 1803. Gift of H. O. Havemeyer, 1888.

OVERLEAF: A bird's-eye view of the inauguration of the Brooklyn Bridge on May 24, 1883, with a display of fireworks, as represented in a lithograph published by A. Major. The Edward W. C. Arnold Collection of New York Prints, Maps, and Pictures. Bequest of Edward W. C. Arnold, 1954.

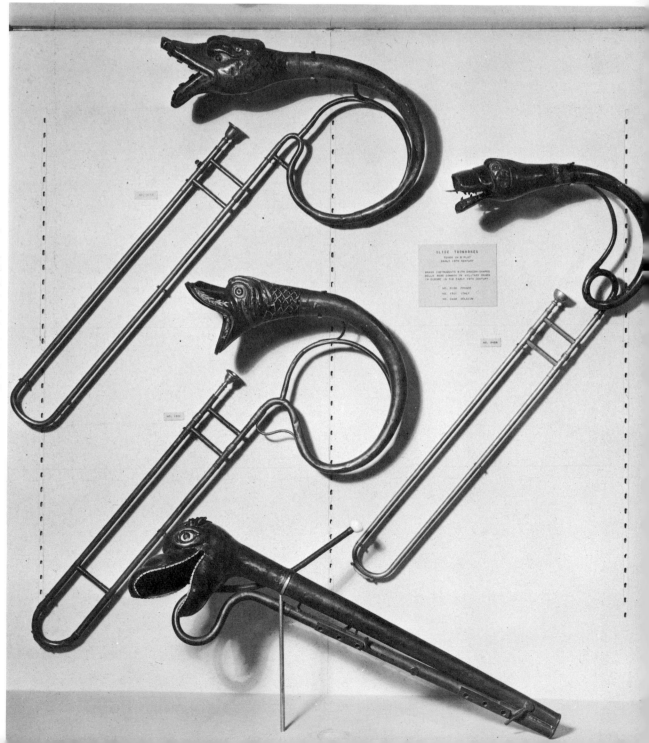

ABOVE: *Pochette d'amore* (detail). German, c. 1700. ABOVE RIGHT: Harpsichord. Girolamo Zenti, Italian, 1658. Purchase, 1886. ABOVE, FAR RIGHT: Harpsichord with gilded figures showing Galatea and Polyphemus. Italian, seventeenth century. RIGHT: A group of early nineteenth-century instruments. The bass horn is French, c. 1800; and the trombones (top to bottom) are French, Belgian, and Italian. All are from the Crosby Brown Collection, gifts of Mrs. John Crosby Brown in 1899.

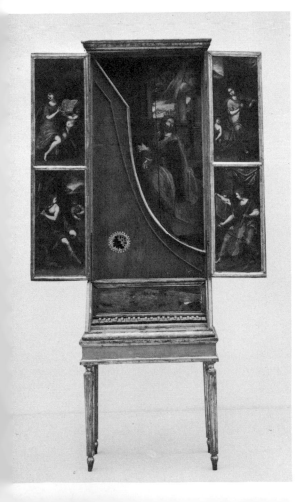

TOP LEFT: Harpsichord. Joannes Couchet. Flemish, c. 1650. CENTER LEFT: Shamanic rattle. Northwest American Indian. BOTTOM LEFT: Clavicytherium. Italian, early seventeenth century. Gifts of Mrs. John Crosby Brown, 1899. BELOW: *James Stuart, Duke of Richmond and Lennox (1612–1655)*. Anthony van Dyck. Oil. Gift of Henry G. Marquand, 1889.

## 1890–1899

Immigrants on the steerage deck of the S.S. Pennland of the Red Star Line, 1893. In one New York institution—the Museum—the new immigrants, the old guard, and the plutocracy were all involved, and even mingled closely. Photograph by Byron, courtesy Museum of the City of New York.

LEFT: *Portrait of a Man*. Rembrandt Harmensz. van Ryn, Dutch, 1606–1669. Oil. Gift of Henry G. Marquand, 1890. ABOVE: *Triumph of Bacchus*. Coptic tapestry panel, third century A.D. From Akhmim. Gift of George F. Baker, 1890. Wool and linen. BELOW: Roman sarcophagus, first century A.D. Marble. Purchase, 1890.

OPPOSITE: Terra-cotta amphora; black-ribbed body; medallions in relief, white ivy bands. Greek (Hellenistic) from Hadra, Alexandria; third century B.C. Purchase, 1890.

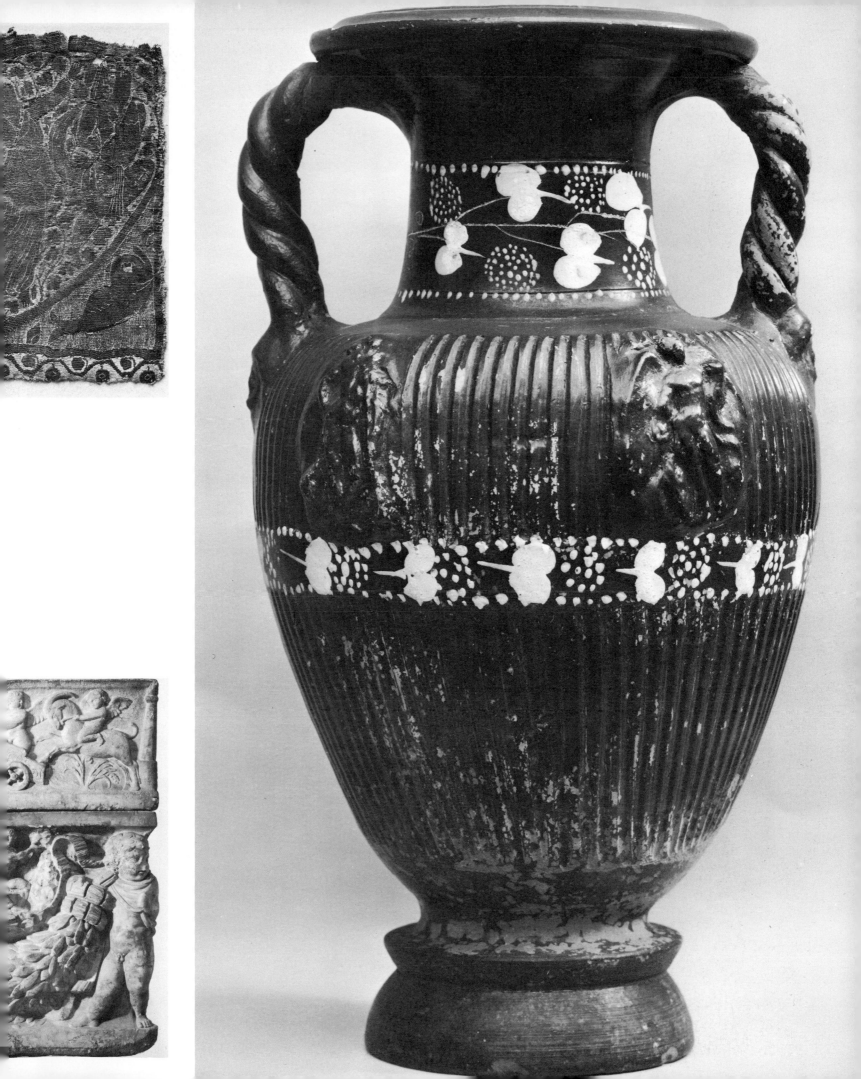

*Simon Lord Lovat*

*Drawn from the Life and Etch'd in Aquafortis by Will.^m Hogarth.*

price 1 Shilling

Publish'd according to Act of Parliament. August 25^th 1746.

BELOW: Brass ewer, inlaid with copper and silver. Egypto-Arabic, Mamluk Period, fourteenth century. RIGHT: Detail of a pair of wood doors inlaid with ivory. Egyptian, late thirteenth or early fourteenth century. Bequests of Edward C. Moore, 1891.

OPPOSITE: *Simon, Lord Lovat*. William Hogarth, English, 1697–1764. Etching, 1746. Gift of Sarah Lazarus, 1891.

ABOVE: *The Music Lesson*. Gabriel Metsu, Dutch, 1629–1667. Oil, dated 1659. Gift of Henry G. Marquand, 1890. ABOVE RIGHT: Tiffany glass vase. New York, 1875–1896. Gift of H. O. Havemeyer, 1896.

OPPOSITE, ABOVE, LEFT TO RIGHT: Iranian seventeenth-century wine bottle, luster on blue glaze. Egyptian fourteenth-century brass stand inlaid with copper and silver. Egyptian fifteenth-century underglaze-painted pottery mosque lamp, signed by Ibn al Gaibi al Tawrizi. All bequests of Edward C. Moore, 1891. OPPOSITE: A view of the Edward C. Moore Collection.

BELOW: Cinerary urn. Etruscan, third century B.C. Purchase, 1896. RIGHT: *Head of a Quarryman.* Alphonse Legros, French, 1837–1911. Red chalk drawing. Gift of the artist, 1892. BELOW RIGHT: Aztec tile. Painted terra cotta. Gift of Frederick E. Church, 1893.

LEFT: Parade in honor of Infanta Eulalia, June 3, 1893. The famous and the fashionable were celebrated on Fifth Avenue, and most of them visited the Museum. Photograph by Byron, courtesy Museum of the City of New York.

ABOVE: Architect Richard Morris Hunt (1827–1895). LEFT: The World's Columbian Exposition in Chicago, 1893, forecast Hunt's taste as it was expressed in the Museum's Fifth Avenue façade (BELOW).

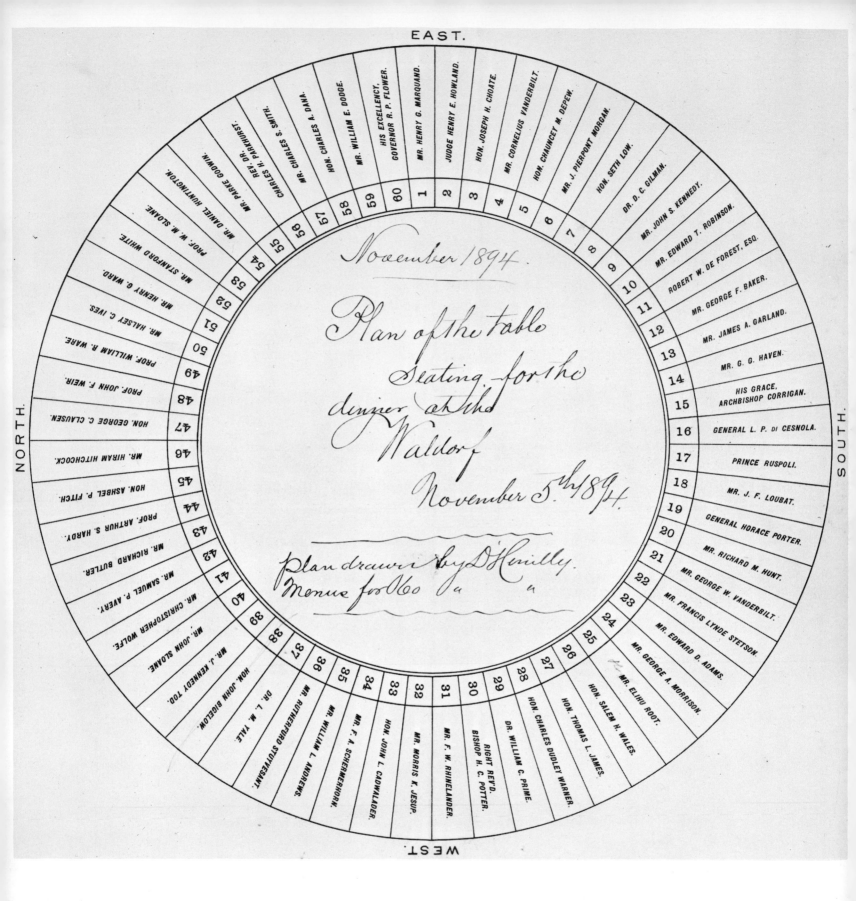

EAST.

MR. PARKE GODWIN.
REV. DR. PARKHURST.
CHARLES H. SMITH.
MR. CHARLES A. DANA.
HON. CHARLES A. DANA.
MR. WILLIAM E. DODGE.
HIS EXCELLENCY, GOVERNOR R. P. FLOWER.
MR. HENRY G. MARQUAND.
JUDGE HENRY E. HOWLAND.
HON. JOSEPH H. CHOATE.
MR. CORNELIUS VANDERBILT.
HON. CHAUNCEY M. DEPEW.
MR. J. PIERPONT MORGAN.
HON. SETH LOW.

DR. D. C. GILMAN.
MR. JOHN S. KENNEDY.
MR. EDWARD T. ROBINSON.
ROBERT W. DE FOREST, ESQ.
MR. GEORGE F. BAKER.
MR. JAMES A. GARLAND.
MR. G. G. HAVEN.
HIS GRACE, ARCHBISHOP CORRIGAN.
GENERAL L. P. DI CESNOLA.
PRINCE RUSPOLI.
MR. J. F. LOUBAT.
GENERAL HORACE PORTER.
MR. RICHARD M. HUNT.
MR. GEORGE W. VANDERBILT.
MR. FRANCIS LYNDE STETSON.
MR. EDWARD D. ADAMS.
MR. GEORGE A. MORRISON.
MR. ELIHU ROOT.
HON. SALEM H. WALES.
HON. THOMAS L. JAMES.
HON. CHARLES DUDLEY WARNER.
DR. WILLIAM C. PRIME.
RIGHT REV'D. BISHOP H. C. POTTER.
MR. F. W. RHINELANDER.
HON. JOHN L. CADWALADER.
MR. MORRIS K. JESUP.
MR. F. A. SCHERMERHORN.
MR. WILLIAM L. ANDREWS.
MR. RUTHERFURD STUYVESANT.
DR. L. M. YALE.
HON. JOHN BIGELOW.
MR. J. KENNEDY TOD.
MR. JOHN SLOANE.
MR. CHRISTOPHER WOLFE.
MR. SAMUEL P. AVERY.
MR. RICHARD BUTLER.
PROF. ARTHUR S. HARDY.
HON. ASHBEL P. FITCH.
MR. HIRAM HITCHCOCK.
HON. GEORGE C. CLAUSEN.
PROF. JOHN F. WEIR.
PROF. WILLIAM R. WARE.
MR. HALSEY C. IVES.
MR. HENRY G. WARD.
MR. STANFORD WHITE.
PROF. W. M. SLOANE.
MR. DANIEL HUNTINGTON.

*November 1894.*

*Plan of the table*
*Seating for the*
*dinner at the*
*Waldorf*
*November 5th 1894.*

*plan drawn by D. Huntly.*
*Menus for 60 " " "*

NORTH.

SOUTH.

WEST.

ABOVE: Seating plan for the trustees' dinner honoring the opening of the North Wing.

OPPOSITE: Above left, *John the Baptist*. Auguste Rodin, French, 1840–1917. Gift of Samuel P. Avery, 1893. Above right, invitation to the inauguration of the new wing. Below, street scene, Riverside Drive, about 1894. Cycling was so popular the Museum opened its own bicycle room.

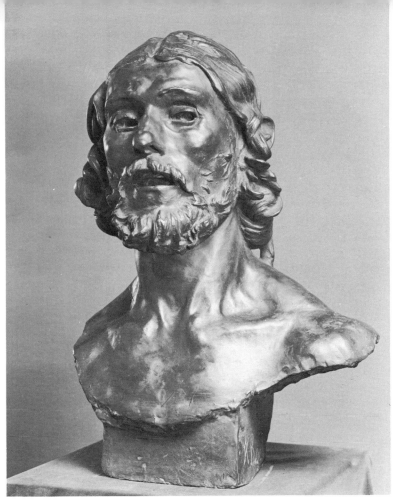

*The Birth of Venus.* Cabanel. Oil, dated 1875. Gift of John Wolfe, 1893.

ABOVE: *The Funding Bill.* Eastman Johnson. Oil, dated 1881. Gift of Robert Gordon, 1898. RIGHT: Antique bronzes given by Henry G. Marquand. Illustrations from *Harper's Weekly.*

LEFT: Onlookers at the Gould-Castellane wedding in 1894. BELOW LEFT: A Havemeyer party arriving at the Claremont Inn. BELOW: Mrs. Cornelius Vanderbilt's house at Fifth Avenue and Fifty-eighth Street. It was a time of great wealth and extravagance. Society was lavish with itself and the Museum.

ABOVE: *In the Catskills*. Thomas Cole, American, 1801–1848. Oil on canvas. Gift in memory of Jonathan Sturges by his children, 1895. BELOW: Ladies' luncheon at Delmonico's, 1902. (Courtesy Museum of the City of New York)

*Peace and Plenty*. George Inness. Oil, dated 1865. Gift of George A. Hearn, 1894. BELOW: Richard Morris Hunt's proposed master plan for the future growth of the Museum.

George Inness (Courtesy The Century Club)

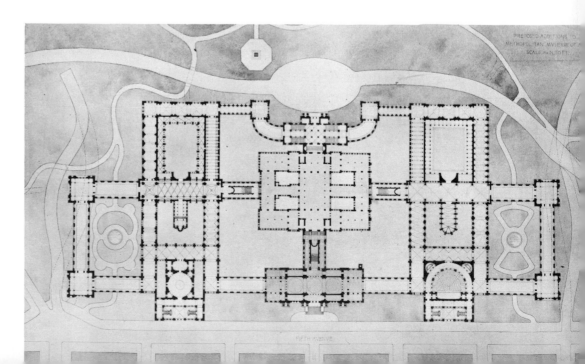

LEFT: *General Andrew Jackson (1767–1845)*. Hiram Powers. Marble, c. 1835. Gift of Mrs. Frances V. Nash, 1894. RIGHT: *Portrait of the Artist*. Thomas Sully, American, 1783–1872. Oil, dated 1821. Gift of Mrs. Rosa C. Stanfield, in memory of her father, Henry Robinson, 1894. BELOW: *The American School*. Matthew Pratt. American, 1734–1805. Painted in 1765 in Benjamin West's London studio. Oil. Gift of Samuel P. Avery, 1897.

*Grand Canal, Venice.* J. M. W. Turner, British, 1775–1851. Oil. Bequest of Cornelius Vanderbilt, 1899.

OPPOSITE: *Last Moments of John Brown.* Thomas Hovenden, American, 1840–1895. Oil. Gift of Mr. and Mrs. Carl Stoeckel, 1897. RIGHT: *A Boat on the Shore.* Gustave Courbet, French, 1819–1877. Oil. Gift of Mary Goldenberg, 1899. BELOW: *Pine Grove of the Villa Barberini, Albano.* George Inness. Oil. Gift of Lyman G. Bloomingdale, 1898.

ABOVE: Stela from the tomb of Zauti, Dendereh. Egyptian, sixth to eighth centuries. Limestone. Gift of the Egyptian Exploration Fund, 1898. RIGHT: *In the Woods.* Durand. Signed and dated 1855. Gift in memory of Jonathan Sturges by his children, 1895. BELOW: A quiet corner of the Museum in the late 1890s with, at right, a partial view of Emanuel Leutze's *Washington Crossing The Delaware*, one of the prize acquisitions of the decade.

*Young Woman with a Water Jug.* Johannes Vermeer, Dutch, 1632–1675. Oil. Gift of Henry G. Marquand, 1889.

ABOVE: The Rospigliosi Cup. Attributed to Benvenuto Cellini, Italian (Florentine), 1500–1571. Gold, enamel, pearls. Bequest of Benjamin Altman, 1913. OPPOSITE: Baptism, detail from The Seven Sacraments. Tournai. The workshop of Pasquier Grenier. Flemish, third quarter of the fifteenth century. Wool and silk tapestry. Gift of J. Pierpont Morgan, 1907.

*Madonna and Child Enthroned with Saints Catherine, Peter, Cecilia, Paul, and the Infant Saint John the Baptist.*
Raphael, Italian (Umbrian) 1483–1520. Tempera on wood. Familiarly known as The Colonna Altarpiece, it was painted for the Convent of Saint Anthony of Padua, Perugia. Gift of J. Pierpont Morgan, 1916.

# III
# THE GOLDEN AGE OF GIVING
## 1900–1939

### 1900–1909

Jacob S. Rogers became a member of the Metropolitan Museum of Art in 1883, paying his $10 fee annually, sometimes appearing in the Museum to do this. He would inquire about how the Museum actually operated, and Director Cesnola, with unusual patience and courtesy, would explain. Then this bearded, quite anonymous person would trudge quietly away. One time, Mr. Rogers asked for a copy of the Museum pamphlet *Charter, Constitution, Lease, and By-Laws*. He received it. On July 5, 1901, he died, and the Museum became the residuary legatee of his estate, estimated at from $5,500,000 to $7,000,000: "The income only of the fund hereby created, or intended so to be, to be used for the purchase of rare and desirable art objects, and in the purchase of books for the Library of said Museum, and for such purposes exclusively; the principal of said fund is not to be sued, diminished, or impaired for any purpose whatever." The mysterious Mr. Rogers, it was now known, came from Paterson, New Jersey, where his locomotive works were established and where he had amassed, by investment, his fortune. He had been a bachelor, and apparently had not owned a single work of art. But by his bequest, he had completely altered the very nature of the Museum.

"It seems like a golden dream," J. Edwards Clarke of the National Bureau of Education wrote to Cesnola. "It is an event on which the whole United States are to be congratulated; for it gives pecuniary independence to the chief art power of the country. What the Trustees and officers of the Museum have already accomplished is like a fairy tale in its splendor. The opportunities that now open before them are simply bewildering." For the first time in its history, the Museum did have millions to spend. And even today the Museum continues to exult in Jacob S. Rogers' unexpected gift. Not so long ago A. Hyatt Mayor, then Curator of Prints, wrote, "It [the Museum] could no longer be managed by a group of art-lovers who gave their time, their money, and their possessions, or persuaded their friends to do likewise. Overnight the Museum found itself a powerful buyer of art, and it had to know what it was buying." Three years after the Museum received its Rogers bequest, on November 21, 1904, John Pierpont Morgan was elected fourth president and the Museum leapt into the vanguard of modern museology.

At sixty-seven, John Pierpont Morgan, reputed to be the richest man in the world, was the most famous American tycoon. He had personally saved the nation from financial catastrophe, and

*J. P. Morgan*
President
1904–1913

he would do it again. The world's most gigantic trust, the billion-dollar United States Steel Corporation, was of his construction. "Pierpontifex Maximus," newspapers named him, while music halls resounded to "Morgan, Morgan, the Great Financial Gorgon." In Europe, they were beginning to call him "The Menace," for in an era when that continent and even Egypt and the East were being pillaged by Americans frantic for art, Morgan was the greatest collector of them all. He sometimes purchased single superb items, but more frequently bought whole collections, because he loved to buy and was especially addicted to the miraculous works created for Renaissance potentates. New England-born, European-educated, raised rich (his father, an Anglo-American banker, had helped arrange the Museum's 1871 paintings purchase), Morgan, even as a very young boy, adored the beautiful and collected bits and pieces of medieval stained glass. Works of unique craftsmanship were his passion, and, after years of acquisition, he could, without exaggeration, tell his son-in-law that the three most costly words he knew were *"unique au monde."* Morgan sought treasures of perfection himself, during his annual London, Paris, and Rome seasons, and later on his Egyptian visits, while masterminding an enormous corps of *cognoscenti:* heads of museums in London and Berlin; dealers; pickers; editors; curators; from 1906 on, his own remarkable librarian and rare-books-and-manuscripts expert, Belle da Costa Greene; and ultimately everyone who worked for the Metropolitan Museum of Art. And it was to that institution he seems to have given his art-loving heart, first as a patron in 1871 and then as a trustee in 1889, almost resigning some years later because of business pressures. Now, as president, he was the most important man in the Museum, and one of the basic motives for his collecting became increasingly evident. "He would gather," writes Aline B. Saarinen in *The Proud Possessors*, "for America an undreamed of collection of art so great and so complete that a trip to Europe would be superfluous. And he would give this vast and splendid compendium to the Metropolitan Museum." He had already started to give in 1897; the final total of his "direct" gifts of objects comes to some eight thousand.

On the evening of November 15, 1905, the autocrat of the Metropolitan Museum stood in the Great Hall of the Fifth Avenue Wing (D), on the huge Oriental carpet laid down for him at all openings and receptions, while over eight thousand people milled about him and the new director, Sir Caspar Purdon Clarke, recently head of London's South Kensington Museum. Nearby was Mr. Robert W. de Forest, a trustee since 1889, soon to be elected Secretary to the Board of Trustees, and the Museum's next president in 1913. He was John Taylor Johnston's son-in-law, and he would, for many years, vigorously link the twentieth-century Metropolitan Museum to its earliest history. The old stalwarts—Cesnola, Marquand, third president Frederick W. Rhinelander, many of the trustees—were as dead as their conservative ways, and the eight thousand had come to view the mighty Morgan and his titled importation. This was the twentieth century, with everything faster, bigger, and richer. The airplane was in the skies; the subway was beginning to clatter beneath the cobbles; some eight thousand automobiles would soon be chugging along roadways; and the First Annual Advertising Show was less than six months away. Saint-Gaudens' naked *Diana* gleamed goldenly from Madison Square Garden's topmost pinnacle, and only fuddy-duddies were shocked. Everyone else said that it was Art and that Mr. Morgan wanted it up there. The Metropolitan Museum, being a Temple of Art, and as Art mirrored Life, as everyone was beginning to believe, it was certain that the Museum under "Pierpontifex Maximus" would become twentieth century more swiftly than many other official or semiofficial institutions. It did.

Morgan ruled the Museum the way he did any of his corporations, involving himself in every executive, organizational, and operational aspect. In the next years, he manned the Board of Trustees with fellow tycoon-collectors: George F. Baker, Henry Clay Frick, George Blumenthal,

Edward S. Harkness, John G. Johnson, and Henry Walters (these last two, along with Charles Freer and Peter A. B. Widener, were thinking about giving their collections to museums in Philadelphia, in Washington, D.C., and in Baltimore). Typical of the Morgan electoral technique was his nomination, in 1912, of Harkness. "I propose," announced "the Great Financial Gorgon," "Edward Harkness. . . . Let's vote on it!" And that election led, within the next twenty years, to the Museum's possession of one of the world's greatest collections of Egyptian art. Existing departments were reorganized, new ones organized. Edward Robinson, much respected archeologist, erstwhile Curator of Classical Antiquities in the Museum of Fine Arts at Boston and then its Director, left Boston to become the Metropolitan Museum's Assistant Director, a new post, and by 1910 its Director. Henry Watson Kent, formerly of the Slater Memorial Museum, Norwich (from which he had helped the Metropolitan Museum assemble its prodigious cast collection), and most recently librarian of the Grolier Club, functioned first as Robert W. de Forest's assistant secretary and then, from 1913 until the 1940s, as Secretary to the Board of Trustees. In 1952 Director Francis Henry Taylor wrote about this bibliophile, typography expert, pioneer in museum cataloguing and other methodologies, this man passionate about American decorative arts long before most collectors were aware of them: "Mr. Kent, despite a certain inflexibility characteristic of his age, had the imagination to devise and put into operation all of the policies of education, as well as the photographic and publication series of the Museum. With little variation they stand today a monument to his vision and determination."

Mr. Kent, in his book of memoirs, *What I Am Pleased to Call My Education*, describes the internal "organization" of the Museum when he went to work in it in 1905: "The Museum had arrived at the point where it did need young men. General Cesnola's staff was made up of men of middle age, without training in museum work. When he died in November, 1904, he left behind him three curators. There was no love lost among these gentlemen . . . one day, one of them invited another to 'come outside,' which he did, but to argue, not to fight. The one chased the other all around through the galleries. I called the policeman at the door, and he stopped the exciting performance. I have never known professional feelings to run so high." When the General's secretary was asked to give the Museum records to Kent he "dumped all the Museum records and letters, which were docketed in the old-fashioned way and bound up with red tape, in a vault helter-skelter," and Kent's first job was to sort them, "flatten them out, and catalogue and file them in new-fashioned filing cases of Dewey's devising. The Registrar was an Irishman, who carried a Latin Bible in his pocket, from which he would ask you to read passages, to test your scholarship." Kent found the Museum's single telephone installed in the library, "to which we had to run when we were called," and the only typewriter was elusive. The Museum restaurant was still famous for its marvelous food, under the supervision of "an Italian of Cesnola's choosing."

Efficiency took over. The Department of Classical Antiquities was organized, and the Department of Egyptian Art, with veteran Egyptologist Albert M. Lythgoe as curator of the latter. A working arrangement was made with the Egyptian government, and for almost four decades the Metropolitan Museum excavated its own treasures from three different Egyptian sites. In 1906 President Morgan gave the Museum the eighteenth-century French decorative-arts section of the Georges Hoentschel Collection, while placing on loan the Gothic decorative art from the same collection. No other American public museum could match this aggrandizement of rooms, architectural details, *objets d'art*, monuments, and furnishings. Hoentschel, an architect, had assembled 505 pieces of woodwork and furniture and 702 pieces of ormolu in the eighteenth-century section alone. Dr. Wilhelm H. Valentiner, one of the world's greatest experts, was brought from Germany

*E. Robinson*
Director
1910–1913

123

to head the new Department of Decorative Arts, and McKim, Mead, and White, who had become the fashionable architects of the new era, were soon designing the Museum's first addition to be planned for a specific collection, Wing F. When it opened in 1910, it was called the Decorative Arts Wing, and after 1918, most appropriately, the Morgan Wing.

Roger Fry, painter, professional connoisseur of paintings, drawings, and works of art by old masters and new, champion of modern art, later to be acclaimed as the "greatest influence on taste since John Ruskin," was imported by Morgan to be the new Curator of Paintings. New York society took to him immediately; the public hated his purchases of El Greco (very daring at this time) and Goya; and soon he was at home again in London, having had a sharp difference of opinion with the fiercely black-eyed, whimsically tempered "Menace," but continuing to act as European advisor.

Something newsworthy happened daily in the Metropolitan Museum of Art. The William H. Vanderbilt Collection of Paintings was on long display. The Heber R. Bishop gift of remarkable jade awaited its debut in the replica of the donor's elaborately gilded and mirrored ballroom, which he had arranged to have constructed in the Museum. The Dino collection was inaugurating the Museum's future world-unique Department of Arms and Armor. Techniques were worked out to involve the city's public schools increasingly in Museum activities. The *Bulletin of the Metropolitan Museum of Art* began publication, first as a quarterly, then as a monthly. The Printing Division was established; the Photograph Division; the Information Desk; a lending collection of lantern slides. Press views were organized, and so was the Office of Superintendent of the Building. The first Supervisor of Museum Instruction was appointed, and the first classroom opened. Money was appropriated for photograph purchasing, and the textile collection became so enormous, with all the new gifts and purchases, that the first Study Room of Textiles was installed. Frederick C. Hewitt of Oswego, New York, not even a Museum member, unknown to the trustees, died, and by 1913 the Museum had received over $1,500,000 from his estate. Second Vice-President John Stewart Kennedy died in 1908, and by 1913 the Museum was richer by over $2,000,000 realized from his estate, with much more to come. And the bequests continued to roll in.

By 1908 the artistic ferment in New York exploded into dramatic, decisive action. The Society of American Artists had merged with the National Academy of Design; while Alfred Stieglitz, of 291 Fifth Avenue, touted photography as fine art, and avant-garde art as the only real paint-pencil-pen-brush-and-sculptor's art. Enemies called Stieglitz and his followers the "Mop and Pail Brigade." Gertrude Vanderbilt Whitney opened her Studio Gallery, presaging the Whitney Museum of American Art, and The Eight held their exhibit at the Macbeth Gallery—Arthur B. Davies, William Glackens, Robert Henri, Ernest Lawson, George Luks, Maurice B. Prendergast, Everett Shinn, and John Sloan. They were the heroes and villains of the day, praised and reviled as the "Ashcan School" and the "Revolutionary Black Gang." George Luks, whose *The Old Duchess* came to the Museum in 1921, summed up what they were about in a single, expletive statement: "Art, my slats! Guts! Guts! Life! Life! That's my technique!" Rosa Bonheurs slumped on the Paris art market, and Millet and the Barbizon school were the accepted modern European masters of the moment. But at the Metropolitan Museum the American realistic wind was blowing strong and clean. Mr. George A. Hearn, the department-store magnate, had, in 1906, established a $100,000 fund whose income's sole purpose was to purchase works by living American artists. In the next decade Hearn doubled this fund by a second. By that time two galleries were completely filled with works he had presented (some of these were European paintings) and a third held the overflow, while the Hearn funds had purchased twenty-six by contemporary Americans. In a half century, Hearn money bought over six hundred American oils and water colors, including Ryder's *Toilers of the Sea*, Homer's *Harvest Scene*, Eakins' *Pushing for Rail*, and Sargent's *Madame X.*

On September 20, 1909, the Metropolitan Museum opened a stupendous two-part loan exhibit as its contribution to New York's Hudson-Fulton Celebration. There were nine days of water pageants; fleets from all over the world anchored in the river while replicas of the *Half Moon* and the *Clermont* wafted and chugged up and down it; continual parades complete with galaxies of costumed Gibson girls on phalanxes of fabulously decorated historic floats rolled along the streets; there were multi-gun salutes; Wright and Curtis flew across the Hudson; and 143 Dutch paintings, valued at $10,000,000, were to be seen in the Museum. This "substitute for a trip to Europe" included thirty-seven supposed Rembrandts, twenty-one Halses, twelve Ruisdaels, and six Vermeers. And also on view was an American exhibit of early paintings and industrial arts. Nothing like the latter had ever before been seen anywhere. Three hundred thousand people came to view it. Henry Watson Kent had been instrumental in the inclusion of this American section. He and de Forest decided "to use the opportunity to test out whether American domestic art was worthy of a place in an art museum." The answer was triumphantly affirmative, and soon after Mrs. Russell Sage bought the entire Eugene Bolles collection of early American furniture, over seven hundred pieces, and presented it to the Museum. With this as a huge beginning, the American Wing was just a little over a decade away.

In 1907, Henry James's *The American Scene* was published, and in it he recorded his visit in the first decade of the century to the Metropolitan Museum: "It is a palace of art, truly, that sits there on the edge of the Park, rearing itself with a radiance, yet offering you expanses to tread. . . ."

## 1910–1919

In 1912, a Leipzig publisher issued a 178-page book by Morton H. Bernath entitled *New York und Boston.* About the art museums of these cities, the little volume was intended to instruct the thousands of Germans who were planning to visit America or make their homes here. "Its publication," exulted the Museum *Bulletin*, "is but a recognition of a situation that has come to exist almost without our consciousness of it. Europe now takes cognizance of America's collections of art, as America has long looked up to the treasures of the Old World." By the end of this decade, *New York und . . .* had become all but obsolete. The Metropolitan Museum was so swollen with treasures that not even the erection of six new wings ("F" through "K," with "I," the Boiler House, and with "K" an empty shell until 1926), designed by McKim, Mead, and White on their usual monumental lines, sufficed. "American generosity seems to set no limit to the growth of our collections, even with the radical suppression of what is inferior and the exhibition of only that which is distinctly superior, which is the policy of the Museum," stated a *Bulletin* of this period, and went on, "The limitations which give us most anxiety are those of exhibition space and increased cost of administration."

What, then, were some of the "distinctly superior" acquisitions of this incredible Museum decade? It is almost impossible to give a sampling of the magnificence that showered like some mythological golden torrent upon the Museum. . . . On April 14, 1913, flags flew at half-mast upon hundreds of New York City buildings; the Stock Exchange shut down for a half day; the Metropolitan Museum of Art closed for the entire day (the first time that had happened in eight years); and memorial meetings were held in Westminster Abbey and in Paris, while in St. George's, New York City, the chancel was almost obliterated by floral tributes more elaborate than the grieving sentiments inscribed upon them by emperors, kings, and governments. Row upon solemn row, the mighty of finance, art, and politics sat contemplating the high summer tide of Jacqueminot roses breaking over John Pierpont Morgan's coffin. Later, in Hartford, his birthplace, he was interred to the pealing of the city's mighty fire bell and the chiming of "Rock of Ages" and "Asleep in Jesus." It was soon known that his net taxable estate came to $68,384,680, and that his son, John Pierpont Morgan, Jr., was to be the sole disposer of the art collections. In addition to the munificent gifts the Museum had already received from Morgan, the Metropolitan's basements and storerooms were glutted with his collections. Having poured in from Morgan's two English houses, the Victoria and Albert Museum, London's National Gallery, and Paris repositories where he had kept them, these treasures, most of them still unpacked, were in the Museum awaiting Morgan's decision. He never saw his collection intact. But after 1917, Museum-goers had the glory of it, for John Pierpont Morgan, Jr., added over 5500 objects (one can only think of them as princely spoils) to such previous gifts as Raphael's *Madonna and Child Enthroned* (the *Colonna*); the *Pietà* and *Entombment* from the Château de Biron; the entire Hoentschel collection (the Gothic and Renaissance section was given in 1916); the antique Chinese porcelains; and the five Sacrament tapestries. "We might say that his loss was irreparable, to the Museum," read a resolution adopted at a special meeting of the Board of Trustees, on April 1, 1913, "but for the fact that his constant and generous efforts in its behalf have placed it in a position where its future among the great art institutions of the world is assured."

When William Henry Riggs of Paris, boyhood friend of the elder Morgan and Museum vice-president from 1870 to 1874, gave his arms and armor collection in May 1913, Bashford Dean, curator of the recently formed Department of Arms and Armor, delightedly reported, "In certain regards it is probably first even among national collections. Its especial interest lies in its great number of historical and decorated pieces and in its arms of high epoch." But "the most splendid gift ever received by the Museum from an individual" (the words are Edward Robinson's, now director) was bequeathed in October 1913. Benjamin Altman, founder of the department store, willed his collection. The Museum could have this spectacular assemblage if it was kept forever intact, and if the estate's executors would have approval of every future detail connected with it. A special keeper, functioning as liaison between the Museum and the estate, was to come along with the collection, making sure that it had as much exhibition space as it had enjoyed in Altman's mansion. The trustees, by this date strongly opposed to restrictions, accepted the bequest immediately. They had no choice, for this native New Yorker, who had had to go to work when he was twelve years old, this frugal bachelor, of whom Duveen said, he "travelled like a Cook's tourist," had acquired, in some eight years, thirteen Rembrandts, four Memlings, a very great Vermeer, an incomparable Ruisdael, an Antonello, a Tura, paintings by Dürer, Titian, Verrocchio, Holbein, Velazquez; a Rospigliosi cup and rock-crystal objects; the rarest of Chinese porcelains; Renaissance sculptures; vintage Oriental rugs; eighteenth-century French decorative arts; tapestries; and unique pieces of European furniture. John G. Johnson, the Philadelphia collector, sourly said of "the wealthy trader," as he nicknamed him, "If the price is sufficiently high, he will buy." In 1915, when the Morgan gifts, the Altman collection, and the first arms and armor exhibit ever held in the United States were displayed under the same roof for the first time, the Museum found it almost impossible to cope with the crowds that came to view them.

The Museum opened its Lecture Hall, ten new Egyptian galleries, an Arms and Armor Hall, and a fine new library—for the little bundle of books and pamphlets, which had come up from Fourteenth Street to the Museum in the Park thirty years before, was burgeoning into one of the world's most important art libraries. President de Forest and his brother had given the Museum a temple from India, other important Indian treasures had accumulated, and so a section of Indian arts was installed. "Did these ugly, even sacrilegious things really belong in the Museum?" some viewers asked. The Museum explained that "a heathen idol can also be a work of art." The course of future collecting could be discerned.

When, in 1913, the Armory Show, formally titled "International Exhibition of Modern Art," shocked America into awareness of French "modernism," the Museum—disregarding outraged shrieks of "Hideous!" "Pathological!" and "Unadulterated cheek!" at Duchamp's *Nude Descending a Staircase*, Picasso's *Les Demoiselles d'Avignon*, the works of Rouault, Redon, and Cézanne—quietly spent some of Catharine Lorillard Wolfe's money and bought *La Colline des Pauvres* by Cézanne, precursor of the Cubists. Three years previously the Museum had acquired a trio of drawings by Matisse. Not only were there revolutions in art, but new art forms were evolving. In 1914 the Museum *Bulletin* published an article on the new verb, "to film," and in 1916 an article on "The Use of Motion Photography in Museums." Soon the Metropolitan Museum was involved in a program of moving pictures—wonderful for people of all ages—and children loved them. The Museum felt strongly that if it did not attract the young, it failed. It not only showed them movies, but held story hours for them, published a special *Bulletin* for them, arranged "treats," and ultimately gave them their own Junior Museum within the Museum.

Specialists and scholars came from everywhere to fill Museum posts. Edward Robinson, Director and Curator of the reorganized Department of Classical Art, was assisted by future Curator of Greek and Roman Art Miss Gisela M. A. Richter from England, who in the early 1950s was the first woman, other than a head of state, to receive from the University of Oxford the degree of Doctor Honoris Causa, in recognition of the collections and publications she had done at the Metropolitan Museum. From Amsterdam came S. C. Bosch Reitz, foremost expert on Chinese porcelains, to head the Department of Far Eastern Art for the next twelve years. When the publisher Harris Brisbane Dick left to the Museum his and his father's trove of prints and a fund for "the purchase of desirable and proper objects of the Fine Arts," the Museum gathered its increasingly remarkable hoard of prints together and asked one of the nation's leading print-collecting amateurs to leave his lucrative law firm to head the Department of Prints. For three decades William M. Ivins was its curator, later becoming Assistant Director and Acting Director of the Museum. Ivins immediately inaugurated very special exhibitions; he soon purchased the Dürer collection of Junius S. Morgan, wrote extensively about his passion for prints, and made the department the envy of all other museums. The Dick fund went on not only to buy prints but to gather such "desirable and proper objects" as the album of fifty drawings by Goya; the harnesses of Henry II of France and Anne de Montmorency, Constable of France; and that superlative set of Greek adornments known as the Ganymede Jewelry.

The Museum stretched a solid thousand feet along Fifth Avenue, from Eightieth Street to Eighty-fourth. It was rich in bequests, usually left for purchases, and very rarely of any help in their maintenance. Over $1,000,000 came from Francis L. Leland, and $500,000 from editor-publisher Joseph Pulitzer. The Pulitzer money ultimately bought such rarities as the Michelangelo drawing for the Libyan Sibyl, and another fund he left did help with the Museum's housekeeping. John Hoge, a man from Zanesville, Ohio, left his valuable midtown Fifth Avenue real estate to the

*R. W. de Forest*
**President**
**1913–1931**

Museum. Mrs. Edward J. Tytus subsidized the publication of the wall paintings the Museum excavations were unearthing in Thebes. Jessie Gillender left money for "the giving of explanatory lectures . . . for the benefit of artisans engaged in crafts demanding artistic study as expressed in contents of The Metropolitan Museum of Art," thereby making the first bequest which would help the Museum's education program. Another educational venture was the loan exhibition of seventy-eight oils sent by the Museum to Washington Irving High School in Manhattan, where twenty thousand viewed it. There were lectures for the deaf and work with the blind. Miss Helen Keller came to the Museum. "My visit . . . last Sunday," she wrote, "was one of the most delightful experiences of my life. 'A thing of beauty is a joy forever' and there were many joys for me in those wonderful collections—miracles of patient, creative hands. I thank you for all the pleasure you gave me, and even more warmly for your kind thought of my blind fellows. I hope you can arrange lectures for them every year."

Trustee John L. Cadwalader left his eighteenth-century English furniture and porcelains, his Chinese ornamental bronzes, and a fund for the purchase of additional English furniture and porcelain, and this legacy doubled the Museum's holdings of those much desired objects. With Mrs. Morris K. Jesup's bequest came seventy-one paintings, chosen by Curator Bryson Burroughs and his staff, and funds for the securing of unusual works and "for the encouragement of American Art in any way the Trustees may think best." Among the results are Dosso Dossi's *Three Ages of Man*, Andrea del Sarto's *Holy Family*, Copley's *Portrait of Mrs. Sylvanus Bourne*, and Inness's *Delaware Water Gap*. The Kennedy fund bought Carpaccio's mysterious *The Meditation on the Passion* and Veronese's opulent *Mars and Venus United by Love*, which had belonged to the Emperor Rudolph II, Queen Christina of Sweden, Cardinal Decio Azzolino, the Duke of Bracciano, Philippe, Duc d'Orléans, and an assortment of notabilities in France, Belgium, and England.

The influx of masterpieces would, it seemed, never end: Leonardo drawings; entire rooms from early American houses; and the Lahun Treasure. These necklaces, girdles, anklets, bracelets, and rings, and their inlaid ebony casket, as well as the toilet set of gold-mounted obsidian cosmetic jars, silver rouge dish, razors undulled by thousands of years, and whetstones, came from the twelfth-dynasty tomb of Princess Sit-Hathor-Yunet. And the piece of greatest splendor is the pectoral, given to the Princess by her father, Sesostris II. The most superb piece of Egyptian jewelry extant, it is intricately fashioned of gold inlaid with over 370 bits of lapis lazuli, turquoise, carnelian, and garnet, and incorporates solar falcons, the kneeling god of "years,"and a royal cartouche, signifying, "the sun-god gives hundreds of thousands of years of life to Sesostris II." A complete Egyptian tomb, almost 4500 years old, was given by Edward S. Harkness. And some four years after he gave the tomb of Lord Chamberlain Peri-nebi, Harkness gave William. This benign, four-and-a-half-inch-high faïence beast, the color of an Egyptian evening sky and delicately patterned all over with his homeland's lotus buds and blossoms, is the most famous, lovable hippopotamus in the world. And in came the parade armor of Galiot de Genouilhac, Louis XII's and Francis I's master of artillery. Resplendently etched and gilded over its entire surface with scenes of the labors of Hercules, this work of high art is probably the most astonishing example of its genre anywhere.

When Isaac D. Fletcher bequeathed 251 *objets d'art* (classical antiquities, paintings, Gothic sculptures, decorative arts, metalwork, Near and Far Eastern ceramics, and Oriental textiles) and a fund of over $3,400,000 (the second largest the Museum had ever had), Robert W. de Forest said of the Fletcher bequest, "It is most notable for the delicate line which he has drawn between his strong desire to make his collection a permanent memorial to his wife and himself by keeping it together, and his recognition of the inexpediency of making the acceptance of his gifts conditional

*The Bullfight.* Francisco José de Goya y Lucientes, Spanish, 1746–1828. Oil. Wolfe Fund, 1922.

ABOVE: Two-fold paper screen; wave design in colors on gold ground. Ogata Korin, Japanese, 1658–1716. Tokugawa period, 1615–1867. Fletcher Fund, 1926. OPPOSITE: Studies for the Libyan Sibyl. Michelangelo Buonarroti, Italian, 1475–1564. Drawing, red chalk. Purchase, Joseph Pulitzer Bequest, 1924.

*Cardinal Don Fernando Niño de Guevara.* El Greco, Spanish, 1541–1614. Oil. Bequest of Mrs. H. O. Havemeyer, 1929.

upon carrying out that desire as a legal obligation." De Forest then went on to make what Winifred E. Howe, the author of the omnivorous *A History of the Metropolitan Museum* (Volume II published in 1946 for the Metropolitan Museum of Art by Columbia University Press), hails as "the Bill of Rights of American museums." I give Mr. de Forest's final paragraph in its entirety, for it sums up the thinking of the Museum about bequests, and lays down sure guidelines for itself and any other mature museum of the future.

It may be pertinently asked how far the Metropolitan Museum of Art, and for that matter any like institution, can recognize the natural desire of donors for some lasting recognition of their gifts without impairing scientific installation, present and prospective. The action of the Metropolitan, taken promptly after Mr. Fletcher's will was made public, indicates this. It can label every object with the donor's name. It can group together objects which naturally belong together and are likely to remain together and give them a group label. It can recognize the donor in its catalogues and handbooks. It can exhibit a new collection as an entirety for a limited time, as it intends to do with Mr. Fletcher's collection. It can even give a donor's name to a gallery, as it has done in the case of Henry G. Marquand. But it cannot wisely prevent the proper arrangement of its growing collections as an integral whole by accepting gifts conditioned on perpetual segregation. There are exceptions to any general rules. Such an exception was made in the case of the Altman Collection. There undoubtedly will and should be exceptions in the future. But these exceptions in the case of a museum so well established as the Metropolitan and with such certainty of continued growth will become rarer and rarer, and when made will be predicated either on the great value of the collection or on its being so homogeneous in character as to fit naturally into any proper prospective installation.

In 1920 the Museum would celebrate its fiftieth birthday, but before that golden anniversary, it would have to weather its first world war.

The war in Europe cut the Museum off from important treasure sources, while making it possible for the Museum to build up its Egyptian resources with greater expediency. But the Museum was more concerned, during these pre-1917 days, with its own economic stomachache than with any foreign disorders. *The New York Times* let the world know about it, on March 1, 1914:

The Metropolitan Museum's Growth too Big for Its Income! Its Running Expenses Have Doubled in Ten Years Because of the Great Collections That Have Been Added Yet the City's Share in Its Up-Keep Has not Proportionately Increased.

By 1915 the Museum was appealing to the public for funds, ruefully reminding that "it costs nearly twelve times as much to administer the Museum today as it did in 1880." It pointed out that the Museum was no longer isolated in the northern suburbs: in 1880, only seven per cent of the population had lived north of Eighty-sixth Street, but by 1910, thirty-seven per cent was living there.

But even the Museum's financial plight lessened in importance, at least temporarily, in 1917 when "the unfortunate conditions in Europe," as the *Bulletin* referred to the war, caught up with the United States. "I Want You for the U.S. Army," an urgent-eyed, grimly determined Uncle Sam declared from James Montgomery Flagg's recruiting poster, and twenty-four Museum men, including Herbert E. Winlock, a future director, were serving their country. More and more women came to be given jobs; Frances Morris, the first to have worked in the Museum, had come in 1896 without

Director Cesnola's complete approval. Attendance in the galleries dropped alarmingly in 1917, but more and more people came to study. Over fifteen hundred annual members withdrew. Sales of postcards, catalogues, everything the Museum sold, dropped. Coal shortages forced economies in light and heat. The Museum decorated itself for visiting foreign delegations, and received these allies to the sound of appropriate music beneath potted palms. It erected towering flagpoles; hung a proud banner upon which, sadly, gold stars increased; ran a *Bulletin* column, "Army Museum Men in Service"; arranged Liberty Loan Drives; intensified its American exhibitions. There was an unprecedented American colonial silver show—the most extensive ever held; and homages to the Hudson River School, Thomas Eakins, Albert Pinkham Ryder, and American sculpture. In 1918 Museum attendance suddenly soared, and more people came than ever before save during the Hudson-Fulton year of 1909 and the Morgan exhibition year of 1914. Soldiers and sailors arrived in battalions. The Museum continued to "do its bit," arranging special tours for them, lectures, and all sorts of diversions. Edward S. Harkness underwrote concerts conducted by David Mannes, and the Great Hall was jammed to overflowing. The number of symphony-orchestra concerts increased, backed by de Forest and John D. Rockefeller, Jr.; they were so popular that Mannes continued to conduct them for thirty years.

The Ordnance Department in Washington was deeply interested in the Museum's Department of Arms and Armor; Bashford Dean, the curator, served six months as Chairman of the Armor Section of the Council of National Research, became a major, and was ordered to proceed to Europe to see how antique means of defense could help twentieth-century warriors. His knowledge was especially needed in developing body protections: the doughboy's helmet resulted, and the Museum eventually received a gift of "modern" arms and "armor" to add to its collection. War not only claimed Museum staff and diminished purchasing, but brought more and more workers in American enterprises of all sorts, especially the needle trades, decoration, and furnishing, to seek sources and inspiration in the Museum's collections. In 1917 the Museum mounted its first exhibition of work by manufacturers and designers showing Museum influence. This was so successful that by 1918 the Museum had appointed an Associate in Industrial Arts; was embarked on lecture programs for salespeople, buyers for stores, and all sorts of kindred workers; and was firmly launched on its long series of annual industrial arts exhibits. Industrial by implication, the 1918 cooperative venture between the New York Botanical Gardens and the Museum was one of the most captivating shows the Museum ever held. With plant forms in ornament as the theme, Museum galleries became gardens wherein Museum treasures reflected the living plant and floral shapes.

Daniel Chester French's *The Victory* stood stalwartly at the head of the great main stair where, during a war two decades away, the Museum's plaster cast of the Victory of Samothrace would gleam as optimistically as her predecessor. A mother wrote to a Museum curator, "I received a letter from my soldier son . . . telling me how nice you were to him and his friends . . . to receive such kindness and be so nicely entertained was such a treat to them. I want to thank you *very* much for your kindness to the boys. It has saddened our home more than I can tell you for us to send that big fine son of ours to war, but that is not all—I have two more sons just as tall and fine as he is that are called. You see I am telling you how fine they are—well, they are my sons. Again I want to thank you for your kindness to my son."

Some time during the morning of November 11, 1918, President Woodrow Wilson wrote his message to the people of America: "My Fellow Countrymen: The armistice was signed this morning. Everything for which America fought has been accomplished. It will now be our fortunate duty to assist by example, by sober, friendly counsel, and by material aid in the establishment of just democracy throughout the world."

The Museum put out more flags, decorated its Fifth Avenue front as it had never before, and displayed, among its recent accessions, its authentic Brueghel, *The Harvesters*, bought for a pittance by Bryson Burroughs, who had immediately known this war refugee to be the real thing. The boys came home along the avenue, singing their hearts out, and hundreds of thousands of happy voices joined in. Everyone believed in the wonderful future. The Museum unveiled a bronze tablet to its staff heroes and took down its banner with the gold stars upon it.

## 1920–1929

At four p.m. on Tuesday, May 18, 1920, in the Lecture Hall of the Metropolitan Museum of Art, a little band of musicians struck up the minuet from Haydn's Quartette op. 76 no. 2, then plunged into the finale of that captivating work, while five hundred specially invited guests ceased their chattering. President Robert W. de Forest, chairing this unique occasion, introduced Commissioner of Parks Francis D. Gallatin, and the formal ceremonies commemorating the Museum's golden anniversary were under way. The President of the University of the State of New York, speaking next, referred to the Museum as "this House of Beautiful Things," stressing "this Museum in its new functioning is primarily an educational institution, a place not simply of conserving or record-ing but of teaching." The Presidents of the Museum of Fine Arts, Boston (also founded in 1870), and the Art Institute of Chicago, founded in 1879, gloried not only in the spectacular half-century history of the Metropolitan Museum but in the "phenomenal development of museums in the United States." Where only five museums, devoted wholly to art, existed in 1870, some ninety-two had been established by 1910, with the greatest museum boom west of the Alleghenies. "The attendance in these Western museums," Chicago's President Hutchinson announced, "is more than double that of the Eastern museums." And he concluded, "Is there any good reason why there should not be another Renaissance of Art?" We are, he affirmed, "already on the threshold. . . . There is an awakening on every hand." There was no reason why the United States should not be in the center of the new Renaissance. And who should lead the new movement? The Metropolitan Museum, "first and foremost of us all."

When Robert W. de Forest stood before the distinguished five hundred, and began quietly, "Fifty years ago the Metropolitan Museum of Art existed only as the vision of a group of public-spirited persons—artists, clergymen, lawyers, men of affairs," he was the embodiment of that original all-for-art and art-for-the-people group. "Those dreamers," he went on, "had 'no building, not even a site; no existing collection as a nucleus; no money.' . . . Today the institution which they founded has a building extending along four blocks of Fifth Avenue; a site on which there is still room for expansion; collections which already rival in extent and surpass in installation those of the great museums of Europe, and money to the amount of more than $16,000,000. True, the Museum is restricted in the use of most of this money but it is nonetheless Museum money."

It is a model address, straight from de Forest's heart, unsentimental and steeped in his life-long Metropolitan Museum experience. After quiet, factual historical recapitulation and homage to those who made the Museum what it was by 1920, the "Founders, and their successors," the donors, the staff, the cooperative city and state governments, members of all classes, and the "great crowds from east side, west side, and every side . . . which throng our galleries," Mr. de Forest defined "the American Museum idea" thusly: "It is a public gallery for the use of all the people, high and low, and even more for the low than for the high, for the high can find artistic inspiration in their own homes. The low can find it only here . . . there are no privileged classes in our Museum unless it be the children, and they are not a class. We are not content simply to show dead things, however beautiful they are and however much inspiration may come from their dead beauty. We seek to make everything in our Museum alive and to enter as a living force into all the interests of our community. This is our contribution toward making art free for democracy. . . .

"And what should be the policies of the Museum in the future, so that our successors, when they come to celebrate its hundredth anniversary, may do so with the same satisfaction with which we celebrate its fiftieth?" Mr. de Forest asked. "Strict adherence . . . to the policies of the past, with possibly some difference of emphasis and an open-minded readiness to meet the changes of public sentiment in the future just as the Trustees of the past generation met the changing sentiment of later times." The Museum must continue to recognize all of the arts equally and be both educational and recreative in direct proportion. "I look," he said, "to greater emphasis being laid on modern art. . . . We are interested quite as much, if not more, in what the art world is doing now as we are in what it has done in the past. Modern art in painting and sculpture is well represented in our Museum. The other forms of modern art are still to be adequately represented." He pointed out that although the Museum had been charged with the neglect of American art, this was no longer true. The 1904 collection of 147 American pictures, representing 83 American painters, and the 48 American sculptures, representing 26 American sculptors, had grown into a permanent collection of 503 paintings by 214 American painters, and 186 sculptures by 91 American sculptors. The paintings alone filled four galleries, and the Museum frequently circulated American works (and others) throughout the nation, under the American Federation of Arts management. For American decorative art, Mr. de Forest hinted a growing Museum in the near future. And looking ahead, he foresaw "but one storm signal" in the Museum's future: "Can and will our city continue to perform its part of our partnership relation?" As Museum expenses mounted, the city's appropriation became less and less adequate. And even though the appropriation had been increased in 1920 to $300,000, Mr. de Forest bluntly warned, on this golden anniversary day, "There will still be a deficit." There always would be a need for maintenance funds, and it would always be met.

So with a salute to the ever-spreading "art museum impulse . . . national in extent," and a "To all we give a hearty birthday greeting," the address ended, the five hundred cheered and the band dashed into Brahms's Waltzes, op. 39.

Then the members of the corporation; benefactors; lenders to the Anniversary Exhibition; the representatives of state, city, and national government; the heads of art societies and the city's higher educational institutions; museum officialdom not only from the Metropolitan Museum itself, but from museums all over the United States (many had also come to the Convention of the American Federation of Arts to be held in the Museum) all trailed into the huge Great Hall. They walked amidst the convoluted garlands and wreaths, the coats of arms and the emblems of the state and city and of the many countries represented in the Museum's collections, with which McKim, Mead, and White had decorated the hall as a gift to the Museum. At the foot of the main stair, two memorial tablets of Botticino marble, after McKim, Mead, and White designs, were unveiled to "THE FOUNDERS OF THE METROPOLITAN MUSEUM OF ART APRIL 13, MDCCCLXX" and "BENE-FACTORS OF THE MUSEUM DURING THE FIRST HALF CENTURY OF STRUGGLE AND GROWTH MDCCCLXX-MDCCCCXX." Said Elihu Root, the Museum's current first vice-president,

It is especially grateful to me, and I know it must be to all of you, that while the first name on the list of the Founders and the first name on the list of Benefactors is that great citizen of New York, John Taylor Johnston, the last names on the list of Benefactors are his daughter, Emily Johnston de Forest, and his son-in-law, Robert de Forest. . . . The spirit of great and noble citizenship lives still in America. The instinct of service, the habit of benevolence, the urge of patriotism, the love of beauty, the devotion to humanity live still in America. And so long as our free republic retains its freedom this institution and all the ranks of other institutions which have come along in the same cause and are inspired by the same spirit will live and increase and be a blessing to mankind.

To the plaintive sounds of Tchaikovsky's "Andante Cantabile," the assemblage dispersed. That evening, seventy-five men (there is not a single woman's name on the guest list) sat down to an anniversary dinner and conviviality in the University Club. And almost all the gala year long the Museum presented, in all of its departments, an exhibition "unequalled in its quality and comprehensiveness by an assembling of the fine arts in America hitherto." To the Museum's permanent displays, some 104 lenders added 1154 objects. In the Room of Recent Accessions the Museum's own memorabilia were displayed, and portraits were hung of the founders, trustees, and Benefactors. In the picture galleries, about fifty paintings bore labels which read, "One of the 174 pictures first purchased by the Museum, 1871." The Gallery of Special Exhibitions housed a lavish loan show of French decorative arts and sculpture. (The Museum received two of its unique pieces of fine French furniture this year with the William K. Vanderbilt bequest: the superb commode of ebony and black and gold lacquer with gilt-bronze mounts and matching *secrétaire* fashioned by Jean Henri Riesener for Marie Antoinette.) . . . In November, when the celebration year was nearing its end, eight Manhattan and Bronx high school pupils won, for their schools, prizes, "framed enlargements from photographs of paintings and sculptures in the Museum collection." Each student had written a winning composition, "A Visit to the Metropolitan Museum" or a closely related subject. And little Eleanor Mann, of Evander Childs High School, took home a photograph prize all her own, for her composition was judged the best of all the winners.

The "greater emphasis . . . on modern art" suggested by Mr. de Forest had already started at the Museum late in 1919. After a delay by dock strikers, a loan show of modern French art, sent by a French government grateful for United States aid during the recent conflict, opened and was on view until February 1, 1920. Among the moderns exhibited were Monet, "whose influence on American landscape has been so peculiarly powerful"; Renoir, ". . . the artist's recent death lends just now a peculiar interest to these pictures"; Besnard; Signac; Bonnard; Roussel; Denis; Vallotton; and a host of lesser "moderns." Harry B. Wehle, later Curator of Paintings, concluded in his *Bulletin* article, "Few paintings in the exhibition, and indeed few pictures by artists of our own America, would have been painted quite as they are if the great so-called Impressionists of France had not lived and labored."

On May 2, 1921, the Museum held a private viewing for its members of its up-coming "Loan Exhibition of Impressionist and Post-Impressionist Paintings," a show planned to run until September 15. Careful to state precisely why it was holding this exhibition, the Museum announced that it was "in response to a wide general interest in the matter and to a particular request of a group of collectors and artists who wish to see these modern pictures in comparison with others of accepted standards." The Museum was swift to acknowledge that the art of Cézanne (his name was "the battle cry of enthusiasts"), Gauguin, Van Gogh, and their followers received extreme praise or excessive abuse, nothing in between. The momentous loan show included significant Courbets; six Manets; a good sampling of Degas race-course, ballet, bath, and milliner's shop scenes; four Toulouse-Lautrecs ("whose sarcastic art grew out of Degas' drawing"—the comments are Wehle's); twelve Renoirs; and not too many pictures by "the impressionist painters of sunlight," Monet and Pissarro, for the Museum felt that the public had had sufficient opportunities to view these. There were at least two Seurats; nine Matisses—even so modern a collector as Sam Lewisohn found some of these "difficult"; a group of Picassos; seven Derains; a Puvis de Chavannes; a handsome representation of Redon's "rare opalescent visions"; a Bonnard; and a Vuillard. But the focus of the whole exhibition was the work "of three artists who have within a few years attained . . . a . . . place among the immortals": seven or eight very late Van Goghs; ten Gauguins (mostly Tahitian); and the twenty-three Cézannes. The latter were especially debated. The works all came out of New York City collections, and there could have been even more on the walls, had there been room. Concurrently Ivins, Curator of Prints, assembled a comprehensive show of the last one hundred years of "French Prints and Drawings."

Some critics praised, declaring that this exhibit was the most useful the Museum had ever held. Everyone in and out of the art-and-museum world argued furiously over "these crazy, modern things," and the first seven weeks nearly forty thousand came to puzzle over them, making an average attendance of some eight hundred a day. Just before the September 15 closing date, Metropolitan Museum members, all sorts of other could-be-interested citizens, and the city's newspapers received, from an anonymous "Committee of Citizens and Supporters of the Museum," a protest urging "that all persons having at heart the welfare of our community and civilization write to the authorities of the Metropolitan Museum expressing their disapproval of the present exhibition." It was, the "Committee" ranted, Bolshevist, degenerate, and consequently un-American! The Museum firmly reiterated its reasons for holding the exhibit, repeated that both admiration and detestation for the modern art was always excessive, and proceeded to make a declaration of independence which set a pattern for the rest of its years: "The Museum knows no partisanship in art nor does it promote any particular school of art, ancient or modern. It seeks to give to the public the opportunity of seeing every kind of art, from everywhere, which any considerable number of people esteem or admire, quite regardless of the particular taste of its officers and trustees."

The September *Bulletin* told its readers that only ten protesting letters had come to the Museum, while the Parisian art dealer René Gimpel, in chatting with Bryson Burroughs in the Museum about this "very fine exhibit of modern art," marveled that "people laughed at the opening of this exhibit . . . I didn't laugh, I'm too afraid that the future will come to laugh at me." Gimpel also noted in his comprehensive *Diary of an Art Dealer* that when one of the Degas paintings was offered for sale to the Boston Museum, which was going to buy it, "Some women were against it, saying the picture was immoral: this couple weren't married [the two figures in the Degas], as the bed was a single bed."

The New York hullabaloo over the "modern" works became international, causing Sir Martin Conway to write, from H. M. Office of Works to the London *Times*, a prescient letter, too long, unfortunately, to quote in full: "It is easy to pour scorn on post-impressionist art . . . it makes its offer not to me and my contemporaries, but to the rising generation, and still more to the generations that are still later to follow. Moreover, the art that is to come is still inchoate, and will no more resemble the post-impressionist work of today than the art of Michelangelo resembles Giotto's. What we now behold is but the germ . . . it is universal. It is appearing in every advanced country, and is finding recognition everywhere." By 1927, Durand-Ruel, the dealer, told Gimpel that he was buying Impressionists in the United States and reselling them to an increasingly eager French market, and a Cézanne was being offered for sale in New York City for almost $112,000, while a Matisse was on the market for $20,000. In January 1929, the year the Museum of Modern Art was founded in New York City, the Metropolitan Museum of Art suddenly became, with one amazing bequest—the H. O. Havemeyer—one of the world's foremost repositories of some of that modern art so much decried at the beginning of the decade.

In this brave new Twenties' world, everything that was not being torn down was going up, up, up, faster and faster: skirts, the stock market, skyscrapers. Woolworth Gothic towers and William Morris Hunt château-*palazzo* mansions were vanquished by structures as cubist in their basic designs as any genuinely vanguard, Cézanne-Picasso-inspired work of art. And everywhere a frosting of "modernistic" decoration gleamed and glittered, especially after the 1925 *Exposition des Arts Décoratifs* in Paris, many of whose Art Déco furnishings and decorative pieces New York saw in 1926 when the Museum exhibited and bought them. When, in 1929, the Museum held its eleventh exhibition of American industrial art, "The Architect and the Industrial Arts: an Exhibition of Contemporary American Design," the most evolutionary creators, asked to form a Co-operating Committee, designed the various installations. What Raymond M. Hood, Ely Jacques Kahn, Eliel Saarinen, Eugene Schoen, Joseph Urban, and others did was a revelation. For the first time, viewers saw a whole series of complete interiors specifically planned by ranking modern American designers who intimately knew American problems and taste. There were 185,256 visitors to the show, which had to be kept open almost seven months. And what they saw in the Museum was reflected vigorously in the city about them. Geometries of silver, glass, and chrome flashed high above Fifth Avenue where so recently the stately homes of Vanderbilts had been erected to last forever. The new, coruscating, ever more commercial city surged at the southern extremity of Central Park, always advancing uptown eastward of Fifth Avenue and the Museum.

By the end of the Twenties the Museum had its largest deficit; the highest attendance in its history; and a decade rich in fulfilled promises, unexpected benefactions, and amazing purchases. Little wonder that European countries begged America's Metropolitan Museum of Art to send exhibits showing how the Museum worked and revealing the virtues of its pioneering museology. Movies became an important part of daily life, and the Museum increasingly made them part of its educational program. As the sound of the radio seeped through the nation, the Museum aired its expertise over WNYC. The X ray helped more and more in matters of authentication. Even Cesnola's *haute cuisine italienne* was supplanted by a self-service cafeteria, and the galleries were furnished with chairs—to ease museum fatigue. The Information Desk expanded; over eight hundred postcards of different treasures and Museum views were for sale. Less and less did anyone argue whether a photograph was a work of art, for the Museum was accumulating its collection of master photographs, urged on by gifts from Alfred Stieglitz and his friends.

Galleries opened, were hung and re-hung: whole epochs moved from one end of the building to another. The 1914 war having deposed monarchs and impoverished European nobility, the Museum was gathering in spoils, while American collectors were a never-ending source of treasure. But what they gave was changing just slightly. Rembrandts and Van Dycks, Italian old masters, eighteenth-century English masterpieces, and other examples of "High Art" still arrived in astonishing numbers, as did early American and European (especially Lamerie) silver, Italian majolica, Renaissance bronzes, antique textiles from Peru and just about everywhere else, Mexican arts and crafts, magnificent Oriental rugs, decorative and other arts of the ancient Near and Far East, medieval splendors of all kinds, and entire architectural units such as the shop front from the

Quai Bourbon and rooms from eighteenth-century French hôtels and American colonial dwellings. William K. Vanderbilt; Edmund Cogswell Converse; James F. Ballard; Reverend Alfred Duane Pell; Collis P. Huntington and his son, Archer; Ogden Mills; and the V. Everit Macys were among the most bountiful donors. And Jean Jacques Reubell, the Parisian collector, gave the Museum the most complete collection of court swords and daggers extant. But the emphasis was increasingly on the decorative arts, both antique and modern, with Edward C. Moore, Jr., even giving an annual sum with which to purchase the modern. And the Museum amassed a fine collection of Twenties-Thirties objects and furnishings of the kind which were to become so popular again in the late 1960s. When Edward S. Harkness topped his long list of splendid Egyptian gifts with the presentation of the entire Carnarvon collection of Egyptian antiquities, over 1400 of the most exquisite such objects ever gathered by one person, the Museum found itself one of the world's greatest repositories of Egyptian art. Even persons remote from any interest in museums were awed, for the name Carnarvon meant the recent discovery of King Tut-ankh-Amun's tomb, and that fabulous event, with its ramifications of legendary riches and curses, had captured the imagination of the first half of the hero-worshipping Twenties as wholly as Lindbergh's flight did in the decade's second half. In 1925 the Museum even refused the extremely valuable Senator William A. Clark bequest because of the restrictions his will imposed.

But when money was the gift, the Museum seems never to have refused. In this decade alone Mrs. Stephen V. Harkness (Edward S.'s mother) gave $1,000,000, as did George F. Baker, the George Blumenthals, and John D. Rockefeller, Jr. The latter, having had a study made of the Museum's "activities and accomplishments," gave his million in the form of sixteen thousand shares of the capital stock of the Standard Oil Company of California, and soon after established a fund for the special purpose of buying George Grey Barnard's "medieval gray stones" and Gothic treasures, the foundation upon which the Museum erected The Cloisters with Rockefeller's constant assistance—but the story of that acquisition will be told later. The most surprising bequest of all came from publisher-financier Frank A. Munsey, a man quite unsuspected of any interest in the Museum. In 1934, nine years after Munsey's death, George Blumenthal, Museum President, announced that the Munsey bequest would come to about $10,000,000, "the greatest single benefaction received by the Museum since its founding," and all of it, principal and income, completely unrestricted. Its sole purpose, Munsey stated in his will, was "to serve the needs of education, enlightenment and culture for the countless generations for all time to come."

And on November 10, 1924, the American Wing opened, the structure itself being a gift from Mr. and Mrs. Robert W. de Forest. He had hinted, in his Fiftieth Anniversary Address, that the Museum would soon have a home for its swiftly increasing collection of American decorative arts, furnishings, and period rooms, and here it was, three whole stories of it, chronologically arranged in seventeen meticulously furnished period rooms (only two of these being reproductions), the earliest (seventeenth century) being at the top of the new wing, and the latest (early nineteenth century until about 1825), arranged on the bottom. The south side of this unique structure incorporated the Tuckahoe marble façade of the United States Branch Bank, the old United States Assay Office, which from 1824 until 1915 had presented its beautiful, severe, landmark face to Wall Street. Robert W. de Forest, seeing this architectural gem about to become debris, asked for it, was given it, and stored it away for the Museum on an empty plot of Museum ground. Now the Assay Office front stood, presumably forever, looking down upon an old-fashioned, sweet-scented garden which, with its flagged, box-bordered walks and huge inset Connecticut millstones, had been specially created to make visitors feel that they were, indeed, having an adventure in some enchantingly appointed American past.

BELOW: *Rehearsal of the Ballet on the Stage.* Edgar Hilaire Germain Degas, French, 1834–1917. Oil colors freely mixed with turpentine, on paper mounted on canvas. Gift of Horace Havemeyer, 1929. The H. O. Havemeyer Collection. OPPOSITE: *Mezzetin.* Jean Antoine Watteau, French, 1684–1721. Oil. Munsey Fund, 1934.

*Max Schmitt in a Single Scull*. Thomas Eakins, American, 1844–1916. Oil, signed and dated 1871 on scull in background. Alfred N. Punnett Fund and gift of George D. Pratt, 1934.

Inside and out, the American Wing was the triumphant realization of a daring dream. Museum Secretary Henry W. Kent had germinated the project: the 1909 Hudson-Fulton Celebration exhibition; Mrs. Russell Sage's purchase and gift of the Bolles collection; and some fifteen years of additional acquisition, mostly through the efforts of Kent, the de Forests, R. T. H. Halsey, and the Department of Decorative Arts curators, had made it come true most brilliantly. "Except for Mr. Halsey," said de Forest in his opening-day address, "You might have had an American Wing, but you never would have had *this* American Wing." Richard T. Haines Halsey, Manhattan broker and indefatigable collector of and lecturer and writer on early Americana, had become a Museum trustee in 1914, almost immediately taking on the chairmanship of the newly formed Committee on American Decorative Arts. For the year preceding the American Wing opening, he had given his entire time to working with Joseph Breck, Curator, and his assistant, Charles O. Cornelius, with whom Halsey wrote the *Handbook of the American Wing*, so swiftly to become a standard text. Halsey, carefully researching each detail, had worked with the architect, Grosvenor Atterbury, and everyone concerned, deciding what colors the walls were to be, how the curtains were to hang, which fabrics to use, where each piece of furniture and decorative object was to be placed. Halsey performed decorative miracles, and Atterbury architectural ones, for the problem of fitting existing rooms of varying shapes and sizes, plus a large exhibition hall on each floor, into a building still to be erected, seemed almost insoluble. It was all well worth the prodigious efforts, the long years of planning and waiting, for from the moment the American Wing opened, it was one of the Museum's most successful divisions. Visitors came from everywhere; articles appeared about the wing's use of wall colors, fabrics, illumination, window hangings; early American decorative arts' and domestic arts' prices soared; Americana gifts to the Museum multiplied: when the wing opened it was able to exhibit the splendid Charles Allen Munn bequest of paintings, silver, and prints. Its existence caused a revolution in interior decoration and domestic architecture and also signaled such future developments as Colonial Williamsburg, Old Sturbridge Village, the Henry F. du Pont Winterthur Museum, and a whole flock of American wings in museums throughout the nation and even, ultimately, an American decorative-arts museum in England. The *New York Tribune*, with great foresight, had summed it all up when, in 1922, the de Forest gift had been announced: ". . . from a certain point of view the most significant piece of good fortune which has ever befallen the Metropolitan Museum."

In 1928, the *New York World* published a cartoon showing a flapperish girl and a dignified older woman peering up at the colossal Richard Morris Hunt façade of the Museum. "This, Aunt Nellie," says the young woman, "is the Metropolitan Museum of Art. I suppose I could spend a whole day looking at the things they have in it." And in it, she would, of course, have found, even in 1929, the original of this Denys Wortman cartoon, for it came to the Museum as a Ralph Pulitzer gift.

## 1930–1939

The decade began with the terror of the Great Depression, and it ended in the horror of Hitler's war. The Museum, while suffering consequences of both the Depression and the war, grew to symbolize for more and more people a monumental affirmation of faith in man and the survival of his highest endeavor. Two blazing beacons in Museum history light the Thirties, one at the beginning of the decade and the other at its end.

On Monday, March 10, 1930, the first of an eight months' total of over a quarter of a million viewers arrived to revel in a six-gallery exhibition of one of the Museum's most magnificent bequests, the H. O. Havemeyer collection, which had been accepted unanimously by the trustees in January 1929. The bequest and its presentation, unusual in its lack of restrictions, were as remarkable as Mrs. Louisine Waldron Havemeyer and her children, Adaline Frelinghuysen, Electra Webb, and Horace. Mrs. Havemeyer willed the gift, her husband, Henry Osborne Havemeyer, the sugartrust founder, having died in 1907: their children not only fulfilled the wise benevolence of their mother's will but exceeded it.

The Havemeyer collection, unique even in this age of giving, reveals the fused interests of two people who, while understanding the taste of their times, were, inevitably, just a step ahead of it. They were not really avant-garde, but they were, as Mrs. Havemeyer loved to put it, "the last word." They owned a profusion of works by Rembrandt, Rubens, Vermeer, Hals, de Hooch, Cuyp, Ostade, van der Goes, Cranach the Elder, Veronese, Bronzino, even by Decamps and Corot. They possessed an even greater number of adventurous works by the Impressionists and their precursors, and spectacular El Grecos and Goyas, which they bought at a time when there was almost no market for them. Mr. Havemeyer began his collecting at the Philadelphia Centennial in 1876, where he became enthralled with the curious art objects from China and Japan: metallic brocades, exotically patterned silks, lacquer boxes, sword guards, and carved ivory inros. He bought in great quantities because, like so many American magnates, he thought in tremendous numbers and had a passion for objects created by masterly hands. The future second Mrs. Havemeyer matched Mr. Havemeyer's passion for craftsmanship. "I prefer to have something made by a man than to have something made by an oyster," she was heard to say during a discussion about the desirability of owning pearls. She, of course, owned pearls, a string of sixty-one matched small moons bought by Mr. Havemeyer at the Centennial.

The Impressionists came into Mr. Havemeyer's life in 1883, after he married Louisine Waldron Elder, of Philadelphia. The twenty-nine-year-old bride, niece of his first wife and daughter of a well-to-do "sugar family," wore pink gingham at the wedding, a clue to her cozy indifference to fashion and her lifelong dedication to independent thinking. And she brought with her a small but incandescent gathering of startling art works, including Degas' La Répétition de Ballet, the first Impressionist work ever to be bought by an American. One day in 1875 Miss Elder, then in Paris to be "finished," and already saving out of her $50 monthly allowance to buy pictures by Monet and Pissarro, was led to a "color shop" by Miss Mary Cassatt of Philadelphia, who had already been in Paris a year and was completely absorbed in Manet, Courbet, and most in Degas. One look at the Degas pastel in the shop window, and Miss Elder knew she must have it. Borrowing a hundred dollars from her sister, Louisine Elder bought the Degas for 500 francs. In 1965 her grandson sold the same Degas at the Parke-Bernet Galleries in New York for $410,000. But back in the late 1870s and thereafter, Miss Elder continued to be frugal in all expenditures save in those concerning her purchase of "modern" works by the new French masters—and Whistler. Meanwhile Miss Cassatt continued to paint, adore Degas, and become more and more the liaison between her Impressionist friends and American art patrons like her own rich Philadelphia family and the Havemeyers and Mrs. Potter Palmer of Chicago.

From 1896 on, when they gave an enormous gift of Japanese textiles and then one of Japanese prints, the Havemeyers lavished benefactions on the Museum. Their town house at 1 East Sixty-sixth Street was nostalgically Romanesque on the outside and the last word in decoration by Louis Comfort Tiffany and Samuel Colman on the inside—even the table silver was Tiffany and Colman in design. This mansion disgorged a succession of splendors, many of them going anonymously to the Museum: collections of Tiffany glass, Courbets, a fine Tiepolo ceiling painting, Oriental and Islamic decorative arts. Along with making a joyful life filled with beauty, Mrs. Havemeyer was a painstaking housekeeper, once even telling Mrs. Jack Gardner of Fenway Court, Boston, that she could not see the Havemeyer house on a Saturday morning: that time was sacred to cleaning. But only a huge tome about the Havemeyers would permit a detailing of their gifts and loans to the Museum and the fascinating chronicle of their very American lives. As early as 1898, Mary Cassatt wrote about her Havemeyer friends, "I consider they are doing a great work for the country in spending so much time and money in bringing together such works of art." And she added, "All the great public collections were founded by private individuals." In 1908, Miss Cassatt firmly advised that the Havemeyer collection not be given to the Metropolitan Museum, for that institution did not exercise "good judgment and taste in its acquisitions." Nevertheless, twenty-one years later the collection, 1967 items strong and then appraised at $2,500,000, was in the Museum.

Louisine Waldron Havemeyer was constant in her belief in the virtues of personal thrift and wide largesse for the public good, especially through the blessings of art. She was steadfast for women's rights, at sixty-four even going to jail for this belief. In her last months this indefatigable woman carefully scored a "Z" on each object she thought Museum-worthy, writing meticulous, voluminous annotations to go along with the gifts. Then she was ready to meet her Maker, hopeful of her deserved heavenly reward, and attired, no doubt, in her best nightdress, held up by the typewriter ribbons with which she had, during her illness, hastily replaced frayed supports. At seventy-four, Mrs. Havemeyer was dead of heart disease. And, of course, she had the last word, at least in her beloved Museum.

The printed catalogue of the H. O. Havemeyer collection is 125 pages long in its 1958 revised edition and includes Horace Havemeyer's 1956 Near Eastern bequest. Here they all are, the wonders that were first seen by Museum members and their friends on that gloomy Depression Monday early in the spring of 1930. Here are the old masters, including thirty-four Rembrandt prints, "the most extraordinary gift this department . . . has ever received"; eighteen Courbets; the Whistlers Mrs. Havemeyer had bought out of her girlhood savings; the light-mad, sun-struck Impressionists, including eight Monets and forty-two Degases, plus sixty-eight of his bronzes; the five Cézannes; the extremely delicate Cassatt color prints, twenty-three of them; and Daumier's supreme *oeuvre*, *The Third Class Carriage*, for which Mrs. Havemeyer had paid $40,000 in 1913, after frugally journeying to the Borden auction in a public conveyance. Nine Manets were in the bequest. "One must turn over a new page in the history of art if one wishes to know anything of the painter Manet," Mrs. Havemeyer wrote of him. One morning, perhaps in 1889, Mr. Havemeyer told his wife that he was off to the Durand-Ruel exhibition at the Academy. "If you find any Manets there, be sure to buy me one," Mrs. Havemeyer suggested. He did; he almost always bought any unusual painting, ancient Mesopotamian pot, antique Chinese screen, or exotic textile his Louisine wanted. He even purchased Courbet's most sensuous nudes, for he never doubted, at least not for long, his wife's taste or his own.

The H. O. Havemeyer collection is of such a lofty level because the Havemeyer children not only added sumptuously to their mother's original bequest, from both their parents' collection and their own, but also asked the Museum's curators to help decide which works should be bequeathed

and which presented as gifts to the Museum. It took Breck (Decorative Arts), Burroughs (Paintings), Ivins (Prints), Priest (Far Eastern), Grancsay (Arms and Armor), Lansing (Egyptian), and Miss Richter (Classical) almost a year to determine this. In 1957, A. Hyatt Mayor, then Curator of Prints, wrote about these extraordinary benefactors, "They had in the highest degree the indispensable requirement for a great collector—the courage of perception—and this rare quality makes a Havemeyer object recognizable no matter where it turns up. Their things do not look rich materially but each one identifies itself in any gallery by its accident of imagination."

In her autobiography, *Sixteen to Sixty: Memoirs of a Collector* (privately printed for the family of Mrs. H. O. Havemeyer and the Metropolitan Museum of Art, New York, N.Y., 1961), an epigraph sums up Mrs. Havemeyer's philosophy of art appreciation and collecting, and it serves also as a testimonial for and to all great art lovers and collectors: "Art [will] hold up her head and say: 'I am a first necessity; all else may be cheap, but I shall ever be in demand. My present owner's fortune may crumble, his title may vanish, his manhood deteriorate, but I shall survive and with proud prestige of fame, pass on from generation to generation, from one great land to another, bearing regardless of race or time my message unto all mankind.' "

There is a pendant to the Havemeyer year in the Museum, another evidence of collectors' hungry determination and art's longevity. William Christian Paul, an utterly obscure insurance clerk of modest means, left 1065 Chinese textiles to the Museum. These treasures came out of his little two-room West Side apartment to make the Museum's Chinese textile collection "the best in any museum in the world, with the exception of the Imperial Palace Museum of Peking." And there were other affirmations to cheer the Museum and its frequenters during this decade when shanty towns of the new poor were mushrooming in the Park, making it look much as it did when the first plans had been made to locate the Museum there some sixty years before. Although the number of paying annual members plummeted during the first four years of the Thirties and general attendance fell off frighteningly, attendance at the Museum's free concerts and lectures soared, with 16,798 coming to a single concert early in 1935.

A whole era passed with the deaths of Robert W. de Forest; Henry Walters; Edward Robinson, director since 1910; Advisory Trustee Daniel Chester French, who had defended Saint-Gaudens' *Diana*; Joseph Breck; Bryson Burroughs; Elihu Root, trustee for thirty-seven years; and Albert M. Lythgoe, who had founded the Egyptian expeditions. In addition to the ever-successful twenty-eight-year-old Egyptian digs, the Museum's Near Eastern expeditions had gone on triumphantly for almost three years. George Blumenthal, banker, long-time trustee, and a voracious collector who lived on Park Avenue in a vast mansion which "seemed the absolute model and epitome of the palace of a renaissance prince . . . one of the most spectacular private homes in the city," became the Museum's seventh president after the death of William Sloane Coffin. There was a sudden sense of newness and energy in the Museum air, with Blumenthal heading a board to which were elected, as the decade progressed, Horace Havemeyer, Myron C. Taylor, Marshall Field, Nelson A. Rockefeller, Roland L. Redmond, Thomas J. Watson, and others important in the Museum's future. Egyptologist Herbert E. Winlock, who came to the Museum in 1905, when the staff numbered 124, was director until ill health caused him to resign in 1939; Harry B. Wehle became Curator of Paintings; and finally Ambrose Lansing took over the Department of Egyptian Art. There were rigid economies, with salaries being lowered for a time and purchases of important treasures being curtailed, but a Department of Near Eastern Art was established, with Maurice S. Dimand as its curator. Then the vast Department of Decorative Arts split into three constantly expanding departments. At least two out of every three objects that come into the Museum are neither paintings nor sculptures. James J. Rorimer, who had come to Decorative Arts in 1927, headed the Department of Medieval Art and The Cloisters; Preston Remington, the Department of Renaissance and Modern Art; and Joseph Downs, the now independent American Wing.

The Depression years spawned museum and art activity. The Whitney Museum of American Art was founded in 1930, and the Solomon R. Guggenheim Museum in 1937. In that same year Aline Bernstein and Irene Lewisohn created the Costume Institute, now unique among world museums. The Frick Collection opened in 1935, and the Museum of Modern Art, in its new building, in 1939. Six years before, the Metropolitan Museum and the Museum of Modern Art had, for their mutual benefit, created a joint committee of the boards of each. And throughout most of the decade, the Work Projects Administration helped the Museum by assigning technicians and office workers to it, while the Museum aided American artists, using Hearn fund money to build up the contemporary American art collection. It was a good American decade at the Museum. The American Wing was enlarged to accommodate the great entry hall from the 1765–1769 Van Rensselaer Manor House, Albany, and the added gifts from Van Rensselaer descendants and others, which included the mansion's original woodwork, its picturesque original 1768 scenic wallpaper, and elegantly paneled doors. The new one-story building also housed the anonymous gift of a fine room from Providence, Rhode Island, and when a second story was added, in 1934, there were two more beautiful rooms in which Curator Downs arranged the profusion of cheery Pennsylvania German decorative arts which had been given to the Museum by Mrs. Robert W. de Forest. Soon the American Wing incorporated the seventeenth-century parlor from the Thomas Hart house, Ipswich, Massachusetts, and the room and two staircases from the 1671 Samuel Wentworth house in Portsmouth, New Hampshire. And by 1939, the American Wing had been given, by John Bayard Verplanck, James De Lancey Verplanck, and other descendants of the original owner, Samuel Verplanck, the furnishings of his and his wife's very fashionable drawing room, in which New York's Tories had gathered when the house was still standing at 3 Wall Street—until 1803.

This was the decade in which exhibitions celebrated George Washington, Benjamin Franklin, S. F. B. Morse, John La Farge, and John Singleton Copley, the latter exhibition being the first in America to which Great Britain's national museums made loans. And furniture fanciers saw a revelatory display of early pieces made by New York craftsmen, while silver lovers enjoyed the serene splendors of a show of early New York-made silver.

The biggest American Wing acquisition came in 1933 when Judge Alphonse Trumphour Clearwater, who for many years had quietly been assembling and putting on loan in the Museum a superlative American silver collection, bequeathed over five hundred pieces. This gracious, humorous, old-fashioned American made his collection so that future generations would have a chance to see that "there existed in the American Colonies, and early in the States of the Republic, and among the members of early American families, not only a refined taste creating a demand for beautiful silver, but an artistic instinct and skill upon the part of American silversmiths, enabling them to design and to make articles of Church and domestic silver which in beauty of line and workmanship, well compares with the work of foreign silversmiths."

Judge Clearwater's belief in American craftsmen pervades the decade's culminating American exhibition, "Life in America," three hundred years of it, as depicted in 290 works by the painters who saw it. It was a special loan show, from 145 collections, held in the Museum during the New York World's Fair, April 24 to October 29, 1939, and no one had ever viewed anything like it. Here was life as Americans had actually lived it, art and history combining to create a new and vivid form of visual documentary evidence. The catalogue, a witty, charming compendium, has become collector's quarry, while *Life in America*, the two-volume, 1076-page social history by Marshall B. Davidson, then editor of the Museum's publications, is a cornerstone in popular American historical studies.

Along with opportunities to rediscover American roots, these Depression years exposed Museum-goers to the evolving idea of using art to promote international understanding and good will. Soviet Russia sent an exhibition of icons; French national museums contributed heavily to a comprehensive showing of French eighteenth-century painting and sculpture; and Dwight W. Morrow, United States Ambassador to Mexico, 1927–1930, and Fred P. Keppel instigated a "Decorative Arts of Mexico" exhibit which enchanted all beholders. There were exhibitions reflecting expanding collecting tastes and amplifying Museum acquisitions. The Depression may have lessened the latter, but collectors continued to assure themselves of at least a little immortality as long as world-wide impoverishment and fascist ravages in Europe were throwing unexpected treasures on the market. The Museum gained some of these glories.

Fifth Avenue jeweler Michael Dreicer's flawless medieval and Renaissance collection, including twenty-four superb paintings, definitely became the Museum's after a decade of wrangling with heirs, as did the Theodore M. Davis bequest after fifteen years of litigation. Here was a museum in itself, 1104 items, and among them, marvelous works of Egyptian art excavated by lawyer-financier-Egyptologist Davis while on digs in Thebes, in the Valley of the Kings. When the bequest of Benjamin Altman's cousin and successor as store president, Colonel Michael Friedsam, came in 1931, the Museum acquired a collection especially formed to "illustrate the art of painting" from the sixteenth to the nineteenth centuries. Strongest in the earlier epochs, it was supplemented by decorative-arts objects of excellent quality in all periods. Colonel Friedsam's underlying aim in making this bequest exemplifies the highest motivations underlying this golden age of Museum giving: ". . . to enrich the City of New York . . . and thus to enhance its prestige as one of the most important art centers of the world; and to make available to students in New York these works of art . . . brought together primarily for their particular study and inspiration."

It is difficult to believe that the Depression actually curtailed Museum acquisitions, for in this decade the Museum acquired not only the intarsia *studiolo* from the ducal palace of Gubbio but the Grinling Gibbons stair from Cassiobury Hall; the stately Landsdowne House room (now one of the most beautiful in America); the Kirtlington Park room; and masterpieces by Hubert van Eyck, Rubens, Titian, Raphael, Mantegna, Fra Filippo Lippi, Watteau, Goya, Henri Rousseau, and George Caleb Bingham. His serene, mysterious *Fur Traders Descending the Missouri* is like a marvelous memory of the American Midwestern frontier fixed forever in the mind. The largest purchase of Romanesque architectural elements was made, and the decorative-arts objects purchased or given to the Museum during these years were, some of them, more splendid than any related treasures in other collections.

On May 10, 1938, the Museum's most monumental affirmation of faith in man and his spirit's survival through art opened its doors. The Cloisters was the many-years-long dream of one man, John D. Rockefeller, Jr. "Thus there is realized today," he told the dignitaries and other guests at the opening ceremonies of this museum of medieval art, "an ideal toward which I have been working for twenty years. . . . If what has been created here helps to interpret beauty as one of the great spiritual and inspirational forces of life, having power to transform drab duty into radiant living . . . those who have builded here will not have built in vain."

George Grey Barnard, an American sculptor of vigorous figures, had an affinity for Romanesque and Gothic sculpture and architecture. Knowing that it was impossible for American sculptors to study these epochs without going to Europe, he sought out such works, especially in southern France, where he was able to find fragments, architectural elements, and sometimes almost-whole structures or complete statues half-buried in barnyards and used to prop up hen coops, or littering the fields. He could, of course, buy these old stones for almost nothing. In 1914, Barnard assembled them in a little red brick building which he had designed and erected on a patch of land near his studio, very far uptown in Manhattan on Fort Washington Avenue. This would be his museum of medieval art, "open to all." To this churchlike structure, always filled with the fragrance of flowers and incense, Welles Bosworth, the architect closest to the Rockefellers during the earlier years of this century, brought John D., Jr., who immediately fell in love with what he saw and bought one hundred objects, both Barnard's own work and that of the anonymous artists of the Middle Ages. A cult was growing in America for the medieval: Henry Adams' *Mont St. Michel and Chartres*, privately printed in 1904, had been publicly published in the previous year (1913), while Mrs. Jack Gardner, even earlier, in the Nineties, had bought Romanesque capitals and Gothic sculpture. But George Grey Barnard and, later, John D. Rockefeller, Jr., gave the medieval cult its biggest impetus.

The cult really found wings when Joseph Breck, Decorative Arts Curator, informed Mr. Rockefeller, already famous for world-wide philanthropies and munificence to the Museum, that Barnard's collection was for sale, and Rockefeller proffered a fund from which the Museum could purchase the trove, and another fund which would care for the maintenance of Barnard's Cloisters as a public museum. And on May 3, 1926, the public began to trek north to the Museum's branch museum. It was an immediate success, for despite lack of transportation (not until 1932 did a subway stop near it, and the Fifth Avenue Coach Company did not arrange a bus route until 1933) over forty-six thousand people came to The Cloisters during its first ten months.

That this sanctuary for the medieval would always be viable was immediately apparent to Breck, The Cloisters' first curator, and to everyone else involved in the Museum. Mr. and Mrs. Rockefeller at once gave The Cloisters a gift of forty Gothic sculptures, while Mr. Rockefeller was already planning a new home for the expanding collection. It would be just to the north, on Manhattan's highest ridge, occupying some four acres of the sixty Rockefeller had bought in the hope that the city would accept this historic ground, the last Indian-owned on the island and a fought-over bastion during the Revolution, for use as a public park. "With Rockefellers," wrote William Manchester in his *A Rockefeller Family Portrait from John D. to Nelson*, "wealth is something you spend on other people."

It took about twelve years of Rockefeller tenacity and personal supervision, and it took more and more Rockefeller millions. In 1934 John D., Jr., gave a "Gothic" fund which enabled the Museum to buy as it built. And at last, there it stood, a monastery-citadel, fashioned of hand-cut blocks of millstone granite from New London, Connecticut, and authentic Gothic architectural elements mostly from southern France. High above the Hudson Valley it loomed, not quite medieval, nor remotely twentieth century, but a happy construction of the simplest Gothic transliterated by twentieth-century minds steeped in medievalism. Breck had instigated it; Rockefeller had paid for it and nourished it; James J. Rorimer, having taken Breck's place after he died, had realized it in its every practical detail, by working ceaselessly not only with Rockefeller, George Blumenthal, a special trustee committee including Nelson A. Rockefeller, John D., Jr.'s second son, and Boston architect Charles Collens, but with hundreds of specialists, craftsmen, contractors, and laborers besides. Always Rockefeller was on hand, with his famous four-foot folding ruler, which he carried in his hip pocket, but never did he interfere: "The decision is yours," he inevitably told Rorimer. But no matter who made the final decision, Rockefeller insisted that the result be even more perfect than had been believed possible. When Aline B. Saarinen was researching *The Proud Possessors*, Nelson Rockefeller reminisced to her, "One of father's favorite expressions is 'The last five percent is what counts.' His whole feeling is that if the last five percent—the finish and the detail—are taken care of, everything else will come out all right." In the first ten months that the new Cloisters was open, 536,551 visitors came, more than in the entire ten years the old Cloisters had been open. So "everything else" did "come out all right." Cloisters visitors not only wandered through the most important collection of its kind in America, which by this time included among Rockefeller gifts "the most superb ensemble of fifteenth-century tapestries in existence," *The Hunt of the Unicorn*. There was also the unexpected beauty of the museum's situation, with its herb garden; its flower-bordered, flagged paths; its fruit trees blossoming seasonally; and its extraordinary vista across the wide river of acres of the Palisades which had been bought by Rockefeller and presented to the Palisades Interstate Park Commission to preserve their beauty forever. And everyone loved the concerts of recorded medieval music—everything from Gregorian chants to country dance tunes—as well as the special beauty of displays and programs at Christmas and Easter and the high springtide garden parties for Museum members. "In a well-rounded life," John D. Rockefeller, Jr., was once heard to say, "beauty plays a real part." For the beauty that is The Cloisters, J. D., Jr.'s, funds have paid some ninety-five per cent of the cost.

On March 13, 1925, René Gimpel noted in his diary, a document of frequent, acerbic, uninhibited assessment, "John D. Rockefeller, Jr., came to see me today. I didn't know him and I found myself confronted with a marvelous creature. He delivers sermons in church on Sunday and has in fact something of the priest about him. This man, the greatest philanthropist the world has ever seen, does so much good on earth, cares so much about all our miseries, that I am not surprised he seems to be somehow of divine origin. This constant occupation, the occupation of goodness, has surely fashioned his face in the likeness of his spirit . . . it is a wonderful thing to see."

The decade of the two great affirmations, the H. O. Havemeyer collection exhibition and The Cloisters' opening, also included, in 1939, the opening on January 18 of the Museum's new Armor Hall, which now housed one of the world's greatest collections. The late Bashford Dean was mainly responsible for this. And, as visitors looked at some of the finest suits of armor extant, on September 3, when Britain and France declared war on Nazi Germany, they found, perhaps, some assurance in noting that these legendary trappings and implements of war had survived as works of supreme craftsmanship. Indeed, the Armor Hall was filled with works of art.

OPPOSITE: Street scene in 1900. Afternoon crowds in front of the Flatiron Building, Broadway and Fifth Avenue at Twenty-third Street.

# 1900–1909

Madison Square in 1901. Looking south from about Twenty-fourth Street. Photograph by Byron, courtesy Museum of the City of New York.

ABOVE: *Florinda*. Franz Xavier Winterhalter, German, 1806–1873. Oil. Bequest of William H. Webb, 1901. Winterhalter, the court painter of his era, used the Empress Eugenie and her maids of honor for several of his most famous canvases. LEFT: The East Wing, opened in 1904.

ABOVE: Etruscan biga from Monteleone, 550–540 B.C. Wood with bronze sheathing. Rogers Fund, 1903. BELOW: Apulian hydria: the abduction of Persephone. Fourth century B.C. Gift of Miss Matilda W. Bruce, 1907. RIGHT: Portrait statue of Trebonianus Gallus (reigned 251–253). Roman. Bronze. Rogers Fund, 1905. OPPOSITE: Jousting armor. German, c. 1500. Rogers Fund, 1904.

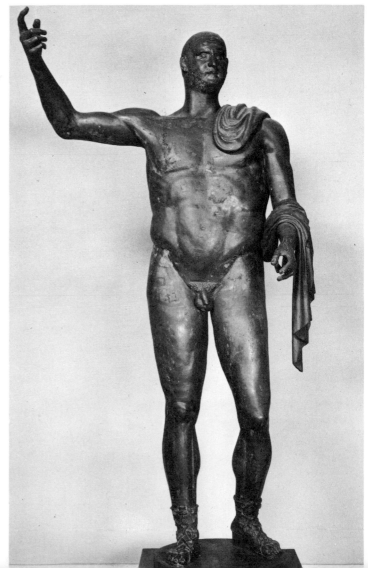

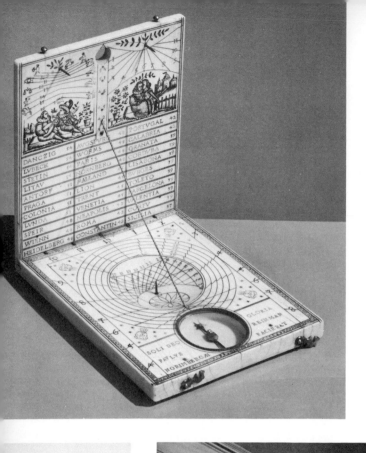

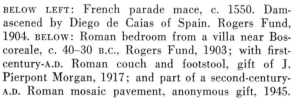

LEFT: Portable compass dial. Paul Reinman, 1578–1607. Ivory. RIGHT: Portable wooden cube dial, paper-faced, with four vertical sundials, one horizontal dial, and a compass on the base. Both German, from Nuremberg. Gifts of Mrs. Stephen D. Tucker, 1903.

BELOW LEFT: French parade mace, c. 1550. Damascened by Diego de Caias of Spain. Rogers Fund, 1904. BELOW: Roman bedroom from a villa near Boscoreale, c. 40–30 B.C., Rogers Fund, 1903; with first-century-A.D. Roman couch and footstool, gift of J. Pierpont Morgan, 1917; and part of a second-century-A.D. Roman mosaic pavement, anonymous gift, 1945.

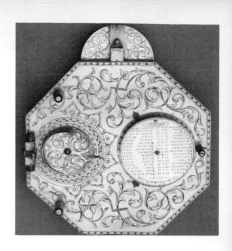

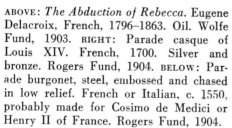

ABOVE: *The Abduction of Rebecca.* Eugene Delacroix, French, 1796–1863. Oil. Wolfe Fund, 1903. RIGHT: Parade casque of Louis XIV. French, 1700. Silver and bronze. Rogers Fund, 1904. BELOW: Parade burgonet, steel, embossed and chased in low relief. French or Italian, c. 1550, probably made for Cosimo de Medici or Henry II of France. Rogers Fund, 1904.

ABOVE RIGHT: Portable compass dial of brass-gilt and silver. Claude Dunod, Düsseldorf. German, dated 1714. Gift of Mrs. Stephen D. Tucker, 1903. RIGHT: Armor of an officer of a Daimyo of Sakai, flame color and gold. Japanese, c. 1550. Rogers Fund, 1904.

BELOW: "Hawk" Panel from the pyramid of Sesostris I. Egyptian, twelfth dynasty. Lisht Excavations, 1907–1934. Limestone.

ABOVE: Bedroom from the Sagredo Palace. Venetian, c. 1718. Rogers Fund. LEFT: *Benedikt von Hertenstein* (1495?–1522). Hans Holbein the Younger, German, 1497–1543. Oil on paper, mounted on wood. Rogers Fund, aided by subscribers, 1906.

ABOVE: Earring from Madytos. Greek. Fourth century B.C. Gold. Rogers Fund, 1906. RIGHT: *The Adoration of the Shepherd*. El Greco (Domenicus Theotocopoulos), Spanish, 1541–1641. Bequest of George Blumenthal, 1941.

ABOVE: Relief from the temple of Mentu-hotep, Deir-el Bahri. Egyptian, twelfth dynasty. Limestone. Gift of the Egyptian Exploration Fund, 1907. BELOW: *The Gulf Stream*. Winslow Homer, American, 1836–1910. Oil, dated 1899. Wolfe Fund, 1906.

RIGHT: *Angelica and Medor*. Jacques Blanchard, French, 1600–1638. Oil. Gift of George A. Hearn, 1906. BELOW: Room from Flims, Switzerland, c. 1682, of carved and veneered wood. Rogers Fund, 1906.

ABOVE: *The Oxbow (The Connecticut River near Northampton)*. Thomas Cole.
Oil, dated 1846. Gift of Mrs. Russell Sage, 1908. LEFT: Relief from the tomb of
Ny-ku-Hor and Sekhem-Hathor. Egyptian, fifth dynasty. Rogers Fund, 1908. BELOW:
Collar of carnelian, green feldspar, gold-leaf on plaster, green faïence from the
tomb of Senebtisy. Egyptian, twelfth dynasty. Lisht Excavations, 1906–1907. Rogers
Fund, 1908.

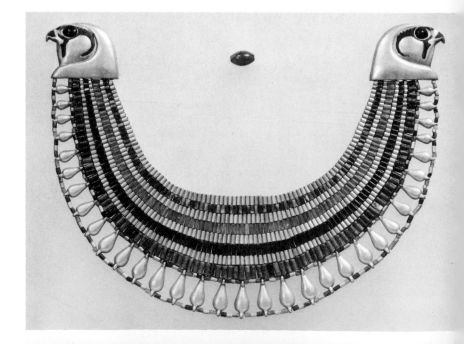

LEFT: Statuette of Tha-hap-emu from Memphis. Egyptian, thirtieth dynasty. Diabase. Gift of the Egyptian Research Account and British School of Archeology in Egypt, 1908. ABOVE: Connecticut-type chest, American, late seventeenth century. Oak top and bottom, pine back. BELOW: Banister-back armchair. American, c. 1700. Maple, ash, and oak. Gifts of Mrs. Russell Sage, 1909.

*The Rocky Mountains.* Albert Bierstadt, American, 1830–1902. Oil. Rogers Fund, 1907.

*Madame Charpentier and Her Children.* Pierre Auguste Renoir, French, 1841–1919. Oil, dated 1878. Wolfe Fund, 1907.

OPPOSITE: The "aristocracy of the pen" cele-brated Mark Twain's birthday at Delmonico's, December 5, 1905. At his table (clockwise) are Kate Douglas Wiggin, Twain, Bliss Carman, Mary E. Wilkins Freeman, and friends. Photo-graph by Byron, courtesy Museum of the City of New York.

RIGHT: Pyxis from Cumae. Pottery. Attributed to the Penthesileia painter. Athenian, c. 465–450 B.C. Rogers Fund, 1907. FAR RIGHT: Calyx-krater. Attributed to the painter of the Berlin Hydria. Athenian, 460–450 B.C. Rogers Fund, 1907.

LEFT: *Mother and Child*. Mary Cassatt, American, 1845–1926. Oil. George A. Hearn Fund, 1909. ABOVE LEFT: Funerary lekythos. Greek, c. 440 B.C. Pottery. Rogers Fund, 1908. ABOVE: Wing E under construction in 1907. BELOW: Courtiers with roses. Franco-Flemish (Arras or Tournai), c. 1435–1440. Wool tapestry. Rogers Fund, 1909.

BELOW: *A Group of Trees*. Titian, Italian, 1485–1576. Pen and ink. Rogers Fund, 1908.

ABOVE: *Landscape*. Thomas Gainsborough. Charcoal and chalk. Rogers Fund, 1907. BELOW: Eighth National Automobile Show, 1907. Photograph by Byron, courtesy Museum of the City of New York.

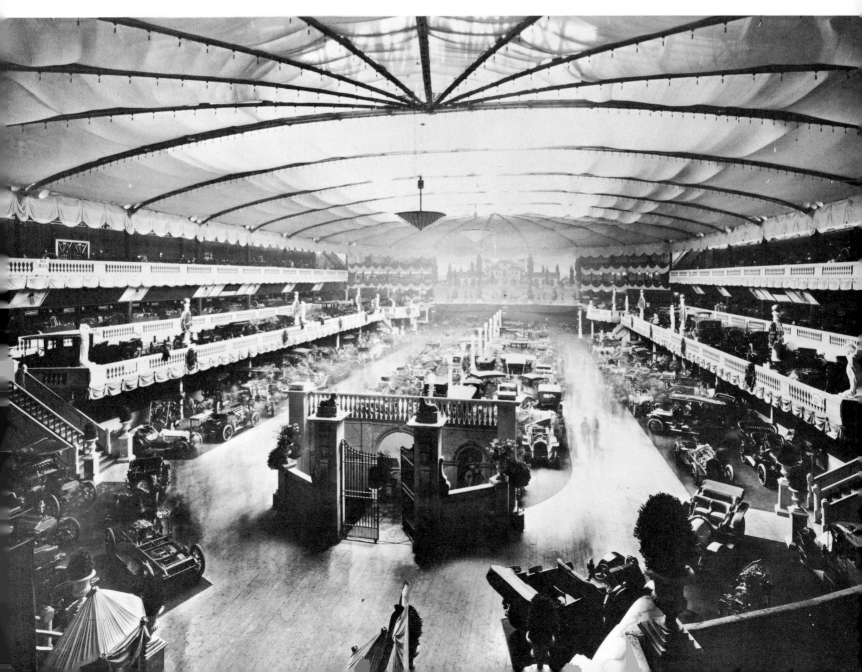

Views of the special exhibitions in the American section of the Museum honoring
the Hudson-Fulton Celebration in 1909 (ABOVE, BELOW, and OPPOSITE PAGE, BOTTOM).

Highlights of the city's Hudson-Fulton Celebration. ABOVE: A gathering of New York State Indians and, at right, Governor Hughes addressing the crowd at Spuyten Duyvil. RIGHT: One of the parades. BELOW: At left, Sailors present the *Clermont*'s bell and, at right, part of the water pageant, showing the replicas of the *Half Moon* and the *Clermont*.

**1910–1919**

The Museum in 1916.

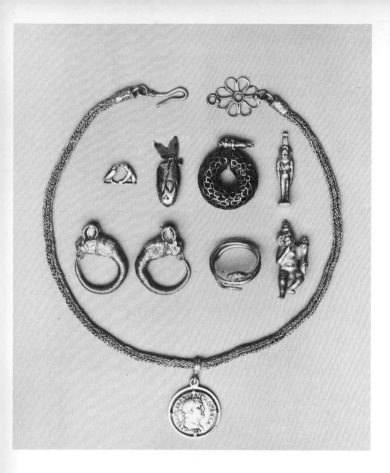

ABOVE: *Madonna and Child Enthroned with Saints*. Taddeo Gaddi, Italian (Florentine), active 1334, d. 1366. Tempera on wood, gold ground. Rogers Fund, 1910.

ABOVE LEFT: Egyptian jewelry of the Ptolemaic or Graeco-Roman period. Third century B.C. Gold. Gift of Miss Helen Miller Gould, 1910. BELOW LEFT: Amphora. Greek, c. 650 B.C. Rogers Fund, 1911. RIGHT: Wood panel. Egyptian, Fatimid period, eleventh century B.C. Rogers Fund, 1911.

BELOW: Rug with design of animals. Persian (Tabriz), sixteenth century. Silk and wool. Hewitt Fund, 1910. OPPOSITE: *Mars and Venus United by Love*. Paolo Veronese, Italian (Venetian), 1528–1588. Oil. Kennedy Fund, 1910.

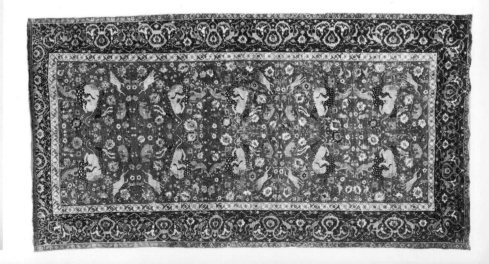

PAVLVS · VERONENSIS · F ·

LEFT: Daybed. American, seventeenth century. Gift of Mrs. Russell Sage, 1909.
BELOW: A section of the Winslow Homer 1911 exhibition.

OPPOSITE: At left, statue of a youth, perhaps Gaius or Lucius Caesar. Roman, Augustan period. Rogers Fund, 1914. At right, carved chest by Thomas Dennis, Ipswich, Massachusetts, c. 1675. Gift of Mrs. Russell Sage, 1909.

*Girl Asleep.* Johannes Vermeer, Dutch, 1632–
1675. Oil. Bequest of Benjamin Altman, 1913.

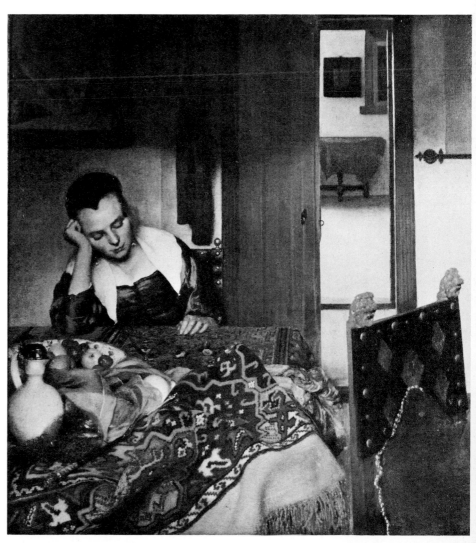

ABOVE LEFT: Japanese mask, fifteenth century. Gift of Bashford Dean, 1914. ABOVE: Paintings in the Morgan Collection, 1913. LEFT: Panel. Italian or Spanish, fifteenth century. Gold on velvet. Rogers Fund, 1915. RIGHT: *The Last Communion of Saint Jerome.* Sandro Botticelli, Italian (Florentine), 1444/1445–1510. Tempera on wood. Bequest of Benjamin Altman, 1913. FAR RIGHT: Statuette. King Sesostris I. From the tomb of Imhotep, Lisht. Egyptian, twelfth dynasty. Painted cedar. Excavations, 1913-1914. Rogers Fund supplemented by contribution of Edward S. Harkness. BELOW LEFT: *Madonna and Child with Scroll*, Luca della Robbia, Italian (Florentine), 1399/1400–1482. Enameled terra cotta. Bequest of Benjamin Altman, 1913. BELOW RIGHT: *The Meditation on the Passion.* Vittore Carpaccio, Italian (Venetian), c. 1455–1523/1526. Tempera on wood. Kennedy Fund, 1911.

OPPOSITE: *Angel of the Revelation.* William Blake, English, 1757–1827. Water color with pen and ink. Rogers Fund, 1914.

180

ABOVE: *Tommaso Portinare*. Hans Memling, Dutch, active c. 1465, d. 1494. Tempera and oil on wood. ABOVE LEFT: *Portrait of a Young Woman*. Rembrandt. Oil on wood, dated 1633. LEFT: *Portrait of the Artist*. Rembrandt. Oil, dated 1660. BELOW: *The Toilet of Bathsheba*. Rembrandt. Oil on wood, dated 1643. Bequests of Benjamin Altman, 1913.

OPPOSITE: *The Virgin and Child with Saint Anne*. Albrecht Dürer, German, 1471–1528. Tempera and oil, dated 1519. Bequest of Benjamin Altman, 1913.

OVERLEAF: Viewing the pictures, 1912.

Two oil paintings by Rembrandt. ABOVE: *Lady with a Pink*. OPPOSITE:
*Man with a Magnifying Glass*. Bequests of Benjamin Altman, 1913.

LEFT: *Arrangement in Flesh Color and Black: Portrait of Theodore Duret*. Whistler. Oil. Wolfe Fund, 1913. ABOVE: Colossal geometric krater. Greek (Attic), eighth century B.C. Rogers Fund, 1914.

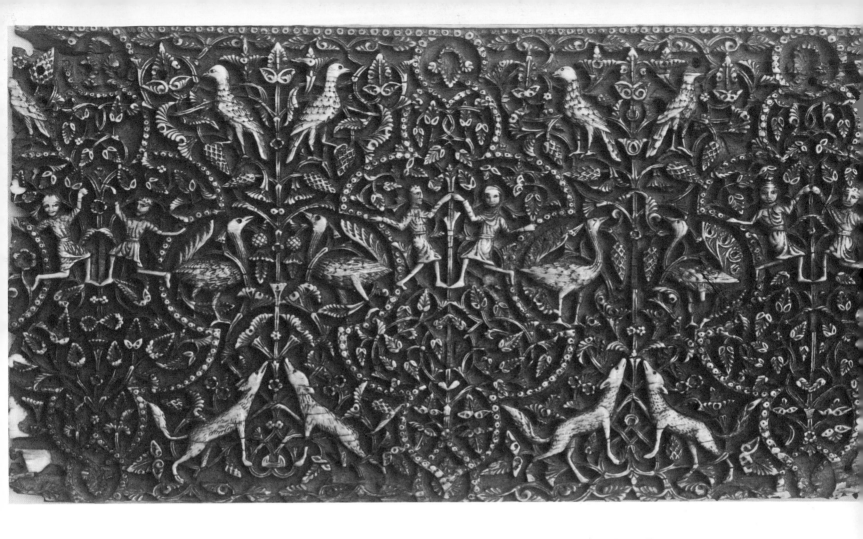

ABOVE: Ivory plaque, carved in deep relief. Hispano-Moresque (Cordova), period of Hakam II, 961–976. Kennedy Fund, 1913. BELOW LEFT: Tomb of Peri-nebi from Sakkara. Egyptian, fifth dynasty. Gift of Edward S. Harkness, 1913. BELOW RIGHT: *The Holy Family with Saint Mary Magdalen*. Andrea Mantegna, Italian (Paduan), 1431–1506. Bequest of Benjamin Altman, 1913.

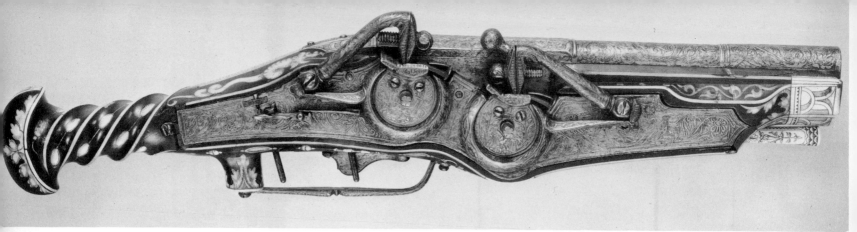

ABOVE: Double-barrel, double-wheel-lock pistol, made for the Emperor Charles V by Peter Peck of Munich. German, 1450. Stock and butt inlaid with engraved ivory. Gift of William H. Riggs, 1913. LEFT: "William." Figure of a hippopotamus from tomb of Senbi, at Meir. Egyptian, twelfth dynasty. Gift of Edward S. Harkness, 1917. BELOW: Ball-butt wheel-lock pistol, one of a pair, with primer-spanner. French, 1580. Gift of William H. Riggs, 1913.

OPPOSITE: Leaf from a Khamsa of Nizami. Persian (Herat), A.D. 1524–1525. Gift of Alexander Smith Cochran, 1913.

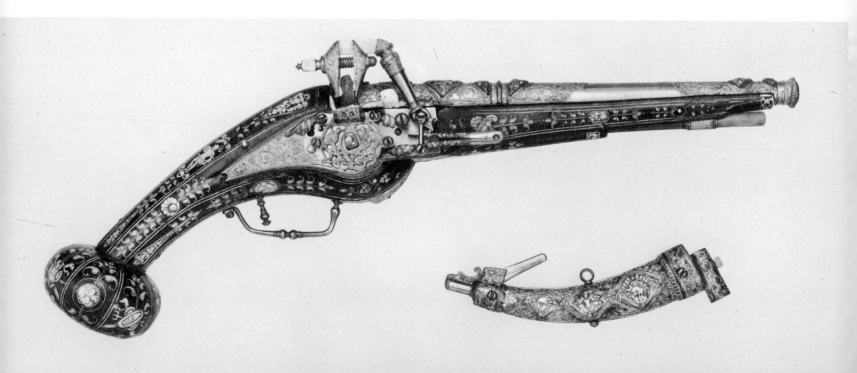

میان جانی و او برنس حبیب
شاه از دیدہ آن بلورکش
پسمن غافل ز نظر ابرشاه
از شرم چشم او و ٔ خیمهٔ آب

زمین مرده ابرا برآسمانست
شده خورشید یعنی وان دلانش
یک پستهٔ سته پُر بزرگ کشن راه
هستے لرزیده جون در خیمه مهتاب

بران خیمه که جای ما کشسته
فشاند از دیده باران ٔ سحابی
جو ماه آمد برون از ابر مشکین
همایے دید بر پشت ٔ درزی

مو پس من کنابی ز رابشته
که طالع شد قمر در برج ٔ آبے
بشاهنشه برآمد چشم شیرین
بابالای خذکی رشته سردی

جزان جاره نبد آن جشمهٔ قند
که کیسور جوشب برمریند
شب خورشید می بوشیدر
عبراف مذبرماه بش فروز
بشب خورشیدی بوشیدرد

ABOVE: Reliquary of the True Cross. Byzantine, eighth/ninth century. Silver gilt with cloisonné enamel. Gift of J. Pierpont Morgan, 1917.

ABOVE, BOTTOM LEFT, and TOP LEFT: Decorative art treasures on display in the J. Pierpont Morgan Wing, 1918. CENTER LEFT: Medallions of the Virgin and Christ. Byzantine, eleventh century. Enamel on gold. Gifts of J. Pierpont Morgan, 1917.

OPPOSITE: Manjusri. Tibetan or Chinese, seventeenth century. Appliqué on satin ground. Kennedy Fund, 1915.

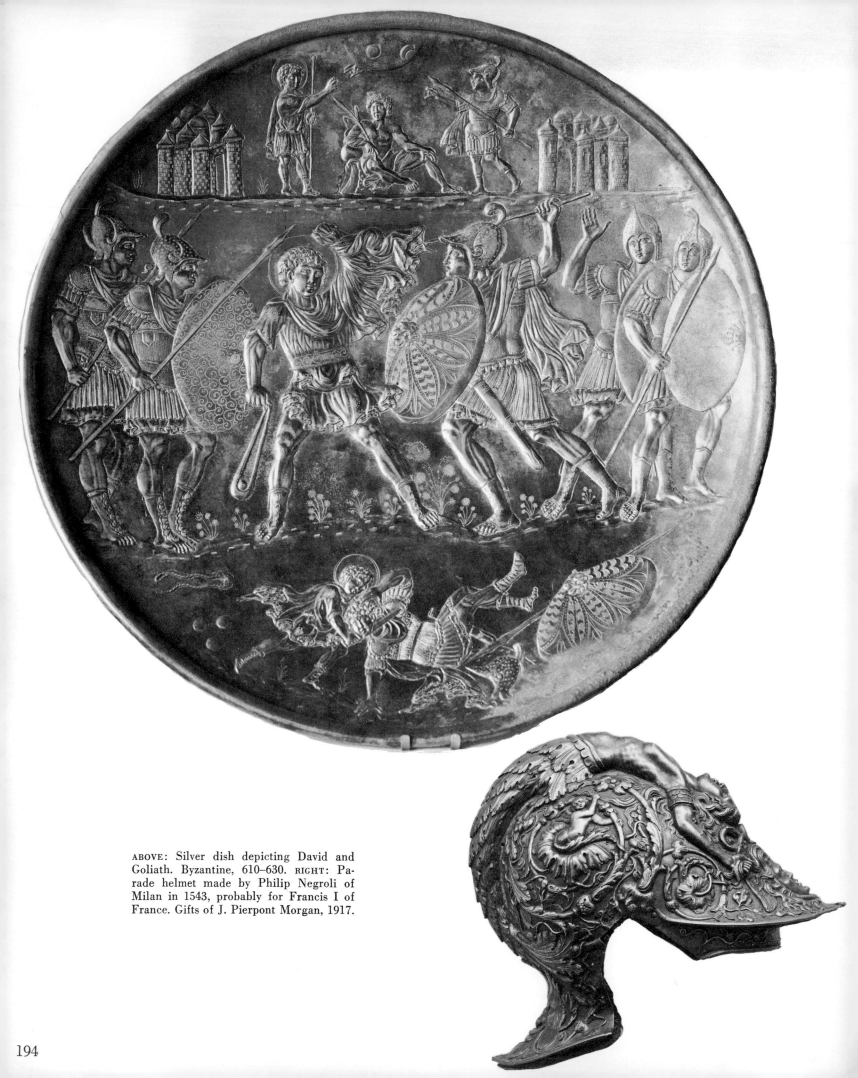

ABOVE: Silver dish depicting David and Goliath. Byzantine, 610–630. RIGHT: Parade helmet made by Philip Negroli of Milan in 1543, probably for Francis I of France. Gifts of J. Pierpont Morgan, 1917.

LEFT: Pectoral with name of Sesostris II, which belonged to Princess Sit-Hathor-Yunet. Egyptian (Lahun Treasure). Contribution from Henry Walters and the Rogers Fund, 1916. RIGHT: Amphora. Attributed to Exekias. Greek, sixth century B.C. Black-figured pottery. BELOW: Porcelain bowl. Chinese, Hsuan Te, Ming dynasty, 1426–1435. Both Rogers Fund, 1917.

ABOVE: *Battle of Naked Men*. Antonio Pollaiuolo, Italian, 1429–1488. Engraving. Purchase, 1917, Joseph Pulitzer Bequest. RIGHT: *Madame X* (Mme. Gautreau). Sargent. Oil, dated 1884. Arthur H. Hearn Fund, 1916.

OPPOSITE: Above left, pottery bowl. Chinese, Sung dynasty or earlier Yüeh yao. Rogers Fund, 1917. Below left, *Wheatfields*. Jacob Isaaksz. van Ruisdael, Dutch, 1628/1629–1682. Oil. Bequest of Benjamin Altman, 1914.

OPPOSITE: *The Letter*. Cassatt. Drypoint and aquatint. Gift of Paul J. Sachs, 1916.

RIGHT: Reliquary from Limoges. French, twelfth/thirteenth century. Champlevé enamel. Gift of J. Pierpont Morgan, 1917. BELOW LEFT: *Descent from the Cross by Torchlight*. Rembrandt. Etching. Gift of Felix M. Warburg, 1917. BELOW: Decorated tester bed from Salem, Massachusetts. Probably by Samuel McIntire, American, c. 1795. Carved, gilded, and painted mahogany. Kennedy Fund, 1918.

ABOVE: *The Four Horsemen of the Apocalypse.* Dürer. Woodcut. Gift of Junius S. Morgan, 1919. ABOVE RIGHT: Gilded equestrian armor made for Jacques Gourdon (called Galiot) de Genouilhac (1466–1546). French or Italian, dated 1527. Rogers Fund and gift of William H. Riggs, 1917. RIGHT: Pier table. American (Philadelphian), c. 1765. Mahogany with marble top. Kennedy Fund, 1918.

ABOVE: Seated Buddha. Chinese T'ang dynasty. Dry lacquer. Rogers Fund, 1919.
RIGHT: "Pompadour" highboy. American, c. 1765. Mahogany. Kennedy Fund, 1918.
BELOW: King Sahu-Re with figure personifying the province of Koptos. Egyptian, fifth dynasty. Rogers Fund, 1918.

Degas

*The Harvesters*. Pieter Brueghel the Elder, Flemish, active 1551, d. 1569. Oil on wood. Rogers Fund, 1919.

OPPOSITE: *Portrait of Edouard Manet (1882–1883)*. Edgar Hilaire Germain Degas, French, 1834–1917. Black chalk. Rogers Fund, 1918.

# 1920–1929

Figures with miniature boats and granary, as found in the tomb of Meket-Re. Egyptian, eleventh dynasty, c. 2000 B.C. Photographed by the Egyptian Expedition at Thebes, 1919–1920.

ABOVE: Carved tablet from a funerary chapel of the Han dynasty 206 B.C.–A.D. 220, said to have stood in the Ching Ping Hsien, Province of Shantung. Chinese, c. A.D. 114. Rogers Fund, 1920. BELOW: *Mrs. Grace Dalrymple Elliott*. Thomas Gainsborough, British, 1727–1788. Oil. Bequest of William K. Vanderbilt, 1920.

OPPOSITE: *The Toilet of Venus*. François Boucher, French, 1703–1770. Oil, dated 1751. Bequest of William K. Vanderbilt, 1920.

LEFT: Funerary model from the tomb of Meket-Re, at Thebes. Egyptian, eleventh dynasty (2131–1991 B.C.). Painted wood. Museum Excavations, 1919–1920. Rogers Fund and contribution from Edward S. Harkness. ABOVE: *Colonel George K. H. Coussmaker, Grenadier Guards* (1759–1801). Joshua Reynolds, British, 1723–1792. Oil. Bequest of William K. Vanderbilt, 1920. BELOW: *Murder in the Rue Transnonain*, lithograph from *L'Association Mensuelle*, 1834. Honoré Daumier, French, 1808–1879. Rogers Fund, 1920.

ABOVE: *Dust Storm, Fifth Avenue.* John Sloan, American, 1871–1951. Oil, dated 1906. George A. Hearn Fund, 1921. BELOW: *The Noble Slav.* Rembrandt. Oil, dated 1632. Bequest of William K. Vanderbilt, 1920.

Shop front from the Quai Bourbon, Paris. French, c. 1785. Gift of J. Pierpont Morgan, 1920.

ABOVE: Funerary models from the tomb of Meket-Re. Egyptian, eleventh dynasty (c. 2000 B.C.). Wood. Museum Excavations, 1919–1920. Rogers Fund and contribution from Edward S. Harkness. LEFT: The "Tree of Jesse" stained-glass window. Probably German, c. 1300. Hewitt Fund, 1922. BELOW: The Rodin Gallery in 1920.

Louis XVI ebony *secrétaire* with black marble top and black and gold lacquer panels, with the cipher of Marie Antoinette. Cabinet work by Riesener, 1735–1806; ormolu mounts by Pierre Gouthière, 1732–1813. French, 1780–1790. Bequest of William K. Vanderbilt, 1920.

213

ABOVE: "The Sculpture of Michelangelo," a special exhibition of casts in Room 6, Wing D, in 1922.

LEFT: Bronze statuette of a horse. Greek. Eighth century B.C. Rogers Fund, 1921. RIGHT: *St. Catherine*. Peter Paul Rubens, Flemish, 1577–1640. Etching (touched counterproof). Rogers Fund, 1922.

OPPOSITE: Above, the "Medici" parade helmet, probably made in the Royal French workshop. French or Italian, c. 1555. Rogers Fund and Joseph Pulitzer Bequest, 1904 and 1922. Below, the busy information desk in 1921.

FAR LEFT: Front view of a stone stele: Maitreya between two Bodhissattvas. Chinese, Wei dynasty (fifth century). Rogers Fund, 1924. LEFT: *The Cup of Tea.* Mary Cassatt, American, 1845–1926. Oil. Anonymous gift, 1922.

BELOW LEFT: Statues of King Amun-Hotpe III from Luxor. Egyptian, eighteenth dynasty. Black granite. Rogers Fund and contribution from Edward S. Harkness, 1921. BELOW: Lion head of copper gilt encasing a steel helmet. Italian (Venetian), 1460. Harris Brisbane Dick Fund, 1923.

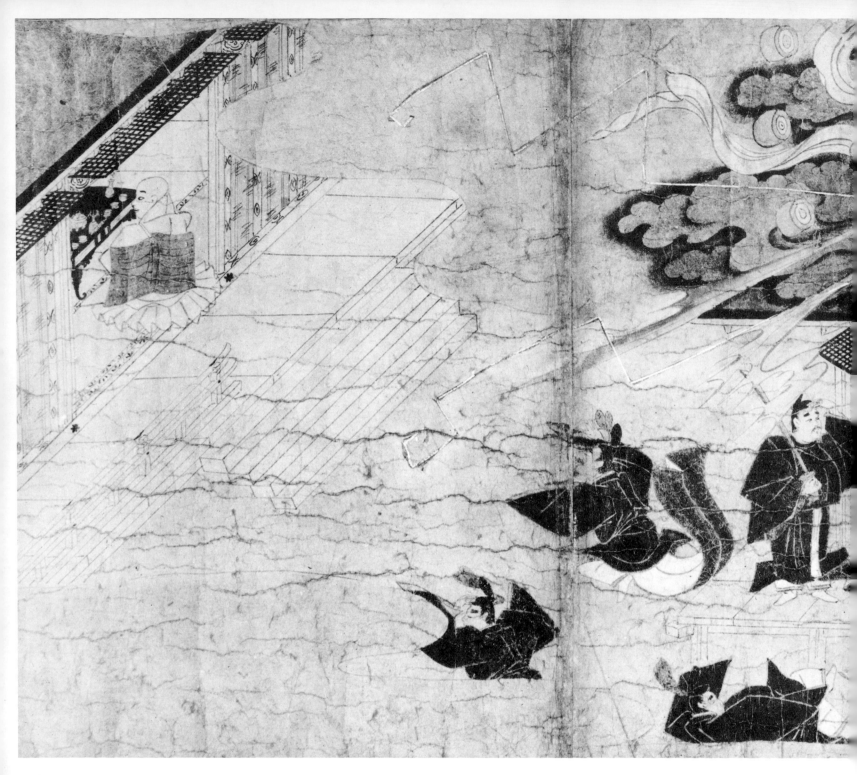

ABOVE: Episode in the *Story of Tenjin*. (Michizane Sugawara, thirteenth century). Detail of a painted scroll by an unknown artist. Japanese, Kamakura period. Fletcher Fund, 1925. LEFT: *A Sacrifice, after Il Rosso*. Antonio Fantuzzi, School of Fontainebleau. Etching. Gift of Miss Georgiana W. Sargent, in memory of John Osborn Sargent, 1924.

LEFT: Sofa made about 1740 for "Stenton," Germantown, the home of James Logan (1674–1751), who was acting governor of Pennsylvania from 1736 to 1738. Rogers Fund, 1925. RIGHT: Crossbow decorated with plaques of bone. Hungarian, dated 1489. Rogers Fund, 1925.

OPPOSITE: Belgian bobbin-lace handkerchief made for Marie Henriette of Austria at the time of her marriage to Leopold II of Belgium in 1853. Gift of the Needle and Bobbin Club, 1924.

ABOVE: Walnut armchair from Philadelphia, c. 1756. Rogers Fund, 1925. RIGHT: Statue of Harmhab, probably from Memphis. Egyptian, eighteenth dynasty (1355 B.C.). Gray granite. Gift of Mr. and Mrs. Everit Macy, 1923.

ABOVE: *Hendrickje Stoffels*. Dated 1660. BELOW: *Flora*. Both by Rembrandt. Oils. Gifts of Archer M. Huntington, 1926, in memory of his father, Collis Potter Huntington. RIGHT: Dagger with sheath. Swiss, 1567. Gift of Jean Jacques Reubell, 1926, in memory of his mother, Julia C. Coster, and of his wife, Adeline E. Post, both of New York City.

LEFT: Ornament of a lady of the Court of Tuthmosis III. Egyptian, from Thebes, eighteenth dynasty, 1501–1447 B.C. Gold circlet and band inlaid with carnelian, turquoise, and green paste. Gift of George F. Baker and Mr. and Mrs. V. Everit Macy, 1920. RIGHT: Statuette of the God Amun, from the precinct of the Great Temple of Amun at Karnak. Egyptian, twenty-second dynasty, c. 900 B.C. The Carnarvon Collection. Gift of Edward S. Harkness, 1926.

ABOVE: Ivory figure of a gazelle, from Thebes. Egyptian, eighteenth dynasty 1375–1350 B.C. Painted wooden base. Both the Carnarvon Collection, Gift of Edward S. Harkness, 1926. LEFT: Statue of Brahma. South Indian, nine/tenth century. Stone. Eggleston Fund, 1927.

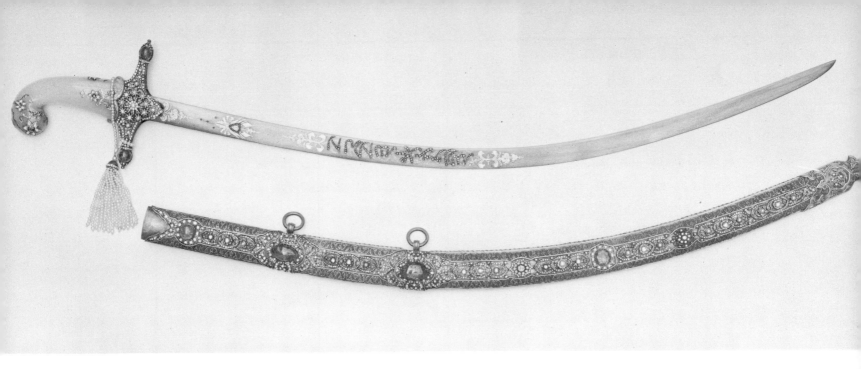

OPPOSITE: Statue of a Lohan. Chinese, Sung dynasty (Liao-Chin), eleventh/twelfth century. Glazed pottery. Hewitt Fund, 1921. ABOVE: Scimitar made for Murad V, who was Sultan of Turkey in 1876. Persian blade dated 1668; fittings later. Jade hilt, chased and jeweled scabbard. Gift of Giulia P. Morosini, 1923, in memory of her father, Giovanni Pertinax Morosini. BELOW: School group studying art in 1924.

ABOVE: Girl with pigeons. Grave stele from the island of Paros. Greek, c. 455–450 B.C. Marble. Fletcher Fund, 1927. RIGHT: Sakijamuni Buddha. Chinese, Wei dynasty, fifth century. Bronze gilt. Kennedy Fund, 1926.

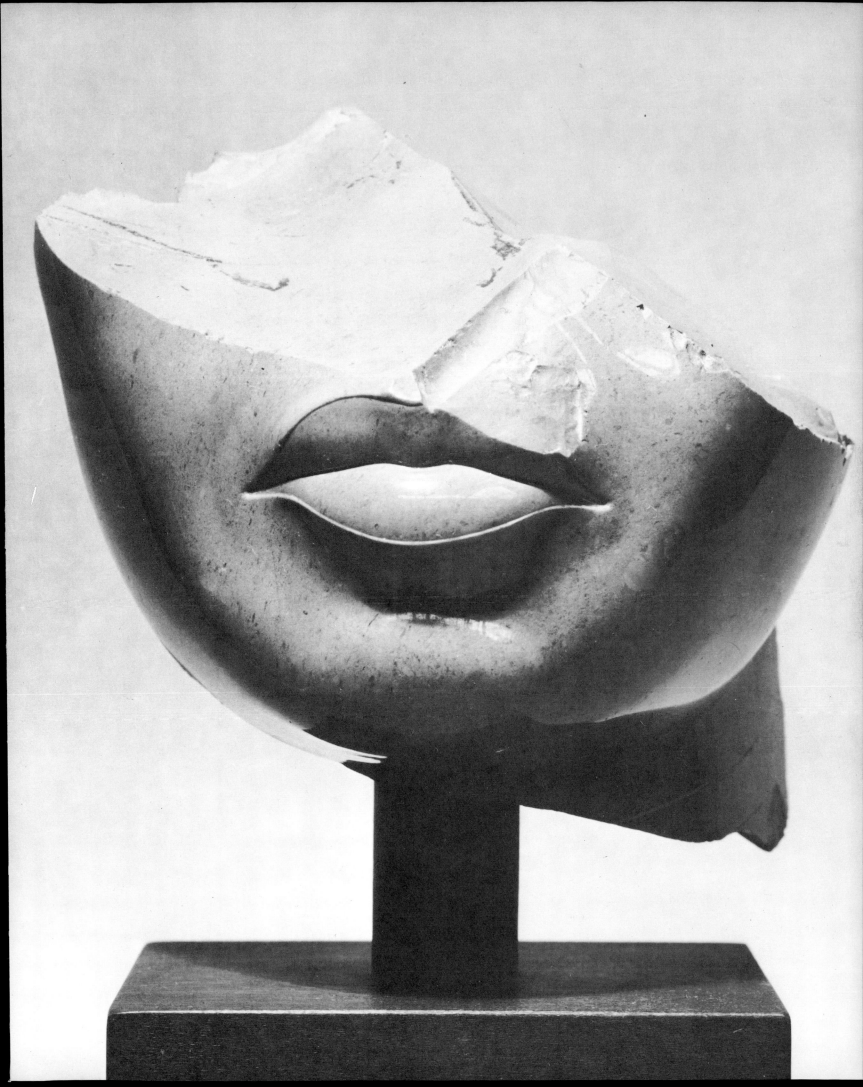

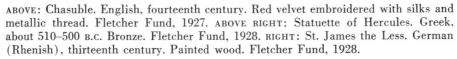

ABOVE: Chasuble. English, fourteenth century. Red velvet embroidered with silks and metallic thread. Fletcher Fund, 1927. ABOVE RIGHT: Statuette of Hercules. Greek, about 510–500 B.C. Bronze. Fletcher Fund, 1928. RIGHT: St. James the Less. German (Rhenish), thirteenth century. Painted wood. Fletcher Fund, 1928.

*Time, Apollo, and the Seasons.* Claude Lorrain, French, 1600–1682. Etching. Harris Brisbane Dick Fund, 1927.

ABOVE: *The Cathedral.* James Ensor, Belgian, 1860–1949. Engraving. BELOW: *Christ on the Mount of Olives.* Lucas Cranach the Elder, German, 1472–1553. Woodcut. Both Harris Brisbane Dick Fund, 1927.

RIGHT: Block-front chest made by John Townsend, Newport, Rhode Island, 1765. Mahogany. Rogers Fund, 1927.

ABOVE: The marble façade of the American Wing, rescued from the 1915 demolition of the United States Branch Bank erected from 1822 to 1824 at 15½ Wall Street, and given to the Museum in 1924 by Mr. and Mrs. Robert W. de Forest. LEFT: *The Letter*. Corot. Oil on wood, painted between 1865 and 1870. Gift of Horace Havemeyer, 1929. The H. O. Havemeyer Collection. RIGHT: Wheel-lock hunting gun bearing the arms of the Duke of Croy. Italian, 1560–1580. Decorated with gold and silver damascening and sculptured ivory. The Bashford Dean Memorial Collection, purchase, 1929, funds from various donors.

OVERLEAF: The Cloisters in Fort Tryon Park, designed by Charles Collens and begun in 1934.

LEFT: Short sword by Matatsune. Gold fittings by Kano Matsuo. Japanese, fourteenth century. Bequest of Mrs. H. O. Havemeyer, in 1929. RIGHT: Double virginal. Hans Ruekers the Elder, Flemish (Antwerp), 1581. Gift of B. Homan, 1929.

BELOW: An accumulation of medieval treasures in the old brick Cloisters structure on Fort Washington Avenue.

Three examples of interior design: A conservatory by Joseph Urban (LEFT), a dining room by Eliel Saarinen (RIGHT), and a child's nursery and bedroom by Eugene Schoen (BELOW), part of "The Architect and the Industrial Arts—An Exhibition of Contemporary American Design" shown at the Museum from February 12 to September 2, 1929.

BELOW: View of the "International Exhibition of Contemporary Glass and Rugs," organized by The American Federation of Arts, as it was displayed at the Metropolitan Museum during November 1929.

*The Gilder Herman Doomer.* Rembrandt. Oil on wood, dated 1640. Bequest of Mrs. H. O. Havemeyer, 1929.

LEFT: *Wife of Cornelis van Beresteyn.* Rembrandt. Oil, dated 1632. Bequest of Mrs. H. O. Havemeyer, 1929. The Museum also has the companion portrait, painted the same year, of her husband, who was Burgomeister of Delft (see page 244).

OPPOSITE: *Joseph Antoine Moltedo.* Jean Auguste Dominique Ingres, French, 1780–1867. Oil. Bequest of Mrs. H. O. Havemeyer, 1929.

RIGHT: *The Wyndham Sisters: Lady Elcho, Mrs. Tennant, and Mrs. Adeane.* Sargent. Oil, painted in 1900. Wolfe Fund, 1927.

RIGHT: *Nathan Admonishing David*. Pen and brown ink, brown wash, white gouache. BELOW: The Hundred Guilder Print: *Christ with the sick around Him, receiving little children*. Etching. Both by Rembrandt. Bequests of Mrs. H. O. Havemeyer, 1929.

*View of Toledo*. El Greco. Bequest of Mrs. H. O. Havemeyer, 1929.

*Boating.* Manet. Oil. Bequest of Mrs. H. O. Havemeyer, 1929.

LEFT: Gothic suit of armor. Italian, c. 1400. The Bashford Dean Memorial Collection, gift of Helen Fahnestock Hubbard, 1929, in memory of her father, Harris C. Fahnestock. RIGHT: *Mont Sainte-Victoire*. Paul Cézanne, French, 1839–1906. Oil. BELOW: *Cornelis van Beresteyn* (1586–1638). Rembrandt. Oil, dated 1632. Both bequests of Mrs. H. O. Havemeyer, 1929.

# 1930–1939

The Museum from the air in the early Thirties.

OPPOSITE: *The Virgin and Child on the Crescent*. Netherlands (?) School, fifteenth century. Bequest of James Clark McGuire, 1931. LEFT: Armor of George Clifford, Third Earl of Cumberland, K.G. (1558–1605). English (Greenwich School), 1590. Steel. Munsey Fund, 1932. ABOVE: *The Death of Socrates*. Jacques Louis David, French, 1748–1825. Oil, dated 1787. Wolfe Fund, 1931.

ABOVE: Column krater attributed to the painter Lydos. Greek (Athenian), c. 550–540 B.C. Fletcher Fund, 1931. BELOW: Chinese robe. Chinese, Ch'ien Lung dynasty, 1736–1795. Emperor's sacrificial robe embroidered in satin stitch; background of darning stitch on gauze. Joseph Pulitzer Fund, 1935.

ABOVE: Thirteenth-century Persian ewer. Underglaze-painted ceramic. Fletcher Fund, 1932. RIGHT: Room from Kirtlington Park, Oxfordshire. English, c. 1748. Both Fletcher Fund, 1932. BELOW: Staircase from Cassiobury Park, Hertfordshire (1677–1680). By Grinling Gibbons, English, 1648–1720. Rogers Fund, 1932.

ABOVE: *The Marriage of Mopsus and Nisa*. Pieter Brueghel the Elder. Pen and brown ink on wood. Harris Brisbane Dick Fund, 1932.

ABOVE LEFT: *The Holy Family with St. Catherine*. Jusepe Ribera, Spanish, 1591–1652. Oil, dated 1648. Samuel D. Lee Fund, 1934. LEFT: Carved lion and bull guardians from the Palace of Ashurnasirpal II at Nimrud. Assyrian, 883–859 B.C. Gift of John D. Rockefeller, Jr., 1932.

LEFT: *La Femme au Brasier (Portia's Suicide).* Jacques Bellange, French, fl. 1602–1617. Engraving. Harris Brisbane Dick Fund, 1930. RIGHT: Sphinx of Hat-shepsut. Egyptian, eighteenth dynasty. Red granite. Rogers Fund, 1930.

253

ABOVE: *Venus and the Lute Player*. Titian. Oil. Munsey Fund, 1936. LEFT AND RIGHT: Two prints from *The Garden of Love* by Christoffel Jegher, 1596–c. 1652, after Rubens. Harris Brisbane Dick Fund, 1930.

OPPOSITE: Above left, *Prudence and a River God*. Tiepolo. Pen and ink, wash, chalk. Rogers Fund, 1937. Above center, *The Swing*. Goya. Gray wash. Harris Brisbane Dick Fund, 1935. Above right, *Adam*. Tullo Lombardo, Italian (Venetian), c. 1455–1532. Marble, c. 1490–1495. Fletcher Fund, 1936. Below, *Fur Traders Descending the Missouri*. George Caleb Bingham, American, 1811–1879. Oil. Morris K. Jesup Fund, 1933.

LEFT: Virgin and Child. French (Ile-de-France), fourteenth century. Painted limestone. The Cloisters Collection, 1937. RIGHT: *Venus and Adonis*. Rubens. Oil. Gift of Harry Payne Bingham, 1937. BELOW: *Giant*. Goya. Print. Harris Brisbane Dick Fund, 1935. BOTTOM: *The Martyrdom of St. Sebastian*. By the Master of the Playing Cards. German. Print. Harris Brisbane Dick Fund, 1934.

ABOVE: *The Birth of the Virgin.* By the Master of the Barberini Panels, Italian (Umbrian), active 1456–c. 1484. Oil and tempera on wood. Rogers and Gwynne M. Andrews Funds, 1935. LEFT: Statue of a youth. Greek, 615–600 B.C. Marble. Fletcher Fund, 1932. ABOVE RIGHT: White porcelain jar with blue underglaze decoration. Chinese, Ming dynasty, Hsuan Te period (1426–1435). Gift of Robert E. Tod, 1937. RIGHT: Altarpiece. Chinese, Wei dynasty (A.D. 386–587). Gilt bronze, dated Cheng Kuang, fifth year (A.D. 524). Rogers Fund, 1938.

Seventh tapestry: The unicorn in captivity, from the Hunt of the Unicorn tapestries.
French or Flemish, fifteenth century. Wool and silk, with silver and silver-gilt. The
Cloisters Collection, gift of John D. Rockefeller, Jr., 1937.

LEFT: *Francesco d'Este* (c. 1430–1474). Van der Weyden. Tempera and oil on wood. The Michael Friedsam Collection, 1931. RIGHT: *Journalists' Café.* Gabriel de Saint-Aubin, French, 1724–1780. Print. Harris Brisbane Dick Fund, 1939.

BELOW LEFT: Parade armor associated with Henry II of France. Made in the Louvre atelier of the Royal Armorers. French, 1550. Harris Brisbane Dick Fund, 1939. BELOW: The Studiolo from the ducal palace at Gubbio. Italian, c. 1479–1482. Rogers Fund, 1939.

OPPOSITE: Mosaic prayer niche from the Madrasa Imami, Isfahan. Iranian, built 1354. Glazed earthenware set in plaster. Harris Brisbane Dick Fund, 1939.

RIGHT: King Ashurnasirpal II and his cup-bearer, from the wall of his palace at Nimrud. Assyrian, ninth century B.C. Alabaster. Gift of John D. Rockefeller, Jr., 1932. BELOW LEFT: Wounded Amazon. Roman copy of a Greek statue of 440–430 B.C. attributed to Cresilas. Pentelic marble. Gift of John D. Rockefeller, Jr., 1932. BELOW RIGHT: Soup tureen, part of a table service ordered by Catherine II of Russia for Prince Orloff. Made by Jacques Nicolas Roettiers, French, 1736–1784? Joseph Pulitzer Bequest, Purchase, 1933.

OPPOSITE: The Roman Court in 1939. Center, the Etruscan warrior, later proved to be a forgery.

*The Crucifixion* and *The Last Judgment*. Hubert van Eyck, Flemish, d. 1426. Tempera and oil. Fletcher Fund, 1933. BELOW: Bobbin-lace flounce. Flemish (Brussels), late seventeenth century. Flounce with medallion portraits and initials believed to represent Maximillian Emmanuel and Thérèse Cunégonde, made for their wedding, 1695. Rogers Fund, 1939.

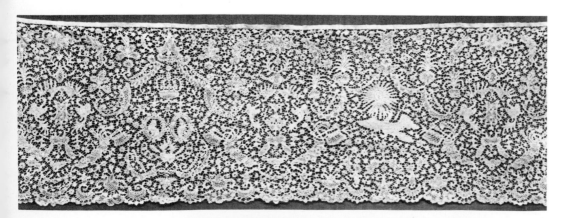

*Moonlight Marine.* Albert Pinkham Ryder, American, 1847–1917. Oil on wood. Samuel D. Lee Fund, 1934.

OPPOSITE: Above, parade shield made for Henry II, King of France from 1547 to 1559. Italian or French, 1550. Steel. Embossed, chased, and damascened on an originally gilt ground. Harris Brisbane Dick Fund, 1934. Below, desk from Mount Mill (Bloomingdale), Queen Anne County, Maryland. Baltimore, c. 1800. Mahogany, satinwood, holly, and ivory. Fletcher Fund, 1934.

267

**1940–1970**

The Great Hall decorated for
a reception in 1941.

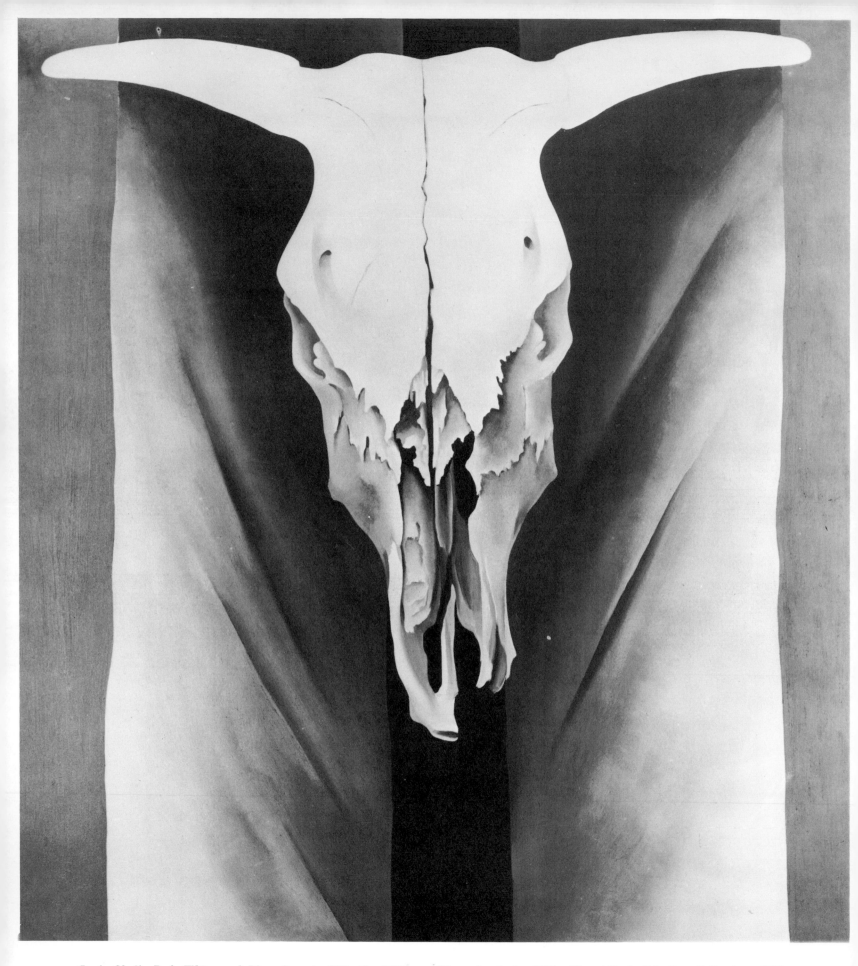

*Cow's Skull: Red, White, and Blue.* Georgia O'Keeffe, 1887— . Oil, painted in 1931. The Alfred Stieglitz Collection, 1949.

# IV
# "PUTTING THE HOUSE IN ORDER"
## 1940–1970

On January 22, 1941, after the Annual Meeting of the Corporation of the Metropolitan Museum of Art, a Museum prize was shown, the *studiolo* from the *palazzo* at Gubbio, a spectacular work of late-fifteenth-century cabinetmaker's art, fashioned in intarsia for Federigo de Montefeltro, the agreeable and intellectual Duke of Urbino. "But this new room," Director Francis Henry Taylor wrote in the *Bulletin*, "has implications which go far beyond its value as an example of fifteenth-century decoration. Both in its conception and in its every detail this tiny scholar's study embodies more than any other monument imported to this country the spirit of Italian humanism." Humanism, trumpeting man's freedom of thought and his fullest self-development, is a most precious heritage. "This mental freedom is by far the most priceless thing that antiquity has handed down to us; more precious than all the riches in our collections. Yet, paradoxically, it is these same treasures of the past, the texts and the works of art, which we must know and study if we wish to preserve that freedom. . . . The Museum is the custodian of something greater than the works of art themselves. It contains the accumulated wisdom through the exercise of which a man may aspire to some degree of humanism."

*W. C. Osborn*
President
1941–1947

By the end of the year, the United States was at war—blacked out, warden-patrolled, stringently rationed. New Yorkers learned what to do if attacked with gas, how to dispose of bodies, and where the swiftly arranged morgues were. Fire-department chiefs brought back from London techniques of handling incendiary bombs, and a huge evacuation camp was built for schoolchildren at New Milford, Connecticut. Air raid drills were held regularly and over a million identification tags were made ready for the children. The Museum's problem was, obviously, that paradoxical one, so succinctly expressed by Mr. Taylor on January 1, 1941: preserving "the treasures of the past" while maintaining an open Museum door to the "something greater," to the affirmations of the free spirit and dignity of man which, somehow, the Museum must continue to offer. In a most brilliantly organized stratagem, planned for fifteen months, a battalion of vans spirited some twenty thousand (the figure is variously put at any number from eighteen thousand up) of the Museum's greatest, most portable glories to a hideaway which was revealed, years later, to have been the Stotesbury mansion at Whitemarsh, Pennsylvania. While the evacuated treasures were on their assiduously guarded country vacation, receiving, in many cases, much-needed overhauling, the Museum galleries were peopled by revenants, and even when these were second best, they were frequently of such unexpected quality and beauty that viewers were astonished.

*F. H. Taylor*
Director
1940–1955

The Museum's venerable collection of casts, especially of the Greek and Roman and the Michelangelo sculptures, came out of retirement. Patinated to approximate the originals, these replicas of some of the world's greatest affirmations of the spirit of man were reassurances and revelations. Beauty, grace, humanism must surely triumph, with Zeus, Apollo, the Risen Christ, Moses, and that most vigorous patron of humanism, Lorenzo de Medici, in the Great Hall and in five major galleries, and the Victory of Samothrace proclaiming freedom at the top of the main stair. There was also a superb original work of religious art. The Museum's enormously tall, Rhenish, thirteenth-century wooden statue of Saint James the Less stood serenely glowing, his seventeenth- or eighteenth-century dull gray (James J. Rorimer called it "battleship-gray") paint removed to reveal his true splendor of gold and red and blue. So war came again to the Museum which, despite a depleted staff, all sorts of crucial shortages and wartime restrictions, and its own particular and peculiar vulnerabilities, became an even greater symbol, an even more potent center, for those who sought to renew their spirits.

In March 1942 the Museum received a letter from a Viennese refugee who had come to New York by way of Paris and Casablanca:

> I should like to convey my thanks and compliments to the direction of the Metropolitan Museum. I am full of admiration of this institution and its staff, of the way they have organized this beautiful building and what they have made of it! You give them [the treasures] really to the public. You really educate the public! Some weeks ago, I was one Sunday in your building, hearing the Fifth Symphony of Beethoven, and I saw the crowd of New Yorkers. Never have I seen such interest. This fine taste to combine great music with the visual arts! And your education for the children! We adults could learn very, very much from this sort of education. When I obtained my U.S.A. visa, I was anxious about the spiritual life here. But what have I met here? A wonderful city, with a spiritual life you don't find anywhere else. New York is now the center of the spiritual world. You can be proud of what you have made and you can be proud of how you made it! A great people like the Americans, who are so hungry for wisdom, knowledge, and progress, must win this war. And we will win it! So help me God. . . .

At one time or another, throughout the war years, every department in the Museum was involved in aiding the prodigious war effort or alleviating its tensions. There were remarkable exhibitions of art works and crafts, both old and contemporary, by nationals of Allied nations. There was a constant flow of Museum-owned or borrowed works on special exhibit. An extravagance of Rembrandts gave specialists on the Museum staff and the viewers an extensive chance to inspect twenty-five of the Museum's Rembrandts, sixteen by his pupils (almost all formerly attributed to the master), and many of his prints and drawings, all Museum-owned and assembled for the first time together. It was a courageous show to put on in time of war, but exactly what the public needed. And there was also reassurance in knowing that the Museum had completely reorganized its personnel. It had its own fire-fighting corps, trained by the New York City Fire Department and on duty round the clock in three eight-hour shifts, and an ear-splitting siren system and other alerting and combatting devices constructed with the aid of expertise from the British Museum. All staff members were assigned air-raid jobs—should there be air raids. There were endless air-raid drills and even alerts, but no raids, so the exhibits continued, and so did the Sunday Victory Concerts; the loan exhibits to army hospitals and installations; and the special events for the armed forces, who thronged the Museum in even greater numbers than they had during the Kaiser's war.

A big Red Cross unit flourished in the Chinese Sculpture Court; the Museum Service Flag was more thickly starred than during World War I; slogans beseeched from the *Bulletin's* pages: "Remember Paper Is War Power," "Good Books for Fighting Men." For United Chinese Relief, a fashion show was held in the Roman Court; for Greek War Relief, a "Greek Islands' Embroideries" exhibit; and for Allied accord, "The Soviet Artist in the War." The State Department sent Mr. Taylor to create good will in Latin America, and the Museum, while giving visitors a chance to see Chilean art, quickened interest in the other America. As it had during World War I, the United States Ordnance Department came for help to the Museum's Arms and Armor Department, where it worked with Stephen V. Grancsay and his staff. After experiments in the Armorer's Workshop of the Museum, an Italian brigandine, dated about 1400, from the Castle of Chalcis in Euboea, became the model for Armor Vest M6, and Air Force Helmet M5 was derived from one of the world's most famous helmets, that of the Galiot de Genouilhac harness, dated 1527.

The Metropolitan Museum of Art was fighting the war by being itself even more variously and profusely than anyone could ever have imagined. New York fashion workers aspired to make the city the fashion center of the world, and the Museum gave them a resounding opportunity to display their talents. For twelve months, committees of New York couturiers and representatives of leading fabric houses worked with the Museum staff to achieve "Renaissance in Fashion 1942," an exhibit which showed what our best-known designers could do. Sometimes of fabrics especially woven for them, but always with Museum Renaissance sources as inspiration, the designers' creations, when displayed with great style in the Museum, helped establish the local couture more soundly than ever before, gave pleasure and assurance to thousands both in and out of the trade, brought the Museum two unique Renaissance costume books, and ultimately were a factor in bringing about the Costume Institute's consolidation with the Museum.

Later in the year, on the first anniversary of Pearl Harbor, the Museum was jammed with crowds who flocked to "the greatest exhibition of contemporary art this country has thus far seen." The "Artists for Victory" exhibit was Francis Henry Taylor's idea. It involved twenty-three nationally known art societies; purchase prizes from the Hearn and Rogers funds and a third Museum fund (the prize money finally came to some $51,000); three selection juries, named by the Artists for Victory organization; an award jury, picked by the Museum; and just about every important painter, sculptor, and graphics artist in the nation. Some fifteen hundred works of art were chosen from the over fifteen thousand sent in, reputations were confirmed or made, and the public found itself at the very heart of the booming American art ferment. The Museum purchased the winners, some forty or more works, ranging from paintings by John Steuart Curry, Peter Blume, Jack Levine, Lyonel Feininger, Marsden Hartley, and Mark Tobey to sculpture by Alexander Calder and graphics by William Gropper and John Sloan.

On April 12, 1945, Franklin Delano Roosevelt died; Hitler was dead on the thirtieth day of that same month; Germany surrendered seven days later; and on August 6, the atomic bomb dropped on Hiroshima. World War II was at its end on August 14, and the world plunged into the Atomic Age. By January 19, 1946, five months and thirteen days later in this improbable new era, the Museum was celebrating its Diamond Jubilee. Most of its treasures were reassembled, unharmed, many of them rejuvenated, and looking as if they had been on a healthful holiday at a spa rather than in exile some three years in a vast country mansion. Almost all of the staff had returned from war and missions of state, while whole complexes of galleries were reinstalled, those containing the paintings having opened with an evening-long, light-blazing victory gala such as had never before been held in the Museum. A radiantly triumphant Princess Juliana of the Netherlands and the

Museum's own glorious returnees, gleaming against adroitly colored walls, were the stars of the incandescent occasion. Even the rich, still fires of the thirteenth-to-sixteenth-century stained glass, over one hundred panels of it, burned again in The Cloisters. The Junior Museum, instituted in 1941, teemed with children and teachers, while the Education and Museum Extension Department, reorganized, was swiftly expanding to involve everyone from preschool children to graduate-level students and highly specialized scholars at Columbia University and New York University's Institute of Art, and to include film-making and radio and television programs, on which the Museum treasures and staff had been intermittently appearing since 1941.

Midst the back-home-again prewar splendors, four collections which had come to the Museum during the war especially echoed the golden age of giving. The Blumenthal collection, bequeathed in 1941 by the Museum's seventh president, brought a wealth of pre-1720 decorative arts, architectural entities, and paintings from what lawyer-collector John G. Johnson had long before called "a unique and very attractive museum home," and others referred to as "*the* palace on Park Avenue." Morganesque in quality if not in numbers, the preponderantly Gothic and Renaissance inheritance ranged grandly through enamels, marbles, bronzes, ivories, majolica, tapestries, textiles, and a group of exceptional medieval furniture; the great patio from the palace of Vélez Blanco (which would be erected in the Museum a quarter of a century later); unique paintings by El Greco and Giovanni di Paolo; and a mysteriously disquieting *Adoration of the Magi* by Joos van Ghent. There was also a purchase fund. To all of this, Mrs. Blumenthal added a multitude of elegant eighteenth-century *objets*.

The bequest of lawyer, humanitarian, amateur painter, and astute collector Maitland F. Griggs gave the Museum at least thirteen of its most captivating, smaller Italian *trecento* and *quattrocento* paintings, including Sassetta's exquisitely pure *Journey of the Magi* and Francesco di Giorgio's heartily symbolic, perhaps unintentionally amusing and worldly *The Chess Players*. With Felix M. Warburg's bequest, and his family's generosity, the Museum gained what William M. Ivins, Jr., called "the most important gift that it has ever received for its Department of Prints": primitive and Renaissance woodcuts; works by Schongauer, Mantegna, Dürer, Marcantonio, Lucas of Leyden; and over forty etchings and dry points by Rembrandt. And banker Jules Bache's collection, installed in the Museum where it would, in 1949, achieve permanent status (arranged, as Bache had instructed, apart and intact from other Museum possessions), included so many French, Italian, Flemish, and Spanish masterpieces of painting that it is impossible to single out, from this Bache museum of remarkable rarities, any one example for special praise. John Pierpont Morgan had collected collections: the Metropolitan Museum of Art had been collecting museums for years. The Museum was now encyclopedic, far beyond the wildest dreams of its original incorporators and, perhaps, even Mr. Morgan. Under the roofs of the Main Building and The Cloisters, the Museum's art showed to the public categories of objects whose exhibition was shared in London by the National Gallery, the British Museum, the Tate, and the Victoria and Albert and in Paris by the Louvre, the Guimet, the Cluny, the Musée des Arts Décoratifs, and the Cabinet des Médailles and Print Room in the Bibliothéque Nationale and the Luxembourg.

"Apparently you are determined not only to exhibit the treasures of the past in a most attractive way, but also to keep abreast and, in fact, ahead of the times by relating this collection to commercial and industrial art, education, and the current problems of the day," said the Honorable William O'Dwyer, Mayor of the City of New York, and, thereby, Trustee Ex Officio of the Museum, to the celebrants at the luncheon given in the Museum on January 19, 1946, for the Seventy-fifth Anniversary Committee. Mayor O'Dwyer continued,

This constitutes the difference between a dead and living institution. It means that you are determined to serve the needs of the New York of the future and at the same time to benefit other American municipalities which look to this great city for inspiration and guidance. One evidence of this is your arrangement with the Costume Museum to include it as an integral part of the Metropolitan. Another thing which interests me tremendously as Mayor, is the fact that you not only have a substantial endowment now, but are preparing to meet the increasing needs of the future and the financial difficulties which lie ahead, by increasing the endowment substantially through private gifts and contributions. In other words, you are not attempting to put all of the burden on the City, which cannot possibly carry it. This city will, of course, carry out its contractual and moral obligations as to maintenance, and it has also agreed to contribute substantially out of postwar capital funds toward your major reconstruction program. I have no doubt whatever that the City, which has supported this great museum so generously in the past, will, in the light of its recent achievements and future plans, contribute even more readily toward its continuance on a sound financial basis.

Here, then, was the pattern of the Museum's future, very much the pattern of its past but ever broadening to encompass, through art, the flux of increasingly complicated life, ever seeking to be the custodian of the best of the times not only in art but in all nourished by art. The Museum would not merely preserve: it would generate, even more than it had in its past. That thriving past was abundantly displayed in the Museum's galleries during this Diamond Jubilee season. An exhibition commemorating the Museum's earliest years, nostalgically titled "The Taste of the Seventies," hung as thickly upon the gallery walls as when the paintings of which it was composed had been first displayed. The statuary gleamed as whitely: "Comestible sculpture—cold forms confected of immemorial marble," wrote Albert Ten Eyck Gardner, Research Fellow. And many who came to laugh remained to marvel at the virtuoso technique so lavishly displayed; at the strength, physical and moral, in these canvases; at the eye for realistic detail; and at this glimpse of not-long-ago life so secure in certainties. And some even found works of art that were beautiful. By the mid-Sixties the Museum itself was seriously collecting Eastlake furniture and other latter-day Victoriana, as it contemplated its Centennial Year.

James J. Rorimer, reminiscing in his ninety-fifth anniversary essay, "Putting the House in Order," in the summer of 1965, took a long look into the last three decades of the continuously evolving "greatest treasure house in the Western Hemisphere." When Rorimer thus characterized the Museum with his favorite phrase of praise for it, he knew more realistically than any other person involved what he was talking about, for he had been close to the heart of Museum matters from 1927, when, at twenty-two, he had come down from Harvard to be assistant to Joseph Breck in the vast Department of Decorative Arts. Taking over the curatorship of the newly formed Department of Medieval Art in 1934, and the tremendous task of building The Cloisters, Rorimer was even closer to the heart. And finally, when in 1955, after he had been director of The Cloisters for six years, he also was elected director of the entire Museum, he was, in a very large sense, the heart itself.

"In 1933 Solomon R. Guggenheim asked me, both as a Museum staff member and friend, what might happen if he were to make a sizable donation toward a new building for the Metropolitan in another location," Rorimer recollected in his 1965 "Putting the House in Order." Then he went on to tell how he and Guggenheim had even doodled "a vast new complex in the southeast corner of Central Park, opposite the Plaza Hotel," a Museum paradise in which every single thing and each

*J. J. Rorimer*
**Director**
**1955–1966**

person had sufficient room. "A central tower would contain offices, workshops, an auditorium, educational facilities, and space for all the other services required by an encyclopedic museum." And from that dream tower would extend, tangent to it, blessed, and apparently inflatable, wings "displaying the art of every major civilization." Maecenas Guggenheim and the Museum, which, of course, also meant the City of New York, would spend thirty million dollars for what would literally be the greatest treasure house not only in the Western hemisphere but in the world. "It was not long, however," Rorimer reported dryly, "before a non-responsive statement by a weary Museum official brought our daydreaming to a close."

There was another relocation fantasy a decade later, during Hitler's war. This time the Museum administration, "exasperated by the deficiencies of the existing plant," hotly pleaded the cause. Robert Moses, Commissioner of Parks, Trustee Ex Officio of the Museum, clobbered that notion immediately. As the voice of the city government, he bluntly told the Museum "that New York had too great an investment in the building to justify starting over, and that moreover, it could serve no other useful purpose if the Museum moved out of it." Mr. Rorimer, a shrewd administrator, incredibly meticulous in any pursuit, and the kind of man who could, by his patience, exhaust victory out of almost any opponent or adverse situation ("I have waited more than twenty years to flush a waiting treasure from its impenetrable surroundings"), in summing up these relocation efforts, converted failure into a sort of victory: "As new solutions to our difficulties have been developed, staying put was probably all for the best."

The job of "staying put" was as delicate and astonishing a feat as walking across Niagara Falls on a tightrope. "Since the first building plans were drawn," Albert Ten Eyck Gardner, Associate Curator of American Paintings and Sculpture, wrote in the ninety-fifth-anniversary-celebration *Bulletin*, "no year has passed when some part of the building was not in the hands of architects. Actually, the building has never been completed. If new construction was not in progress, interior reconstruction or rearrangement was under way. It might reasonably be considered as a sort of cultural coral reef, always growing and changing."

Rorimer, who became director of the "cultural coral reef" in 1955, could be grateful to his predecessor, Francis Henry Taylor. At thirty-seven, the youngest man ever to guide the Museum, Taylor came to this job, the most important of its kind in the country, from nine newsmaking museum years as director of the Worcester Art Museum and previous curatorial experience in the Pennsylvania (since 1938, the Philadelphia) Museum of Art. Taylor was robust in everything that he did: talking, writing, administration, and expertise. He had imagination, flair, lusty humor, erudition, and style, and he needed them all in the tireless, canny wars he waged against museum and other art pedants, against hoity-toity value judgments on works of art and what he termed "cut-rate aestheticism." He could no more run a museum without getting into scrapes with academics and trustees than he could resist anything which he thought would make that museum into a vital, sentient voice for art, and for life. The American museum "is the child of nineteenth-century liberal thought . . . developed by the people, for the people and of the people," he said. A museum's "only hope for survival in the modern world" is "by honestly contemplating and interpreting our resources in the light of their potential usefulness to society." He respected traditions, but he was never fettered by them. "The dilemma of the modern museum is a dilemma produced by [the] eternal conflict . . . between the forces of synthesis and the forces of dissipation. We in the art museums of America have reached a point where we must make a choice of becoming either temples of learning and understanding . . . or of remaining merely hanging gardens for the perpetuation of the Babylonian pleasures of aestheticism and the secret sins of private archaeology."

OPPOSITE: *Two Tahitian Women (Femmes aux Mangos)*. Paul Gaugin, French, 1848–1903. Oil, signed and dated 1899. Gift of William Church Osborn, 1949.

Domine ad adiu
uandum me festia.
Gloria pri et filio
et spiritui sancto.

sicut erat in prin
cipio et nunc et sem
per et in secula seculo
rum. amen. Inuitat.

ABOVE: *Aristotle Contemplating the Bust of Homer.* Rembrandt Harmensz. van Rijn, Dutch, 1606–1669. Oil, signed and dated 1653. Purchased with special funds and gifts of friends of the Museum, 1961. OPPOSITE: *The Kiss of Judas,* from *The Belles Heures of Jean, Duke of Berry* (folio 123v), enlarged one-third. Pol, Jean, and Herman de Limbourg, French, fifteenth-century. Manuscript, c. 1410–1413. The Cloisters Collection, Purchase, 1954.

*Terrace at Sainte Adresse.* Claude Monet, French, 1840–1926. Oil. Contributions from Various Individuals Supplemented by Museum Purchase Funds, 1967.

In Rorimer, Taylor knew that he had a brilliant colleague who could, and most certainly should, eventually become director of the Museum. "A museum man," said Rorimer, "must love works of art with a passion. And in so doing he wants to share his enthusiasms with others." This was also Taylor's credo. And he was, of course, already successfully pioneering, during the war years in the Museum, the basic program Rorimer expounded to W. G. Rogers in an interview published in the *Sun* in Baltimore on November 15, 1959. "The collections come first—the objects, the paintings. We must make these objects intelligible to the public. We must make them intelligible even if that calls for a smoking room here and there in this great building covering four city blocks. Or if it calls for a good restaurant. We don't want the public to think a visit to the museum is a painful ordeal. If more decent toilets make it easier to see Titians, let's have more decent toilets. With accessibility to our objects comes understanding. Somehow art on a pedestal must be brought nearer to the visitor. If we take our collections for granted, we risk becoming a static museum." They were much alike in many professional and even personal ways, these first of the Museum's really new museum men. Addressing the Food Editors' Dinner on October 5, 1960, Rorimer gave his fascinated listeners a glimpse into the blither side of a museum director's life: "In my profession it is said that you cannot be a good director without liking food and knowing about it. Both my predecessor in office and I wanted to cook our own favorite dishes for the openings. I have even wondered whether a gourmet could be a gourmet without being a gourmand— most museum administrators are portly, or at least always dieting." Taylor and Rorimer could have been painted by Domenico Ghirlandaio in fifteenth-century Florence, or have stepped out of Benozzo Gozzoli's *Journey of the Kings* frescos in that city's Medici Palace.

In 1946, when Rorimer returned to the Museum from his three years of intensely active duty in the United States Army (he went in as an infantry private and emerged as Chief of the Monuments, Fine Arts and Archives Section, Seventh Army, Western Military District), Taylor asked him "to serve as chairman of the Staff Architectural Committee" as well as reassume the curatorship of Medieval Arts and The Cloisters. In 1965, Rorimer could honestly, and with satisfaction, say,

> I have been grappling with them ever since, in collaboration with my colleagues, and with . . . architects. . . . The difficulties in planning a reconstruction program for the Museum were not—and are not—confined to finding current solutions to current problems; one must take into consideration what will happen years ahead . . . every change that is made has consequences far beyond the change itself. To close, say, a few galleries for construction means finding space elsewhere for their contents, and probably relocating several service facilities as well. The interlocking relationship of space and activity within the Museum makes planning all the more difficult, and scheduling, very often, a nightmare.

Taylor had been riding the nightmare since 1941, a year after he became director, when he instigated the complete review of the Museum's patchwork structure, which in 1946 was now leading, it was hoped, to the overhauling and reorganization of the entire "coral reef"—not only the sprawl of buildings, parts of which were fragile to the point of danger, but what and whom they housed. The war years had seen the birth of the public's zooming involvement with art: the Museum must be ready to accommodate new acquisitions—and the voracious hordes—with adequate space, services, and amenities still unknown in most museums. As a Museum fund-raising pamphlet of the early Sixties firmly stated, "the extraordinary development of American society has created a demand that is out-running the present capacity of the Museum." Francis Henry Taylor retired in 1955 to return to the Worcester Art Museum and other interests, and by the time Rorimer made his ninety-fifth-anniversary *Report*, a year before he died suddenly on May 11, 1966, the dreams both directors had had for the Museum had transported it triumphantly out of a pre-World War II world as lost and remote as ancient Tyre to anyone born after 1945. A whole repertory of brilliant solutions saw the Museum into the Atomic Age, through the Korean War, when the treasures again stood ready to be evacuated, and through the Cold War into the Space Age.

"To catalogue all that has been accomplished in the past ten years would be both difficult and dull," Rorimer wrote in 1965. But what were some of the high spots? Exhibition areas increased some forty-two per cent, while service areas added twenty-two per cent, including a seven-story service building, one of the Museum's major nerve centers. This one houses facilities for the care of works of art, for the maintenance of Museum buildings, for the comfort and health of the employees as well as, at last, air-conditioning machinery for at least portions of the Museum. Installed with a fund from Trustee–Vice-President Stephen C. Clark (who also bequeathed some of the Museum's finest Impressionist paintings and drawings and representative American and English works), air-conditioning made viewing in forty-two paintings galleries the delight for which both Taylor and Rorimer had labored. A seismographic smoke-detection system could warn almost instantly of the slightest evidence of smoke in any of the Museum's many storage areas. Whole galaxies of period rooms (the Samuel H. Kress Foundation gift, the Croome Court tapestry room; the Landsdowne room; the many fine French rooms given by Mrs. Herbert N. Straus) were revealed in all their splendor. Departments shifted the length of the enormous building, so that the collections could become ever more sequentially logical and thus more useful to viewers. The North Wing was torn up and rebuilt to make more space and to make it safe for its visitors and the weight of its treasures—for example, Queen Hat-shepsut, one of the great eighteenth-dynasty statues, is a four-ton Museum beauty. The new Junior Museum, in the South Wing, could now try to accommodate its thousand visitors a day, for it was complete with its own work and exhibition rooms, library, and restaurant, and with casts from the collection which had, over the years, come and gone in the Museum like ghostly reminders of early Museum aims and ambitions. And where once the Greek and Roman Court had drowsed around its shallow central pool (tempting small children to wading exploits), a self-service restaurant bustled and clattered around its large, deepish pool, rampant with gregarious Carl Milles nudes and plashing fountains. The Museum also had escalators in it, new elevators, and the best of the city's smaller auditoriums, the Grace Rainey Rogers. Named after its donor, a woman who also gave the Museum such treasures as a rich collection of Ingres drawings, the auditorium, designed by Frank Vorhees and Ralph Walker in pale, freshly gleaming wood, is acoustically controlled and equipped with broadcasting and telecasting facilities. Hundreds of thousands of people fill it annually, sometimes to view movies on art subjects, more frequently to hear the world's greatest musicians and internationally famous art savants, such as Sir Kenneth Clark and John Pope-Hennessy, Director of the Victoria and Albert Museum, both scholars appearing as part of the Charles B. Wrightsman endowed series held in conjunction with the New York University Institute of Fine Arts.

When it came to building a new library, Rorimer's architectural sensitivity led to one of the Museum's most effective juxtapositions. The Thomas J. Watson Art Reference Library was erected with funds supplied by the man who founded International Business Machines and was one of the first to help make industry conscious of what it could do for art and what art could do for it. "Art breaks the monotony of life," he once said. "Monotony would drive the world insane. Art is an antidote." Modern in its every detail, from its glass-and-anodized-aluminum International Style façade to its air-conditioned facilities within, this structure, designed by Brown, Lawford and Forbes, houses about 170,000 art-reference items, some of them works of incredible bibliographic art, one of the world's most prodigious collective antidotes against that monotony which Mr. Watson feared would "drive the world insane." And this aggrandisement, born of a handful of pamphlets and books, some 450 items in all, and "sometimes referred to as the heart of the institution which it serves," is now the Western Hemisphere's most exhaustive art and archeological reference library. It is entered from the Museum through the two-story-high, sixteenth-century patio from the castle of Velez Blanco in Spain. Row upon intricately carved row, the venerable marble arcades of George Blumenthal's bequest serenely tie the monumental pre-World-War-I architectural grandeurs of the Museum halls to the necessary but inviting functionalism of the Watson Library. There is even deeper accord when the patio space is utilized for exhibitions of sixteenth-century sculpture, silver, and gold, and for very special concerts and intimate gatherings. And above the library sit, most appropriately and usefully, the Department of Prints and the Department of Drawings, with their own galleries at last, and study rooms, storage space, and offices. Situated in a single building, the three departments that cope daily with works of art involving the use of paper pool their conservation and other technical problems, utilizing the paper-care-and-maintenance laboratory on the top floor of the library building. Here, indeed, is a model museum within the vastness of the Museum. And that is how Francis Henry Taylor, years before, envisioned his Museum of tomorrow: a series of museums interrelated within the colossus of the Museum.

Save for the Mary Stillman Harkness bequests, exhibited in 1952 in all of their splendid profusion, the post-World-War-II decades did not frequently bring bequests or gifts of objects on the scale of those which seemed to flow with never-diminishing vivacity into the Museum during the heyday of the golden age of giving. Still the twenty-five years or so of Taylor's and Rorimer's directorships saw such a plethora of remarkable treasures bequeathed or given to, or purchased by, the Museum—such as Samuel A. Lewisohn's and former Museum President William Church Osborn's paintings and Mr. and Mrs. Charles B. Wrightsman's French rooms—and such a spate of spectacular money gifts—such as the $1,000,000 received from Thomas W. Lamont in 1948 and the surge of corporate giving—that it is impossible to list even a sampling.

The most sensational acquisition was made on a Wednesday evening in November 1961, during the auction at Parke-Bernet in Manhattan of the twenty-four paintings collected by advertising mogul Alfred William Erickson and his wife, Anna. It took precisely four minutes of calm cocked-thumb-and-wink signals for James J. Rorimer, representing his Museum, to outbid dealers Rosenberg and Stiebel, representing Rorimer's home-town museum, the Cleveland Museum of Art. For $2,300,000 the Metropolitan Museum of Art now owned Rembrandt's *Aristotle Contemplating the Bust of Homer*, also known as "The Million-Dollar Rembrandt." Breaking all painting-purchase price records (the next highest was the $1,166,400 United States Secretary of the Treasury Andrew Mellon gave Soviet Russia in 1931 for Raphael's *Alba Madonna*, now in the National Gallery of Art, Washington, D.C.), the Museum had bought, with money from many of its most nourishing bequest funds and trustee and private-individual contributions, an acknowledged masterpiece and a major attraction. When *Aristotle* was exhibited in the Great Hall it was almost impossible to get within proper viewing distance of it. One day a small boy who was trying to get close enough to touch the canvas was yanked back by his mother, who screamed, "Don't bang on the work of art, Maurice!" Over five million people came to the Museum in 1961, the highest attendance record in its ninety-two years, and most of them came to see "The Million-Dollar

Rembrandt," commissioned 309 years ago by a Sicilian nobleman who agreed to pay its painter five hundred florins, an estimated $7800. The painting had been repurchased by Erickson in 1936, for $590,000 (he had first bought it in 1928 for $750,000 and then had had to sell it back to Joseph Duveen in 1929). The Metropolitan Museum's price was also evidence of the rocketing interest in paintings and the astonishing market for them in 1961. "I'm a believer in fate," said Rorimer, "and the picture has come to us, even if the hard way. . . . It would have been heartbreaking, with Wall Street so close, to have lost out on it." The Museum was praised for its enterprise and chided for its flabbergasting expenditure and what some felt was its greed: it reputedly even lost two superior Goyas to Washington's National Gallery because of the Rembrandt purchase. In an interview with Aline B. Saarinen, published in *The New York Times Magazine*, August 14, 1955, Rorimer had said, "If a wonderful object comes along, we should get it even if we are strong there. I'd rather see a masterpiece by an artist already represented in the collection than a second-rate picture by a painter who isn't." He had also told the *Times*, ten days previously, when interviewed on becoming director, "I'm going to have fun in this job because I like works of art."

Having fun in "this job" definitely included acquiring the most famous Rembrandt of the day for the Museum, but Rorimer found no fun during November of that year, when one night he heard the thump and blare of Joey Dee and his Peppermint Lounge quintet beating it out in the Museum's restaurant while 750 spectacularly gowned and suited guests gyrated in the Twist during the Party of the Year, the fashion industry's annual and always successful fund-raising gala for the Museum's Costume Institute. Gay Talese reported in *The New York Times* on November 21 that Director Rorimer "shook with dismay" as he shouted, "I did not invite them. . . . I was not aware of this!"

But he quivered with quiet joy when, two years later, from February 7 to March 4, 1963, 1,077,521 people moved, like a well-drilled army, in and out of the Medieval Sculpture Hall where they stood, for a brief few minutes, hushed to speechlessness by a single, solitary painting on loan from the French government. They had waited, many of these viewers, for hours, standing, some with small children in their arms, for blocks along Fifth Avenue, exposed to the rigors of a harsh New York winter, and each and every one of them seemed to find some reward in the most famous face in the history of art, Leonardo's *Mona Lisa*. "In modern times, by means of countless reproductions, it has become better known than any picture ever painted," wrote Theodore Rousseau, then Curator of European Paintings, now, in 1969, Vice-Director and Curator in Chief of the Museum. "Perhaps the most significant modern tribute to its fame was the attack made upon it in the 1920s by the Dadaists, who ridiculed it as the greatest symbol of the traditional Western culture they wished to destroy. Their attack was, needless to say, unsuccessful, but their appraisal was just, for, as the interest generated by its unprecedented and epoch-making visit to this country confirms, to the people of the world this painting is one of the finest achievements of our civilization." In 1963, the Museum was visited by 6,968,673 people, membership jumped to a new high, and the building had to stay open until nine o'clock at night most of the time while *Mona Lisa* was in residence: the giantism which was afflicting the world had come to the Museum.

But neither the spectacular purchase of Rembrandt's *Aristotle* nor the overwhelming good will created for the Museum by the visit of *Mona Lisa* were James J. Rorimer's most enduring monuments. "The Cloisters is the perfect expression of James Rorimer's great contribution to our lives," said Sherman E. Lee, Director of the Cleveland Museum of Art, at the memorial service held high up in that monument several days after Rorimer's death. "It was his creation, his dearest treasure, his unique vision of a union of history, art and nature that has given so much to all of us—knowledge and, even better, pure delight. He proved that, given enough money (John D. Rockefeller, Jr., had donated an additional $10,000,000 in 1951, the largest gift ever made to the Museum), time, patience, taste, knowledge, and good fortune, one could creatively display the best of the Middle Ages in an alien climate and environment so that one believed—was convinced of—its truth. Foreign skeptics were put to rout—even better, converted. One can truthfully say that The Cloisters reversed the line of giving from the Old World to the New, and gave to the lands of its origin a museum standard, a new benchmark to be envied, emulated, and, more rarely, equaled."

Arthur A. Houghton, Jr., succeeding Roland L. Redmond as President of the Metropolitan Museum of Art's Board of Trustees, reflected upon the trustees' unanimous selection of thirty-five-year-old Thomas P. F. Hoving (after more than 120 other candidates had been considered) and categorized the Museum's most recent Directors. Houghton, head of Corning Glass and a connoisseur of books, art, and men, concluded that Francis Henry Taylor had been a "fire of genius"; Rorimer, "a sound housekeeper"; and that what the Museum needed was another "fire of genius" —hence, Hoving. Here was a young man triumphantly successful in the museum world and outside it. Erstwhile Curator of Medieval Art and The Cloisters, his daring, persistence, and expertise had brought into the collections such treasures as the twelfth-century walrus-ivory cross of Bury St. Edmunds; the Romanesque doorway from the church of San Leonardo al Frigido, in Massa Carrara, Tuscany; the holy-water font beside the doorway; and the St. Thomas à Becket reliquary. As Commissioner of Parks and Administrator of Recreation and Cultural Affairs, Hoving was, in 1966, not only the most uninhibited, iconoclastic, inventive, and popular Parks Commissioner the city had ever had but also a Museum Trustee Ex Officio. In effect, he was the Museum's landlord. Among his duties had been "the expediting of capital improvements to the City's museums and institutions." In twelve of the fifteen front-page months that he held his city office, Commissioner Hoving had expedited $2,752,075 worth of much needed "capital improvements." He was now the first Director the Museum had ever had with one audacious hand in the city government and the other in the Museum's administration and its world of arcane knowledge. Indeed, until medievalist-curator Hoving had relinquished his Museum post, he had been thought of increasingly as medievalist-Director Rorimer's heir apparent, if not definitely his designate.

Rorimer had decided that Hoving was of Museum caliber when, in 1958, he heard the twenty-seven-year-old Princeton Ph.D. lecture at the Annual Student Symposium of the New York University Institute of Fine Arts. At this showcase event, Hoving discoursed upon "Antique Repertory in Annibale Carracci's Galleria Farnese." And that was most fortuitous since the Museum had recently purchased the huge marble table Vignola had wrought for the Farnese. Hoving soon went to work in Rorimer's office, meteorically rising to the highest Medieval Art–Cloisters position while also serving as a hard-working, intrepid, continent-hopping link between the Museum's Director and the world art market. Hoving's special area was the discovery and authentication of art of the early fourth century to about 1500. His renown in the museum world rested securely, and still does, upon his remarkable flair for detection, especially among art objects of his chosen field. Rorimer's dicta, ". . . you've got to get right to a thing. You can't do it from a distance. You've got to touch it," and "You must begin and end with the work of art itself," are also Hoving's. "You peel a work of art like an onion. Shred every layer from it," Hoving told John McPhee for *The New Yorker* profile published in the May 20, 1967, issue of that magazine and later in McPhee's *A Roomful of Hovings and Other Profiles* (New York: Farrar, Straus & Giroux, 1969).

Parallels, parallels, always seek parallels. Use scientific means—ultraviolet light, X rays, and so forth—but always in context with your eye. Scientific analyses can be used

*R. L. Redmond*
President
1947–1964

*A. A. Houghton, Jr.*
President
1964–

*T. P. F. Hoving*
Director
1967–

for or against a work, like statistics. Your eye is king. Get in touch with other scholars—everybody you think is expert. . . . Learn the history of the piece. . . . Then get the work of art with you and live with it as long as you possibly can. You have to watch it. Watch it. Come across it by accident. . . . A work of art will grow the more it is with you. It will grow in stature, and fascinate you more and more. If it is a fake, it will eventually fall apart before your eyes, like a piece of plaster.

It is the first impression that counts, he believes. "Always trust your immediate kinetic reaction."

In December 1966, when Hoving was elected Director of the Museum, his nationwide, and fast becoming international, fame (some thought of it as notoriety) was rooted in the catchword phrase "Hoving happenings." By the thousands people came to the city's parks to fly kites; to join together to express themselves by painting a tremendous canvas (105 yards); to attend a Gay Nineties party for a Goldman Band opening (35,000 gaily crushed together, giving Hoving a twenty-minute standing ovation); to watch a meteor; to fashion plastic foam into dream castles; and to bicycle on roadways forbidden to motorized traffic. Hoving's concern was not only to encourage the citizenry to have joy in their parks and to feel free to come and go happily in them but to help those parks become, in the fullest sense, the works of art he deeply believes them to be. "I want to make the Parks Department's work the absolute highest quality in the United States," he said. He also opined at various times that both art and action are a way of life and that a work of art teaches, enriches, relaxes, and inspires. To implement his convictions, Park Commissioner Hoving established a full-time architect in a department given to employing highway engineers on re-habilitation projects; he also arranged for an artist-in-residence. He lured advice from such practical visionaries as Philip Johnson, Marcel Breuer, Kenzo Tange, Felix Candela, Morris Lapidus, and others—the entire range of environmental experimentors, International Style men to Brutalists—involving them in his plans for sports parks, underground stables, vest-pocket and portable parks, and all sorts of other recreation centers. Sometimes Hoving even went out and found the money with which he helped finance his revolutionary thinking: an exploit he would have to repeat later when the Museum purchased Monet's *La Terrasse à Sainte Adresse* for $1,411,200, the highest auction price ever paid for a "modern" picture. Hoving has a heady talent for fund raising, seeming to know where the available money is, whether it be with a corporation, private individual, foundation, or government.

In retrospect, Hoving's program as Commissioner of Parks and Administrator of Recreation and Cultural Affairs seems a pilot for his activities as the Museum's Director. Both his Parks and Museum endeavors spring straight out of Francis Henry Taylor's sibylline appraisal of what possible hope museums have of survival in the modern world. Their only hope, Taylor affirmed, was "by honestly contemplating and interpreting our resources in the light of their potential usefulness to society." It was his constant preoccupation with how the Parks, and now with how the Museum, could be most useful to society that apparently motivated Hoving's direction. One hundred incredible years separate the Museum's founding fathers from today's Director and his Board of Trustees, but the 1870 motives for creating the Museum and the 1970 motives for carrying on this Museum and even recreating it are basically identical, firmly linked by the century-long concern with the Museum's "usefulness to society." Chronology transposes emphasis.

Today's Museum stress is best summed up in Grace Glueck's "The Total Involvement of Thomas Hoving," published in *The New York Times Magazine*, December 8, 1968, almost two years after the Board elected the Museum's new Director: "These are revolutionary times," Hoving said.

"The social order is in flux, and we must be relevant to it. The question is not *whether*, but exactly *how* we're going to get into the swim. The alternative is the possibility of being pushed in." Earlier in 1968, on April 1, Hoving was quoted in a *Newsweek* article titled "Hoving in the Metropolitan":

> Art can't be detached from the people. . . . I want people to look at art, without embarrassment, without awe, without peering over their shoulder and wondering if there's a professor lurking around to tell them what it's really like. It's a place for the people to battle against the blows of technology and the miseries of life, a place where you can have your mind expanded, not by drugs, but by seeing things in a way you had never seen before.

Relevance, involvement, scholarship, joy: these are Hoving's tenets.

Hoving's wife, Nancy, told *Newsweek* that her husband thought that the Museum's selection committee would turn him down for the Director's job because of his "flamboyance and brashness" while humanizing the Parks. Since April 15, 1967, when "In the Presence of Kings" held its initial preview, followed by a reception for the new Director, Museum attendance and membership have soared, often to unprecedented numbers. Dramatically staged, with special spot-lighting and pavilion settings, "In the Presence of Kings" paraded, mostly from the Museum's own riches, objects commissioned by or associated with royalty. It was essentially a serious exhibition, most extraordinary in its profusion and variety of treasures of superb quality and in its unintentional recapitulation of the Museum's prime donors throughout its ninety-seven-year history. The works of art included some of the Museum's finest and some of its most enchanting: the diorite statue of Gudea, ruler of Lagash, about 2150 B.C.; jewelry from the Tomb of the Three Princesses; the silver gilt royal Sassanian head, portrait of a king who ruled Persia sometime in the late fourth or early fifth century, A.D.; the late-fourth-century-B.C. Apulian volute krater known as *Il Gran Vaso del Capo di Monte*, one of the largest extant; the fourteenth-century *Hours of Jeanne d'Evreux*, one of the two landmark treasures of this genre from the Duke of Berry's library and now in The Cloisters collection; the ravishing fourteenth-century reliquary shrine reputedly fashioned for Queen Elizabeth of Hungary; the parade shield of Henri II of France, which allegorically depicts the battle of Cannae; Lemoyne's marble portrait bust of Louis XV, once owned by Madame de Pompadour; fine furniture once owned by Marie Antoinette, as well as a kennel made for one of her pet dogs; an astronomical globe resting upon Pegasus, which, along with Veronese's *Mars and Venus United by Love* (also in this exhibit), was looted from Prague by Queen Christina's troops; oriental porcelains, scroll paintings, jades of the highest lineage; Rembrandt's *The Noble Slave;* the fabulous Anhalt carpet; and the state sword of the Sultan Murad V, who, in 1876, ruled Turkey for less than a year. The Sultan's sword is so thick with precious jewels and so elaborate with gold that it does not seem a lethal weapon. Its handle is so fragile that a single blow could shatter its magnificent jade.

Lists and catalogues possess a magic of peculiar potency: they can intoxicate. To read a complete itemization of "In the Presence of Kings" and to contemplate how much more is on display permanently—the mysterious Mérode altarpiece; the Antioch Chalice, once thought to be the Holy Grail; the eight-hundred-year-old apse from Fuentidueña, Spain, whose 3300 limestone blocks are now a part of The Cloisters; the giant wrought-iron choir screen from Valladolid, Spain, given by The Hearst Foundation in 1956; the winged, human-headed ninth-century-B.C. lion and bull guardians (over ten feet high) from the palace of Ashurnasirpal II, and the alabaster relief of a winged genie from that same palace at Nimrud, these three mythological creatures having been bought by John D. Rockefeller, Jr., from Kelekian when the Benefactor and the dealer happened to meet one day in 1919 on a Madison Avenue street corner—to contemplate all this and to consider the over 400,000 objects which presently make up the collection, some 75,000 usually being on view, is to become quite drunk with pleasure, pride, and awe. Unlike many older European museums, the Metropolitan, in its brief one hundred years, did not acquire its treasures by looting or war.

So there she stands, the Museum, banners flapping, crackling with innovations, chockablock with plans. Her constitution and bylaws have been revised to bring more trustees on board, to create much-needed Honorary Trusteeships, to provide the Corporation not only with a president but also with a chairman of the Board of Trustees—the first to hold the new office was Robert Lehman. At last the director is the Chief Executive Officer of the Museum, and a portion of his travail is diminished by vice-directors Joseph V. Noble and Theodore Rousseau. Noble, the director's administration aide, is a well-known educational and documentary film maker, photographer, and ceramic archeologist; he has the largest private collection of ancient Greek vases in America. Noble is also a forgery detector, and it was he who proved that the Museum's three Etruscan terra-cotta warriors and the Greek horse were impostors.

The Museum's spectacular, experimentally produced exhibitions like "Harlem on My Mind," "The Art of Fashion," "F-111" bring violent reactions; while "The Great Age of Fresco: Giotto to Pontormo," "Mediaeval Art from Private Collections," "Art of Oceania, Africa, and the Americas" (which presaged Nelson A. Rockefeller's gift of the Museum of Primitive Art), and flotillas of smaller scholarly exhibits, bring adulation. The Museum is criticized and praised for what it does and for what it does not do. But no matter what the reactions are, there are more Benefactors than ever before in Museum history, although the cost to each of them is now $100,000; and the Membership Office and Visitor's Center, manned by student volunteers, have to be open seven days a week. Concert audiences frequently flow over onto the stage, and Museum openings and other festive or organizational events are so gala and so numerous that they are often commented upon in the press. Russel Lynes reported in his "S.R.O. at Mr. Hoving's Met," published in *The New York Times Magazine*, January 1, 1967, that one morning when the Curator of European Paintings was going to work he asked a taxi driver, "Why do you suppose all those people are waiting on the steps to get into the Museum?" The cabbie responded, "It's a new kind of status."

But, in 1969, with a wise eye on the last decades of the twentieth century, that marvelous example of perpetual motion, the Museum, is reaching out far beyond the status seekers. It is reaching into the city's ghettos, hiring an exploratory corps of young people, forming a Department of Community Relations, discussing the feasibility of transporting segments of the collections into the communities themselves. A teen-age advisory panel is considered. The Education Department is now active on all levels of instruction. The Museum is developing high-school-age programs, and graduate-level projects such as curator training and expertise; it offers many new lectures, seminars, and conferences, such as those on forgeries, porcelains (with the many R. Thornton Wilson gifts and loans, the Museum collection can illustrate almost any ceramic series), and on the practical application of computers to Museums. There are computer pilot projects in the Department of Drawings, and a computerized data bank is evolving which should make available information of the most esoteric varieties. The 1870 Museum charter promised that the Museum would encourage and develop "the study of the fine arts, and the application of arts to manufacture and practical life," and that the Museum would advance "the general knowledge of kindred subjects and, to that end" furnish "popular instruction and recreation." In 1908, "recrea-

tion" was excised, being replaced by "education." The words "practical life" shone above the Museum in 1870 like a lodestar: they seem even more effulgent in 1970.

So there the Museum stands like some great historic keep, complete with dozens of specialized workshops, stores, kitchens, offices, and over a thousand people servicing, furbishing, and protecting it. Looking into the future, already transforming her physical being and her intellectual basis, the Museum dreams of many things: Departments of Architecture, of Photography, Departments of . . . but these are the kinds of everyday dreams which, this being the Museum, will come true. And so will the master dream, a twenty-five-year plan to completely rehabilitate and reorganize the Museum's physical structure and its collections—possibly on a chronological basis. Kevin Roche, John Dinkeloo and Associates, who fuse architecture and nature into late-twentieth-century descendants of mid-Victorian Wardian cases, have devised the physical plan. Its display is one of the high-spots of the Centennial Celebration. The renewed Fifth Avenue front and Main Hall were conceived by the same firm, which has also designed the huge glass vitrine to house the Temple of Dendur, given by the United Arab Republic to the United States and awarded to the Metropolitan Museum. As Roche told a *Vogue* reporter, the architects aim is to "make a backyard of Central Park in an attempt to unify the whole thing." They also aim to expand the Museum's American Wing and reconstructed Costume Institute and Textile Study Room; the new André Mertens Galleries for Musical Instruments; the new Pre-Columbian Gallery with its collection of Peruvian ceramics (given by Nathan Cummings) and the Museum's own hoard of Peruvian textiles (started during the hundred-year-old institution's childhood); and the swiftly accumulating contemporary decorative arts, paintings, and sculptures. ". . . I'd like to get a complete Gothic Chapel," the Museum's Director daydreams, "maybe even a Roman catacombs. I'd like to raise $50,000,000. . . ."

"The quality of the Temple isn't high," Hoving told *The New York Times* interviewer about Dendur, "but don't knock it. Its impact is extraordinary. It's an environment, something you can walk into. It puts together a piece of the past. Any work of architectural sculpture I can get my hands on, I'll buy."

And any work he buys will be unified into the Museum, as will New York, Painting and Sculpture 1940–1970 and the other four gigantic main Centennial exhibitions and the Centennial itself; for the Museum, which began with a dream in the Bois, is one hundred years of dreams, and each of them has always been a beginning.

*Remember*

**PAPER IS WAR POWER**

*Use Less Paper—Save All Wastepaper*

# 1940–1949

*The Adoration of the Magi.* Joos van Ghent, Flemish, active 1460–c. 1480. Tempera on linen. Bequest of George Blumenthal, 1941.

ABOVE: Fowling piece made for Napoleon I by Nicolas Noël Boutet at Versailles. French, c. 1810. Harris Brisbane Dick Fund, 1942. RIGHT: Woodwork from the chapel of the Château de la Bastie d'Urfé, St. Etienne, France, 1545–1550. Gift of the children of Mrs. Harry Payne Whitney, 1942, in accordance with the wishes of their mother.

OPPOSITE: Above center, *Witches' Sabbath*. Hans Baldung, German, 1480–1545. Engraving. Gift of Felix M. Warburg and his family, 1941. Above right, statuette from Tell Asmar: Shrine II of the Square Temple. Sumerian, c. 2600 B.C. White gypsum. Fletcher Fund, 1940.

ABOVE: Bronze vessel. Chinese, Shang dynasty, 1766–1122 B.C. Rogers Fund, 1943. RIGHT: *Christ Presented to the People*. Rembrandt. Etching, first state. Gift of Felix M. Warburg and his family, 1941.

ABOVE: Enameled glass bottle. Syrian, fourteenth century. Rogers Fund, 1941. RIGHT: Patio from the Castle of Los Vélez, Vélez Blanco, Almería. Spanish, 1506–1515. Bequest of George Blumenthal, 1941. Erected in 1964 with the Ann and George Blumenthal Fund. (Photograph by Ezra Stoller) BELOW: *Les Demoiselles de Village*. The three sisters of the artist, Lélie, Juliette, and Zoé. Gustave Courbet, French, 1819–1877. Oil. Gift of Harry Payne Bingham, 1940.

OPPOSITE: *The Drowning of Britomartis*. French tapestry, c. 1550–1555. Gift of the children of Mrs. Harry Payne Whitney, 1942, in accordance with the wishes of their mother. LEFT: "Bat Medallion" robe of embroidered satin, believed to have come from the tomb of Kuo Ch'ien Wang (died 1738), seventeenth son of K'ang Hsi. Chinese, early eighteenth century. Anonymous gift, 1943.

RIGHT: Highboy. American (Boston), 1735. Maple and white pine with japanned decoration. Purchase, 1940, Joseph Pulitzer Bequest. BELOW LEFT: Flute in six sections. South German. Probably French or Italian origin, c. 1760. Hardpaste porcelain. Gift of R. Thornton Wilson, 1943, in memory of Florence Ellsworth Wilson. BELOW: *Burial*. Bradley Walker Tomlin, American, 1899–1953. Oil, painted in 1943. George A. Hearn Fund, 1943.

LEFT: Seated Buddha. Chinese, T'ang dynasty (618–906). Gilt bronze. Rogers Fund, 1943. RIGHT: Spangenhelm. Frankish, seventh century. Iron and bronze. Harris Brisbane Dick Fund, 1942.

Painting of tribute horse with escort proceeding through a mountain landscape by an unidentified artist, probably tenth century. Chinese, early Sung dynasty (A.D. 960–1280). Colors on silk. Rogers Fund, 1941.

ABOVE: Head of Bodhissattva, from the cave temples of T'ien Lung Shan. Chinese, T'ang dynasty (A.D. 618–907). Gray sandstone. Gift of Mrs. John D. Rockefeller, Jr., 1942. RIGHT: Plaque from a quiver from the region of Kuh-i-Dasht, Luristan. Iranian, ninth/tenth century B.C. Bronze. Rogers Fund, 1941.

LEFT: South Indian lute or tamboura, inlaid with ivory. Gift of Alice E. Getty, 1946. BELOW: Seated statue of a man with a harp. Cycladic, c. 2500 B.C. Marble. Rogers Fund, 1947.

OPPOSITE: Above left, harpsichord with paintings by Gaspard Dughet, French, probably 1613–1675. Anonymous gift, 1945. Above right, Virgin and Child, German School, fifteenth century. Woodcut. Gift of Felix M. Warburg and his family, 1941. Below left, detail of rug presented by Peter the Great of Russia to Leopold I of Austria. Persian (Herat), sixteenth century. Rogers Fund, 1943. Below right, *Portrait of a Lady with a Fan*. Rembrandt. Oil, dated 1633. Gift of Helen Swift Neilson, 1943.

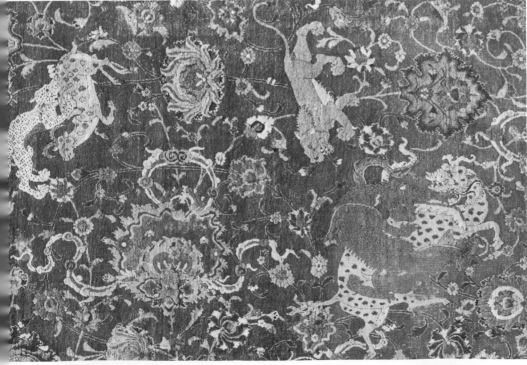

ABOVE: *The Rape of the Sabine Women.* Nicolas Poussin, French, 1594–1665. Oil. Harris Brisbane Dick Fund, 1946. BELOW: Clasp. Attributed to Nicholas of Verdun. Mosan, thirteenth century. Gilt bronze. The Cloisters Collection, 1947.

Head of King Philip Augustus (?), 1165–1223, probably from The Portal of the Virgin, Notre Dame, Paris. French, c. 1210–1220. Limestone. Fletcher Fund, 1947.

LEFT: *Midshipman Augustus Brine* (1770–1840). John Singleton Copley, American, 1738–1815. Oil, dated 1782. Bequest of Richard De Wolfe Brixey, 1943. ABOVE: Mayuri, or long-neck lute, with peacock belly. Indian. Gift of Alice E. Getty, 1946. BELOW LEFT: Ewer with medallions of the signs of the zodiac. Persian, early thirteenth century, Khurasan. Bronze inlaid with silver and engraved. Rogers Fund, 1944. BELOW: *George Washington* (1732–1799). Gilbert Stuart, American, 1755–1828. Oil, painted 1800–1803. Bequest of Richard De Wolfe Brixey, 1943.

OPPOSITE: At left, *Nude Woman*. Picasso. Charcoal. The Alfred Stieglitz Collection, 1949. At right, head of a man from Tikhon Teppeh, Azerbaijan. Iranian, late second millennium B.C. Bronze. Rogers Fund, 1947.

ABOVE: *Gertrude Stein* (1874–1946). Pablo Picasso, Spanish, 1881–    . Oil, painted in 1906. Bequest of Gertrude Stein, 1946. LEFT: Beaker from the region of the Iron Gates of the Danube. Scythian, c. fourth century B.C. Embossed and chased silver. Rogers Fund, 1947. RIGHT: Figure of a bull. Archaemenian period, Sabaean, sixth century B.C. Bronze, with red patina. Rogers Fund, 1947.

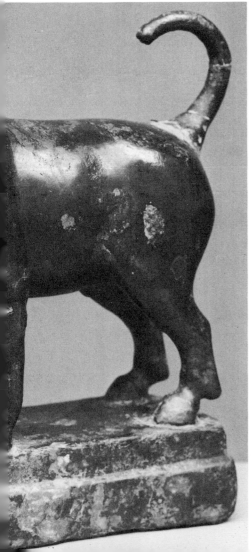

OPPOSITE: At above left, *Melancholia I*. Dürer. Harris Brisbane Dick Fund, 1943. At below left, Joshua and David, detail of the Hebrew tapestry, one of the Nine Heroes tapestries, probably by Nicolas Bataille, Paris. French, c. 1385. The Cloisters Collection, gift of John D. Rockefeller, Jr., 1947. At right. statuette from Gizeh, of the Steward Memy-Sabu and his wife, c. 2420 B.C. Egyptian, late fifth/early sixth dynasty (2500/2400 B.C.). White limestone, originally painted. Rogers Fund, 1948.

RIGHT: *The Muse—Susan Walker Morse* (1819–1885). Samuel F. B. Morse, American, 1791–1872. Bequest of Herbert L. Pratt, 1945. BELOW: Figure of Eros sleeping, said to have come from Rhodes. Greek, Hellenistic period (250–150 B.C.). Bronze. Rogers Fund, 1943.

ABOVE LEFT: *The Standard-Bearer*. Rembrandt. Oil, dated 1654. The Jules S. Bache Collection, 1949. CENTER LEFT: *The Guitarist* (The Spanish Singer). Manet. Oil, dated 1860. Gift of William Church Osborn, 1949. LEFT: *Christ with a Pilgrim's Staff*. Rembrandt. Oil. The Jules S. Bache Collection, 1949. RIGHT: *Sun Spots, 1920*. John Marin, American, 1870–1953. The Alfred Stieglitz Collection, 1949.

OPPOSITE: *Portrait of an Ecclesiastic*. Jean Fouquet, French, c. 1420–1477/81. Metalpoint and black chalk on white prepared paper. Rogers Fund, 1949. RIGHT: *Red Cabbages, Rhubarb, and Orange*. Charles Demuth, American, 1883–1935. Water color. The Alfred Stieglitz Collection, 1949. BELOW: *Blowing Bubbles (Les Bouteilles de Savon)*. Jean Baptiste Simeon de Chardin, French, 1699–1779. Oil. Catherine C. Wentworth Fund, 1949.

LEFT: *Le Billet Doux*. Jean Honoré Fragonard, French, 1732–1806. Oil. The Jules S. Bache Collection, 1949. BELOW: *The Mountain*. Gaston Lachaise, French, 1882–1935. Bronze, dated 1924. The Alfred Stieglitz Collection, 1949. Gift of Georgia O'Keeffe, 1949.

OPPOSITE: *Portrait of Ralph Dusenberry*. Arthur G. Dove, American, 1880–1946. Oil on canvas, with applied ruler, wood, and paper. The Alfred Stieglitz Collection, 1949.

**1950–1959**

*Box Lobby Loungers.* Thomas Rowlandson, English, 1756–1827. Etching, dated January 5, 1811. Purchase, Whittelsey Fund, 1959.

BELOW: Statuette of Athena flying her owl. Greek, fifth century B.C. Harris Brisbane Dick Fund, 1950. RIGHT: Three Sèvres vases. French, 1757–1763. Soft-paste porcelain. Gift of R. Thornton Wilson, 1950, in memory of Florence Ellsworth Wilson. OPPOSITE: *Portrait of a Member of the Wedigh Family*. Hans Holbein the Younger. Tempera and oil on wood. Bequest of Edward S. Harkness, 1940.

ANNO.1532.                    ÆTATIS.SVÆ.29

ABOVE: Enjoying the new Junior Museum: At left, in the snack bar on opening day, October 11, 1957; at center, examining I. Rice Pereira's *Shooting Stars* and Thomas Wildfred's *Counterpoint in Space, Opus 146* at the exhibition "How to Look at Paintings," which was on view from September 1958 to June 1959; and, at right, discovering exploration routes on a map in the special exhibition, "The Age of Discovery—by Caravan and Caravel," which opened the new Junior Museum.

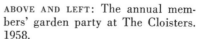

ABOVE AND LEFT: The annual members' garden party at The Cloisters. 1958.

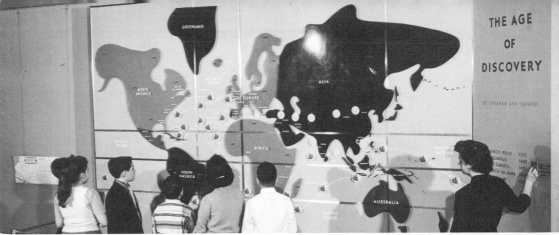

RIGHT: *The Drummond Children*. Henry Raeburn, British, 1756–1823. Oil. Bequest of Mary Stillman Harkness, 1950. BELOW: Director Francis Henry Taylor faces the cameras during filming of his introduction to the English-language version of Pictura Films' *Leonardo da Vinci*.

ABOVE: Leaf from a Shak-nama. Mongol School. Persian, c. 1330. Purchase, 1952, Joseph Pulitzer Bequest. LEFT: Table from Essex County, Massachusetts. American, 1675–1700. Oak and maple. Gift of Mrs. J. Insley Blair, 1951. RIGHT: Banjo back. Wood with ivory inlay. Bequest of Mary Stillman Harkness, 1950.

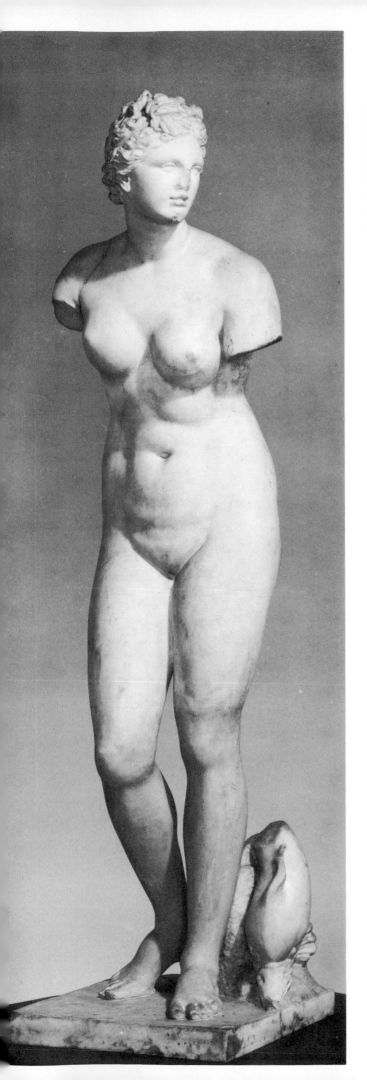

LEFT: Statue of Aphrodite. A copy, probably Hellenistic, of a fourth-century Greek work. Marble. Fletcher Fund, 1952. ABOVE: *Elizabeth Farren, Countess of Derby* (c. 1759–1828). Thomas Lawrence, British, 1769–1830. Oil, painted in 1790. Bequest of Edward S. Harkness, 1940.

319

Incense burner, signed by Jafar ibn Muhammad
ibn Ali. Persian (Seljuk), 1181–1182. Rogers
Fund, 1951. RIGHT: *The Musicians*. Michelangelo
Merisi da Caravaggio, Italian (Roman), 1573–
1610. Rogers Fund, 1952.

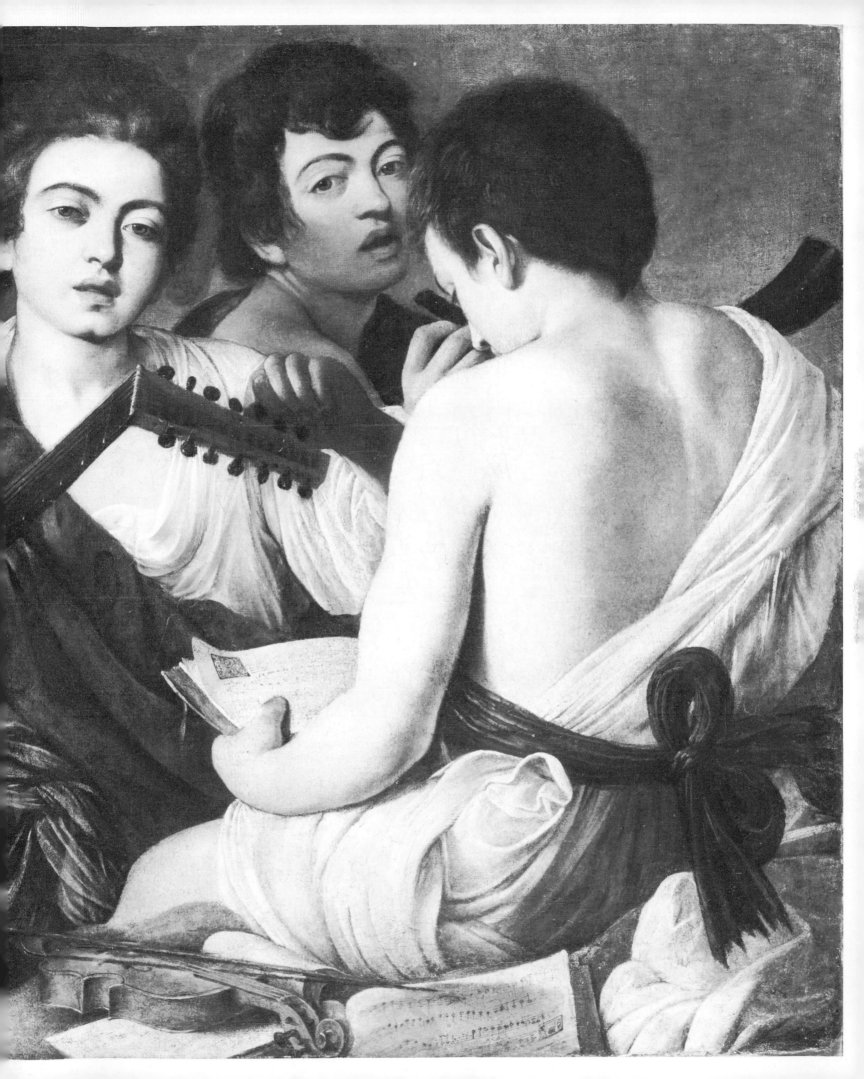

ABOVE: The Arms and Armor Collection in the Morgan Wing. RIGHT: *Christ before Pilate* and *The Visitation*, folios 34 and 35 from *The Hours of Jeanne d'Evreux*, 1325–1328. Jean Pucelle, French. The Cloisters Collection, 1954. BELOW: The restaurant, which was formerly the Roman Court. In the pool, the Aganippe fountain, by Carl Milles (1875–1955).

OPPOSITE: At above left, *No. 11*. Bradley Walker Tomlin, American, 1899–1953. Oil, painted 1952–1953. Arthur Hoppock Hearn Fund, 1953. At right, *crecelle* (rattle). French, fifteenth/sixteenth century. Oak. Gift of Blumka Gallery, 1954. Below, *The Good Samaritan*. Rodolphe Bresdin, French, 1825–1885. Lithograph. Gift of F. H. Hirschland, 1952.

RIGHT: Detail of a yellow satin panel embroidered with scenes from Ovid. After Bernard Salomon. French, 1560–1570. Rogers Fund, 1956. BELOW: Spinettino. Italian (Venetian), 1540. Purchase, 1953, Joseph Pulitzer Bequest.

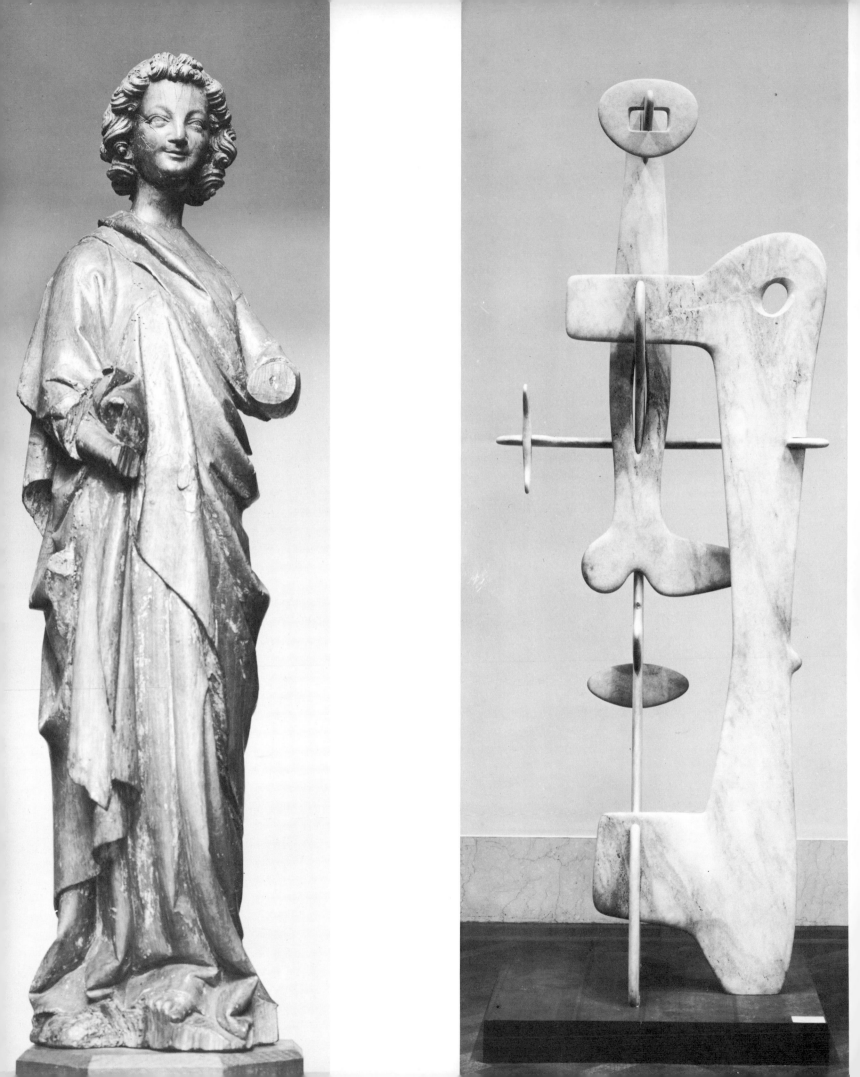

Around the circular engraving:

NON AMBIRE PROBAT SAPIENS, SED LAVDAT HONORES, LAVDAT, CONTINGANT SI TAMEN ILLA PROBIS. SIC PHAETONTAEVS NIMIVM TEMERARIA LAPSVS VOTA DOCET TANDEN FINE CARERE BONO.

C.C. Pictor. Inuc. HG. sculp. 3.

LEFT: Statuette of an angel, one of a pair. Rheims School. French, thirteenth century. Oak. The Cloisters Collection, 1952. RIGHT: *Kouros (in 9 parts)*. Isamu Noguchi, American, 1904–      . Pink Georgia marble, slate base. Fletcher Fund, 1953. ABOVE: *The Fall of Phaeton*. Engraving after Cornelius Cornelisz., by Hendrik Goltzius, Dutch, 1558–1617. Harris Brisbane Dick Fund, 1953.

327

ABOVE: Red-figured amphora, said to be from Nola Berlin painter. Greek (Attic), c. 490 B.C. Terra cotta. Fletcher Fund, 1956. RIGHT: Statuette of a man, from Iraq. Sumerian, c. 2700 (early dynastic period). Copper. Harris Brisbane Dick Fund, 1955. OPPOSITE: Head of ibex. Iranian (Achaemenian), fourth/fifth century B.C. Bronze. Fletcher Fund, 1956.

LEFT: Mahogany cupboard, c. 1760, probably made by William Vile, English, d. 1767. BELOW: Sarcophagus with relief of Dionysos, the Four Seasons, Pan, and other figures. Roman, c. A.D. 220–230. Purchase, 1955, Joseph Pulitzer Bequest.

RIGHT: Gold rhyton. Iranian (Achaemenian), fifth century B.C. Fletcher Fund, 1954.

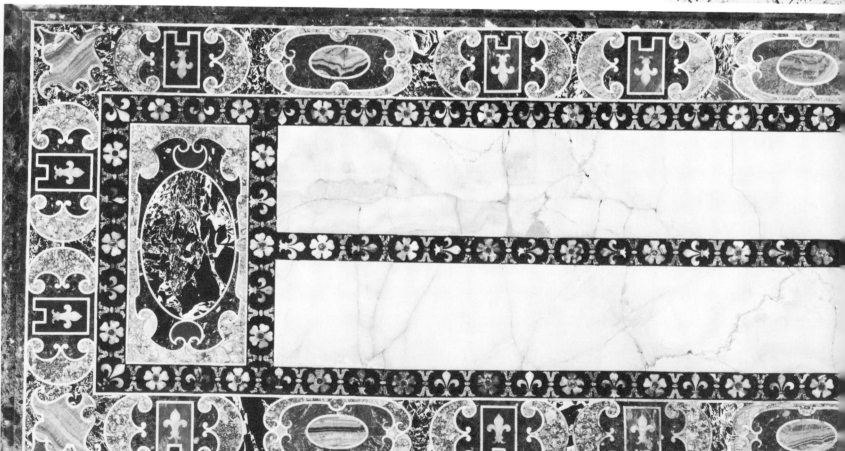

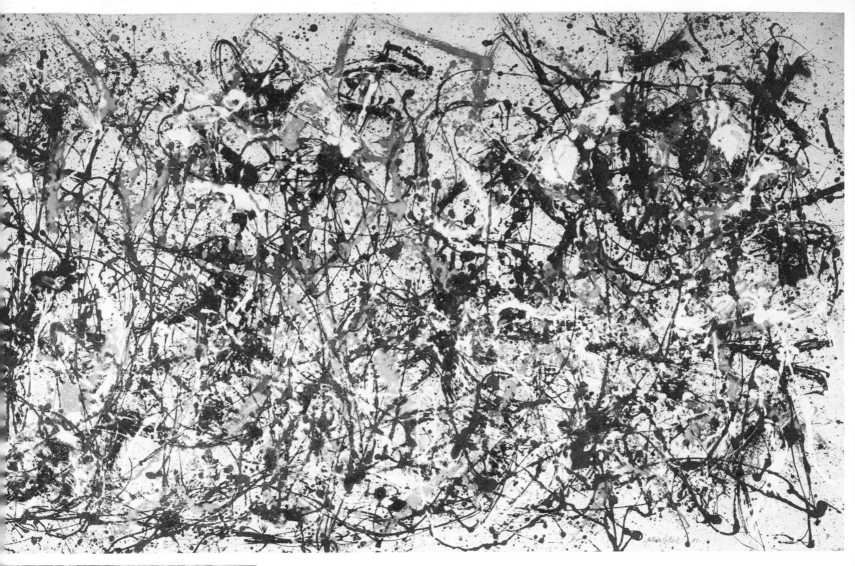

ABOVE: *Autumn Rhythm*. Jackson Pollock, American, 1912–1956. Oil, painted 1950. George A. Hearn Fund, 1957. RIGHT: *Percolator*. Stuart Davis, American, 1894–1964. Oil, painted 1927. Arthur Hoppock Hearn Fund, 1957.

OPPOSITE: Above, *Water of the Flowery Mill*. Arshile Gorky, American, 1904–1948. Oil, dated 1944. George A. Hearn Fund, 1956. Below, The Farnese Table, designed c. 1565–1573 by Jacopo Barozzi da Vignola, Italian, 1507–1573. Marble, alabaster, and precious stones. Harris Brisbane Dick Fund, 1958.

OPPOSITE: *The Crucifixion with the Virgin and St. John.* Hendrick Terbrugghen, Dutch, 1588–1629. Purchase, 1956, funds from various donors. ABOVE: Reja made by the master ironworker Pedro Juan for the Cathedral of Valladolid, Spain, begun in 1668. Iron and limestone. Gift of the Hearst Foundation, 1956.

Tapestry Room from Croome Court, Warwickshire, designed by Robert Adam (Scottish, 1728–1792) and decorated 1760–1761 with Gobelin tapestries commissioned by Lord Coventry. Gift of the Samuel H. Kress Foundation, 1958.

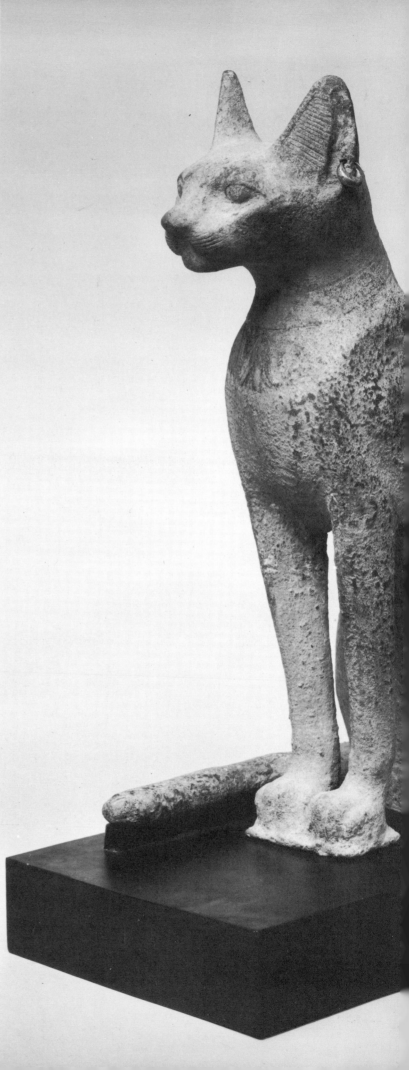

ABOVE: "Pity like a naked babe . . . ." William Blake. Color print. Gift of Mrs. Robert W. Goelet, 1958. BELOW: Figure of Gudea. Neo-Sumerian, c. 2150 B.C. Diorite. Harris Brisbane Dick Fund, 1959. RIGHT: Statue of the Cat Goddess Bastet. Egyptian, late dynastic, ninth to third centuries B.C. Bronze with one gold earring. Purchase, 1958. Funds from various donors. OPPOSITE: Turkish rug. Ushak, sixteenth century. Gift of Joseph V. McMullan, 1958.

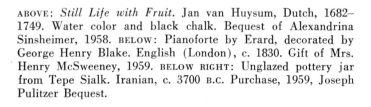

LEFT: Harp. Austrian, probably eighteenth century. Rogers Fund, 1958. BELOW: Settee from the workshop of Duncan Phyfe, American, 1768–1854. Gift of C. Ruxton Love, 1959. OPPOSITE: *Black, White, and Gray.* Franz Kline, American, 1910–1962. Oil, painted 1959. Arthur Hoppock Hearn Fund, 1954.

ABOVE: *Still Life with Fruit.* Jan van Huysum, Dutch, 1682–1749. Water color and black chalk. Bequest of Alexandrina Sinsheimer, 1958. BELOW: Pianoforte by Erard, decorated by George Henry Blake. English (London), c. 1830. Gift of Mrs. Henry McSweeney, 1959. BELOW RIGHT: Unglazed pottery jar from Tepe Sialk. Iranian, c. 3700 B.C. Purchase, 1959, Joseph Pulitzer Bequest.

LEFT: *The Annunciation, with Donors and St. Joseph.* Triptych known as The Merode Altarpiece. Robert Campin, Flemish, active 1406–1444. Oil on wood. The Cloisters Collection, purchase. BELOW: *Irises.* Vincent van Gogh, Dutch, 1853–1890. Oil. Gift of Mrs. David M. Levy, 1958.

*Thrust.* Adolph Gottlieb, American, 1903–      . Oil. George A. Hearn Fund, 1959.

343

# 1960–1969

Masks, spears, and canoe prows from the Asmat tribe of New Guinea, in the loan exhibition "Art of Oceania, Africa, and the Americas" from the Museum of Primitive Art, May 10 to August 17, 1969. The event presaged the welcoming of all the Museum of Primitive Art collections into the Metropolitan Museum—a gift from Honorary Trustee Nelson A. Rockefeller, President and Founder of the Museum of Primitive Art.

OPPOSITE: *Portrait of Edmond François Aman-Jean* (1860–1936). Georges Seurat, French, 1859–1891. Conté crayon. Bequest of Stephen C. Clark, 1960. RIGHT: Figurine of a Nubian, tribute bearer from Shalmaneser, Nimrud. Assyrian, eighth century B.C. Rogers Fund, 1960.

ABOVE: *A Wind-God*. Study for a ceiling fresco figure in the Sala di Apollo of the Pitti Palace, Florence. Pietro da Cortona, Italian, 1596–1669. Chalk. The Elisha Whittelsey Fund, 1961. RIGHT: *The Fortune Teller*. Georges de La Tour, French, 1593–1652. Oil. Rogers Fund, 1960. BELOW: *Christ and the Woman of Samaria*. Rembrandt. Oil. Bequest of Lillian S. Timken, 1959.

OVERLEAF: *La Promenade Publique*. Philibert-Louis Debucourt, French, 1755–1832. Colored aquatint. The Elisha Whittelsey Fund, 1961.

LEFT: *Still Life*. Patrick Henry Bruce, American, 1881–1937. Oil, c. 1928. George A. Hearn Fund, 1961. BELOW: *Invitation to the Side Show (La Parade)*. Seurat. Oil. Bequest of Stephen C. Clark, 1960. OPPOSITE: *Madame Cézanne in the Conservatory*. Cézanne, French, 1839–1906. Bequest of Stephen C. Clark, 1960.

353

ABOVE LEFT: Figure of Vishnu. South Indian, early Chola period, tenth century. Bronze. Purchase, 1962. John D. Rockefeller III gift. ABOVE: Gold plaque from Zawiyeh. Iranian, eighth/seventh century B.C. Harris Brisbane Dick Fund and Rogers Fund, 1954 and 1962. LEFT: Gold cup. Iranian, c. 1000 B.C. Rogers Fund, 1962. OPPOSITE: Gold libation bowl. Greek, third century B.C. Rogers Fund, 1962.

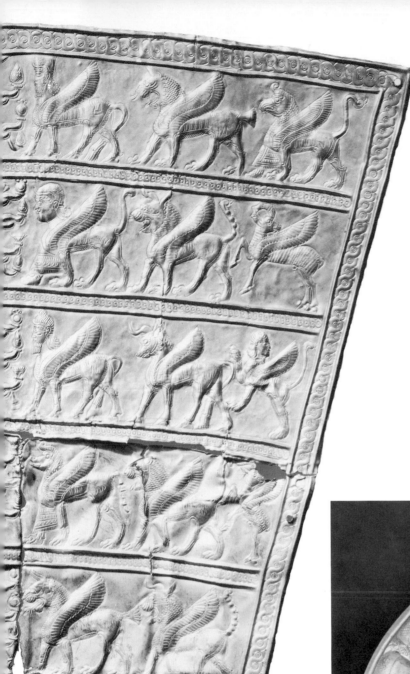

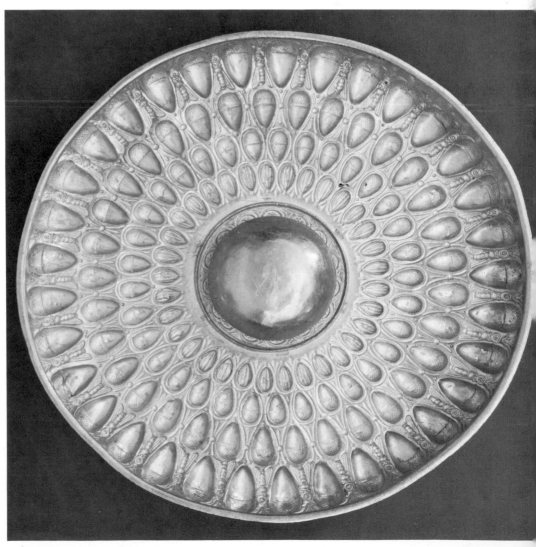

OPPOSITE: At left, *boiserie* from Palais Paar, Vienna, 1769. Austrian. Funds given by the Charles B. Wrightsman Foundation, 1963. At above right, miniature, a leaf from the Mantiq al-tayr. Probably by Mirak. Persian (Herat School), 1467. Fletcher Fund, 1963. Below, side chair, c. 1795. Carving attributed to Samuel McIntire of Salem, Massachusetts. The Friends of the American Wing Fund, 1962.

Above, below, where'er the astonished eye
Turns to behold, new opening wonders lie,

With uproar hideous first the *Falls* appear,
The stunning tumult thundering on the ear.

This great o'erwhelming work of awful Time
In all its dread magnificence sublime,

Rises on our view, amid a crashing roar
That bids us kneel, and Time's great God adore.

RIGHT: *The Falls of Niagara.* Edward Hicks, American, 1780–1849. Oil. Gift of Edgar William and Bernice Chrysler Garbisch, 1962. BELOW: *Musical Angels.* Dürer. Pen and ink. Gift of Mrs. William H. Osborn, 1961.

RIGHT: *The Concourse of the Birds*. Miniature, a leaf from the Mantiq al-tayr, by Habib Allah. Persian, c. 1600. Fletcher Fund, 1963. BELOW: *Study of Stratonice*. Ingres. Chalk. Gustavus A. Pfeiffer Fund, 1963.

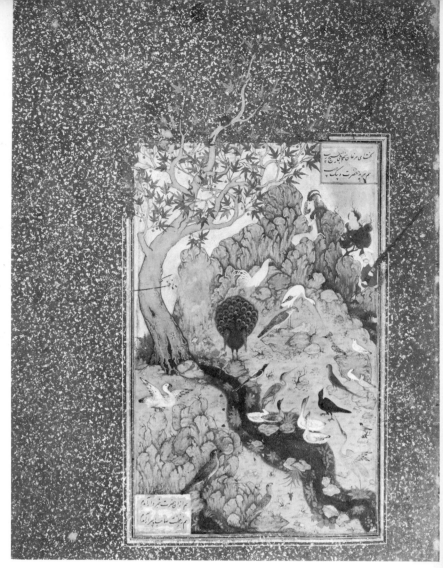

OPPOSITE: French court gown of the period of Louis XV, a gift of Fédération de la Soirie, 1950, in the exhibition "Costumes—Period Rooms Re-occupied in Style," November 27 to December 22, 1963. Portrait of Louis XV as a boy was painted in 1715 by Hyacinthe Rigaud, French, 1659–1743. Purchase 1960, Mary Wetmore Shively Bequest. The setting is the French Alcove, with carvings attributed to François Antoine Vasse, French (1681–1736). Gift of J. Pierpont Morgan, 1906.

ABOVE: *Coney Island*. Joseph Stella, American, 1880–1946. Oil. George A. Hearn Fund, 1963. RIGHT: *Second Theme* (1937–1938). Burgoyne Diller, American, 1906–1965. Oil. George A. Hearn Fund, 1963. OPPOSITE: Siva as Lord of the Dance. South Indian, early Chola period, c. 1000 A.D. Purchase, 1964, Harris Brisbane Dick Fund.

"Guests for Tea," one of the scenes from the 1964 Costume Institute exhibition, "Vignettes of Fashion," shown on this and the following three pages. The tea gowns, from left to right, are American, c. 1903, gift of Mrs. J. N. Thorne, 1953; American, c. 1897, gift of Mrs. I. A. Simon, 1939. Tablecloth of Italian needlepoint and bobbin lace and embroidered linen, c. 1900, is a gift of Mr. and Mrs. Edward S. Burch. The painting is *Tea Leaves* by William Paxton, American, 1869–1941. Oil. Gift of George A. Hearn,

RIGHT: "A Visit to the New Baby—The Victorian Era." Mother's dress is American, c. 1860, gift of Colonel L. E. de Forest, 1951. Christening dress, French, c. 1860, gift of Mrs Adele Kaufman, 1955. Little girl's dress, French, c. 1869, was the first Paris gown of Harriet Hyatt Mayor, mother of the donor. Gift of A. Hyatt Mayor, 1956. Girl's dress, American, 1869, gift of Mary Louise Deming. The paintings, each entitled *Head of a Child*, by William Page, American, 1811–1885, bequest of Emma A. Fortuna, 1925. Rosewood settee, attributed to John Henry Belter, New York, mid-nineteenth century, gift of Mr. and Mrs. Lowell Ross Burch and Miss Jean McLean Morron. BELOW: "The Visit." Left to right: Empire dress (gift of Ethel Frankau, 1939) with spencer (gift of Lee Simonson, 1939) both French, 1804–1814. Small child's dress, American, early nineteenth century, gift of Mrs. John Cattus, 1948. Cap gift of Mrs. DeWitt Clinton Cohen, 1939. Spanish ribbed-silk dress, 1807–1812, gift of Mary Van Kleeck, 1951. Viennese Empire dress, 1804–1814, gift of Lee Simonson, 1939.

BELOW: "The Morning Stroll." Boy's outfit, American, c. 1829, coat gift of Mrs. M. A. Gordon, 1948; cup gift of Mrs. John J. Gibson, 1946. Man's habit, Viennese, 1825–1829, gift of Lee Simonson, 1939. Little girl's pelisse, American, c. 1836, gift of Mr. and Mrs. Willis Reese, 1955, was worn by Mr. Reese's great-aunt, Fannie Willis. Cap gift of Mrs. Albert S. Morrow, 1937.

ABOVE: "A Walk in the Garden." Lady's afternoon dress, American, c. 1860, gift of the Misses Faith and Delia Leavens, 1941. Parasol gift of Agnes Miles Carpenter, 1955. Girl's summer dress, c. 1855, gift of Mrs. Charles D. Dickey, Mrs. Louis Curtis, Jr., and S. Sloan Colt, 1957. LEFT: "Informal Dress." Seated man's attire Italian/Spanish, late eighteenth century, Irene Lewisohn Bequest, 1956. On figure at right, shirt, waistcoat, and breeches Spanish, 1775–1790, gift of Lincoln Kirstein, 1937. Viennese silk day cap, c. 1720, gift of Lee Simonson, 1939.

OPPOSITE: "Family Musicale." Left to right, French eighteenth-century dress and petticoat, gift of Mrs. Robert Wood Bliss, 1943. Man's French Louis XVI velvet suit, Irene Lewisohn Bequest, 1961. Girl's dress, French, Louis XVI. Little boy's Viennese suit, gift of Lee Simonson, 1939.

ABOVE: Mahogany sideboard, attributed to the workshop of John and Thomas Seymour, Boston, 1800–1810. Gift of the family of Mr. and Mrs. Andrew Varick Stout, in their memory, 1965. LEFT: *Pastoral Landscape —The Roman Campagna*. Claude Lorrain. Oil. Bequest of Adele L. Lehman, in memory of Arthur Lehman, 1965. OPPOSITE: *Allegory of Air*. François Boucher, French, 1703–1770. Chalk. Louis V. Bell Fund, 1964.

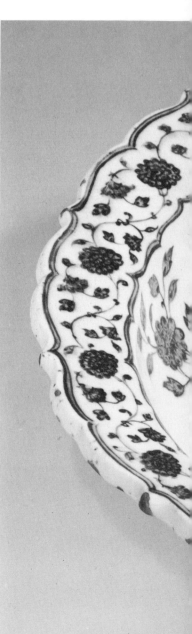

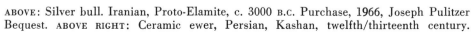
ABOVE: Silver bull. Iranian, Proto-Elamite, c. 3000 B.C. Purchase, 1966, Joseph Pulitzer Bequest. ABOVE RIGHT: Ceramic ewer, Persian, Kashan, twelfth/thirteenth century.

RIGHT: Statuette of a recumbent lion. Egyptian, late predynastic/early dynastic. Quartz. Purchase, 1966. BELOW: Glazed earthenware bowl. Turkish, Isnik, late fifteenth/early sixteenth century. Harris Brisbane Dick Fund, 1966.

ABOVE LEFT: *Study of Saint Domitilla.* Rubens. Wash and chalk, with pen and ink. Rogers Fund, 1965. ABOVE: *Dream of Aeneas.* Salvatore Rosa, Italian (Neapolitan), 1615–1673. Rogers Fund, 1965. LEFT: *A View of Venice from the Sea.* Guardi. Oil. Bequest of Adele L. Lehman, 1965, in memory of Arthur Lehman. OPPOSITE: Bust of a Sasanian King. Iranian, c. fourth century A.D. Silver gilt. Fletcher Fund, 1965.

LEFT: *Basket of Flowers* (1848–1849). Delacroix. Oil. Bequest of Miss Adelaide Milton de Groot (1876–1967), 1967. OPPOSITE: *Adam and Eve.* Dürer. Etching. Gift of Mrs. William H. Osborn, in memory of Johnston L. Redmond, 1967.

Carved and gilded beechwood armchair by Nicolas Q. Foliot, French, c. 1754.

OPPOSITE: *Thomas Willing.* Charles Willson Peale, American, 1741–1827. Oil, painted 1782. Anonymous gift, 1966. ABOVE: Ivory fragment. Assyrian, ninth/eighth century B.C. Harris Brisbane Dick Fund, 1967. RIGHT: *Garden Scene.* Jean Demosthene Dugoure, French, 1749–1805. Gouache. Rogers Fund, 1966. BELOW: *Cider Making.* William Sidney Mount, American, 1807–1869. Oil. Charles Allen Munn Bequest, 1966.

OPPOSITE: *Ugolino and His Sons*. Jean Baptiste Carpeaux, French, 1827–1875. The marble sculpture was executed in Paris 1865–1867, after a model completed in Rome 1860–1861. Funds given by the Josephine Bay Paul and C. Michael Paul Foundation, Inc., and Charles Ulrick and Josephine Bay Foundation, Inc., 1967.

LEFT: Silver ewer. Sassanian, sixth/seventh century A.D. Mr. and Mrs. C. Douglas Dillon gift and Rogers Fund, 1967.
ABOVE: *The Fear of Cupid's Darts*. Jean Louis Lemoyne, French, 1665–1755. Funds given by the Josephine Bay Paul Foundation and the Charles Ulrick and Josephine Bay Foundation, Inc., 1967.

OVERLEAF: *The Three Living—The Three Dead*, pages from the Psalter of Bonne of Luxembourg, c. 1345. Illuminated by Jean Pucelle. The Cloisters Fund, 1969.

I apres commence une
moult meruelleuse et loz
uble exemplaure que len
dit des .uj. uis z des .uj. moz.

378

Si com la matiere no' conte
Sil furent li co duc ou conte.
Auis noble home de grãt auoir
Et de gentil com fil a roy.

THIS AND OPPOSITE PAGE: Views of the Costume Institute exhibition, "The Art of Fashion," in 1968 in the Harry Payne Bingham Special Exhibitions Galleries. The Scottish bustle costume (opposite, above left), worn with a kilt of the Carnegie tartan, was made in Scotland in 1888 and worn by Mrs. Andrew Carnegie, and was a gift to the Museum of her granddaughter, Mrs. James G. Flockhart.

LEFT: Wedding dress worn by Eliza Mier Lorillard at her wedding in 1839 to Nathaniel P. Bailey. Gift of Mrs. Peter McBean and Mrs. E. M. Smith in memory of Natalie Lorillard Bailey Morris, 1968.
ABOVE: Detail of a North African hanging. Sixteenth century. Woven silk with metallic thread. Rogers Fund, 1968.

RIGHT: Eagle lectern from the Collegiate Church of St. Peter, Louvain, Belgium. Mosan, c. 1500. Cast and chased brass. The Cloisters Collection, The Cloisters Fund, 1967. BELOW: Pier table, labeled by Charles-Honoré Lannuier, New York, New York. American, c. 1815. The Friends of the American Wing Fund, 1968.

LEFT: Benin bronze head from Nigeria. The Museum of Primitive Art Collection, 1969. RIGHT: *The Apocalypse.* Page from an illuminated manuscript. English (?). Early fourteenth century. The Cloisters Fund, 1968.

BELOW: A few of the treasures in the Robert Lehman Collection, given to the Metropolitan in September 1969, in their original setting in the Lehman mansion. Two Rembrandts, *Portrait of an Elderly Man* (left) and *Portrait of Gerard de Lairesse,* hang on either side of *St. Jerome as Cardinal,* by El Greco. One of the most important privately gathered collections in the world, it includes nearly 3000 objects of Western European art.

The photographs on the following pages were taken especially for this book by Richard Kalvar.

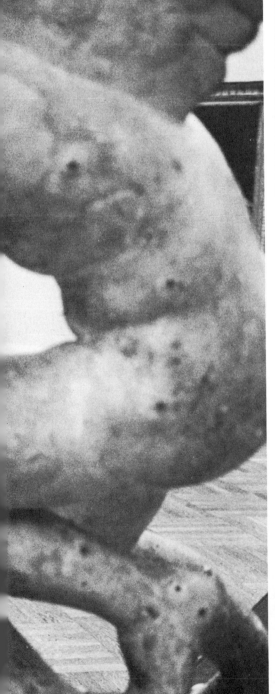

LEFT: The Museum's Fifth Avenue front of the future. © Ezra Stoller, ESTO.

BELOW: The Temple of Dendur within its inflatable tent awaits its glass house.

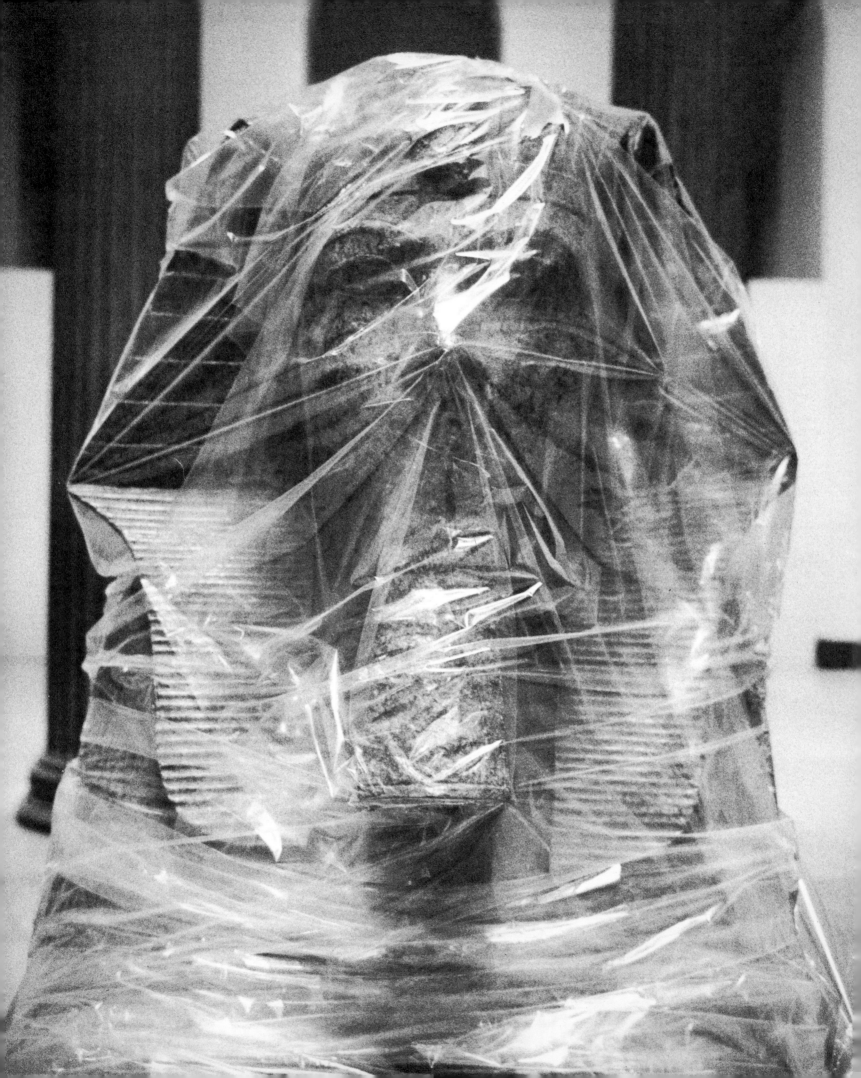

# ACKNOWLEDGMENTS

My gratitude is boundless to the many who have encouraged me and given me practical assistance in the writing of this book. Without the aid of the Metropolitan Museum of Art's Administrative, Curatorial, Departmental, and Service Staffs my book would not exist. I am especially obligated to the chairmen and curators of each department, for they made the basic lists of Museum treasures from which the objects in the Museum's collections illustrated in this book were finally chosen. I wish to thank Thomas P. F. Hoving for his Introduction and for his attentiveness to the book while it was being planned and written. I am also indebted to George Trescher, Secretary of the One Hundredth Anniversary Committee, and most specially to Linda R. Hyman, Research Assistant in that department. Miss Hyman has been a constant source of information and cheer. Archivist John Buchanan opened his meticulous office and files to me and patiently answered all queries. And Katharine Warwick of the Department of Public Relations and her co-workers Dale Weinstein and Elaine Hudson have been of the greatest assistance, supplying me with a ceaseless flow of materials. I also thank Margaret P. Nolan, Chief Librarian of the Photograph and Slide Library (an institution unique in the museum world), and Emily Humberger of the Museum's Photo Sales Department for their help.

Anyone who writes a history of the Museum must build upon Winifred E. Howe's exhaustive two-volume work, *A History of the Metropolitan Museum of Art*, the 1913 volume published by the Museum and the 1946 volume published by Columbia University Press for the Museum. The massive foundations upon which a history of the Museum must rest are the profuse and fascinating publications of the Museum itself, most important of which, to a historian, is *The Metropolitan Museum of Art Bulletin*, now almost sixty-five years old. I am most indebted to the contents of the *Bulletin* and the Museum's annual reports, for it was in these Museum publications and catalogues that I found much of my source material. A special word of thanks to A. Hyatt Mayor, former Curator of the Department of Prints, for his articles in the *Bulletin* and his verbal memories of his long Museum life, and gratitude to Lillian Green, former Public Relations head who helped start me on this history many years ago. Two splendid special catalogues have been of assistance: *Decorative Art from the Samuel H. Kress Collection at The Metropolitan Museum of Art*, by Carl Christian Dauterman, James Parker, and Edith Appleton Standen (New York: Phaidon Press for the Samuel H. Kress Foundation, 1964), and *The Wrightsman Collection*, Vols. I and II, by F. J. B. Watson (New York: The Metropolitan Museum of Art, distributed by the New York Graphic Society). Lousine W. Havemeyer's *Sixteen to Sixty: Memoirs of a Collector* (privately printed for the family of Mrs. H. O. Havemeyer and the Metropolitan Museum of Art, 1961) is a perpetual delight and a well of information, as is Henry Watson Kent's *What I Am Pleased to Call My Education* (edited by Lois Leighton Comings, New York: the Grolier Club, 1949), and the catalogues of the Irwin Untermyer Collection (Cambridge, Mass.: Harvard University Press).

It is impossible to list all of the sources which have contributed to this book, but I was helped by *The New York Times'* and *Time's* and *Newsweek's* coverage of the art and museum world; by articles in magazines and newspapers by John Canaday, Milton Esterow, Rosamund Frost, Emily Genauer, Grace Glueck, Russel Lynes, John McPhee, W. G. Rogers, and Aline B. Saarinen. I must also express my gratitude to the following sources that have furnished me with information or confirmation, and, if not in all cases, with actual quotations: *A History of the Union League Club of New York City*, William H. Irwin, Earl C. May, Joseph Hotchkiss (New York: Dodd, Mead and Co., 1952; thanks also are due to Margaret Lippincott, Librarian of the Union League Club, and to the club itself for its great help); the various volumes of *Century Memorials* (and Andrew Zarimba, assistant librarian of the Century Association, and to the Century Association itself for its needed help); *The Proud Possessors*, Aline B. Saarinen (New York: Random House, 1958); *The Columbia Historical Portrait of New York*, John A. Kouwenhoven (Garden City, New York: Doubleday & Co., Inc., 1953); *America's Taste*, Marjorie Longley, Louis Silverstein, and Samuel A. Tower (New York: Simon & Schuster, 1960); *The Epic of New York City*, Edward Robb Ellis (New York: Coward-McCann, Inc., 1966); *Incredible New York*, Lloyd Morris (New York: Random House, 1951); *A Rockefeller Family Portrait from John D. to Nelson*, William Manchester (Boston and Toronto: Little, Brown & Co., 1959); *The Life of Thomas J. Watson: The Lengthening Shadow*, Marva R. and Thomas G. Belden (Boston and Toronto: Little, Brown, 1962); *Diary of an Art Dealer*, René Gimpel (New York: Farrar, Straus & Giroux, 1966); *The American Scene*, Henry James (New York: Charles Scribner's Sons, 1946); *The Age of Innocence*, Edith Wharton (New York: Appleton-Century-Crofts, Inc., 1950); *The Saga of American Society*, Dixon Wecter (New York: Charles Scribner's Sons, 1937); *"Our Crowd,"* Stephen Birmingham (New York: Harper & Row, 1966); *The Two Lives of James Jackson Jarves*, Francis Steegmuller (New Haven: Yale University Press, 1951); *Art News Annual*, 1945–1946; *Once Upon a City*, Grace M. Mayor (New York: The Macmillan Co., 1958); and *Metropolitan Seminars in Art*, John Canaday.

Nicolas Ducrot, of The Viking Press, has not only designed this book but editorially held my nonwriting hand throughout the monumental pleasure and agony of assembling and writing it. I can best thank him by wishing him on anyone headstrong enough to embark on a similar project: with Nicolas guiding, the shoals will seem less dangerous, the waters friendly indeed. I thank Mary Kopecky, of The Viking Press, for her editorial assistance and Vicki Fox and Cornelia Hice. Bookman Edwin V. Halbmeier has unflaggingly found obscure material for me, as has specialist in art Americana James F. Carr, whose edition of Tuckerman's *Book of the Artists* is a treasure: I thank Mr. and Mrs. Daniel Rose for their gift of *Valentine's Manuals*, and book and gallery man J. N. Bartfield for the gift of the missing *Manual*. I also thank the New York Society Library for permitting me to use their library extensively. I thank, for clippings, unpublished material, and books, Irving Kolodin, Betsy Thurman, Paula Lawrence, Joan Simon, and my brother, Jerome B. Lerman, who discovered for me, amongst other details, that the tax measure providing deductions for gifts was first introduced in 1913. To Betsy Talbot Blackwell, editor in chief of *Mademoiselle*, I unexpectedly owe information on Thomas J. Watson: I am also thankful to Mrs. Blackwell for her constant understanding and encouragement, which have helped to make this project possible. I thank Joan Rubin, Mary Cantwell, Martine La Tour, and Amy Gross, who aided and abetted in various practical ways. I cannot end these acknowledgments without sending the happiest thank you of all to my late father, who, when I was three years old, first took me into the Metropolitan Museum of Art and so began a love affair with it which has gone on for over half a century.

LEO LERMAN

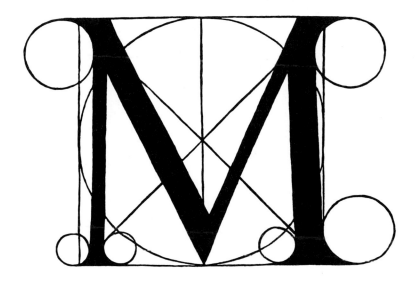

# INDEX